AWARENESS CENTERED TRAINING -

A   C   T

Education, Relationship, Well Being, Choice!

Simply Amazing!

BY
MAUREEN ROSS, MA, NCC, CPDT-KA, RYT

Joyful, Easy Training and Wellness
for a Happy, Healthy and Confident Dog
Reduce Stress and Create Positive Change in Your Life Too!

Enjoy the Journey!

BALBOA.
PRESS
A DIVISION OF HAY HOUSE

T0369049

Cover Photo by Gary Ross
Photography by Gary Ross, Kath DeLong, Liz Harrington

Balboa Press books may be ordered through booksellers or by contacting:

Balboa Press
A Division of Hay House
1663 Liberty Drive
Bloomington, IN 47403
www.balboapress.com
1-(877) 407-4847

ISBN: 978-1-4525-5754-0 (sc)
ISBN: 978-1-4525-5755-7 (hc)
ISBN: 978-1-4525-5753-3 (e)

Library of Congress Control Number: 2012916173

Because of the dynamic nature of the Internet, any web addresses or links contained in this book may have changed since publication and may no longer be valid. The views expressed in this work are solely those of the author and do not necessarily reflect the views of the publisher, and the publisher hereby disclaims any responsibility for them.

The author of this book does not dispense medical advice or prescribe the use of any technique as a form of treatment for physical, emotional, or medical problems without the advice of a physician, either directly or indirectly. The intent of the author is only to offer information of a general nature to help you in your quest for emotional and spiritual well-being. In the event you use any of the information in this book for yourself, which is your constitutional right, the author and the publisher assume no responsibility for your actions.

Any people depicted in stock imagery provided by Thinkstock are models, and such images are being used for illustrative purposes only.
Certain stock imagery © Thinkstock.

Printed in the United States of America

Balboa Press rev. date: 09/18/2012

All the Pets
To all the pets I've loved,
to all who taught me how to live.
You are in my heart and soul,
not forgotten, keeping me whole.
~ Maureen Ross

With Gratitude

I extend my heart-centered embrace to the dogs, (all pets), visionaries, mentors and great friends, for giving me the pleasure and privilege of living and learning with them.

This is dedicated to my life partner and best friend, Gary, who supports my endeavors through peaks and valleys.

I bow in admiration, and get inspiration from passionate people, who dedicate their time, enhancing well being and education with pet assisted therapy. We are forever changed, forever connected. You make a difference.

I treasure seductive, simple moments, when the dogs
come running, after eight seconds, as if I am special.
My hair is not on fire. Dogs give appreciation, attention
and affection freely, without judgment. Wagasana!

CONTENTS

❧ PAWT 8 – Prevention, Management, Solutions (PMS) 275

❧ PAWT 9 – Pathways of Grief—Celebrating Life 311

FOREWORD

"Nothing fuels the creative process like an open mind, an observant heart, and the freedom to express yourself without fear. Have you experienced those moments when inspiration strikes? Suddenly, you find yourself writing, creating, redesigning or exploring a new and challenging territory with your dog.

A spark of inspiration ignites, like a dog digging for buried treasure. You had a vision, plus optimism and enthusiasm, even a sense of urgency. If you stop, listen and observe, as the idea takes shape, you'll notice that your mind, in these moments, feels relaxed and spacious.

Awareness Centered Training (ACT) is about cultivating awareness as you move through living and learning with dogs. You begin to notice your expectations, reactions, desires and all kinds of emotional and behavioral patterns. Over time, as you observe these patterns that contribute to your well being, and as this awareness (practicing in the moment) flows over into the rest of your life, you will find yourself making healthier choices.

We are all on a road to somewhere. ACT, and our dogs, can be powerful vehicles for change. Fortunately, it can only take you in the direction you are steering. It is essential to reflect on where you want to go. Where is your dog taking you? Where are you taking your dog?" Breathing in ~ Exhaling ~ Creating Space, Maureen

"It is not often in this world that we run into a person whose personality rings so true as to be called authentic. Maureen Ross I am proud to say is one of those people. She is truly a WYSIWYG kind of person. No hidden agendas, no ulterior motives when she says something it is from the heart pure and honest. I met Maureen shortly after relocating my Veterinary Practice to New Hampshire. And she has become a friend, a client and a colleague I can entrust with the training of my other client's four legged fur children. I am proud that she asked me to do an endorsement for her new book ACT—Awareness Centered Training. This book like her others is full of heart filled stories and a wealth of wisdom. Enjoy the journey." Dr. Daniel A Cirnigliaro, DVM, CVA, Dr. Dan's Integrative Pet Hospital.

"Maureen Ross is the most creative person in the doggy world. She is a most passionate advocate for the well-being of dogs. ACT is one seriously interesting book, literally overflowing with oodles of heart-felt, fun, practical, how-to advice that is so different from anything else that you have ever read. ACT is about enjoying living with dogs, learning from dogs, and even more—learning about you. ACT is a must read for every dog owner that wants to explore new horizons, simplify sensory overload, joyfully train their dogs, and get fit too." Dr. Ian Dunbar, PhD, BVetMed MRCVS, Founder of the Association of Pet Dog Trainers, Sirius Pup and James and Kenneth Publishing, Author of numerous books on dog training and behavior.

"I will always remember the first time I met Maureen & Gary; November, 1994 in Orlando, Florida. This was my first seminar with the APDT. Their laughs and kindness attracted me to them. I think they couldn't resist my French accent!

We had a wonderful time! Our training techniques and philosophies were similar and they had Jon-Luc, a Newfoundland dog, who they say, "rescued them." At this time, I owned 6 Newfies. We kept in touch. In November '95 in Chicago, at another APDT seminar, they met my new boyfriend and 2 of my dogs: Bronco & Flash. They fell in love with Flash "The Wonder Dog!" They decided to reserve a puppy out of Flash's next litter. Their dream came true in December 2, '95. Flash had 6 puppies; one of the girls was Sage, who became Moe's pet partner friend and loving companion for 13 years.

They drove from New Hampshire to St. Lazare (near Montreal) to pick up Sage. It was fantastic to share our training tips, ideas, jokes and philosophies.

Maureen and I stay in close touch. Since, we have shared many happy memories at APDT conferences through-out the USA. Presenting a workshop at their training sanctuary, gave me the opportunity to share what I know is true; it is all about relationship.

Since I moved to British Columbia, Maureen and I have helped each other through a lot. Whenever I need them, they are helpful and I feel the same way. Their friendship is a very precious gift.

Train Your Dog, Change Your Life, their first book, should be in every trainer's and dog owner's library!

I know this new edition by Maureen will surpass the first because of life experiences. We live, learn and change. Enjoy your dogs." Monique Charbonnier, Professional Dog Trainer and Behaviorist, Gentle Puppy Training, British Columbia."

"All of my life I've wanted my own German Shepherd dog. When I got Bear, I thought love and basic training was what he needed. I'd never heard of socialization. By age 1, he was a wonderful, loving, well-trained dog. The only problem was that he was aggressive with, and intolerant of any person, or animal, outside of the household. I couldn't take him anywhere for fear I wouldn't be able to control him. After months of searching for a trainer I could trust, I found Maureen and Gary. They have taught me with patience, kindness, support and encouragement.

Through behavior modification, using positive reinforcement, understanding and lots of love and respect, I was able to teach Bear that the world is full of friends for us to meet. I learned to pay attention to Bear's body language as he does to mine. We've met many wonderful people, and accomplished things I never dreamed we could. Bear and I were a Registered Pet Partner Team, followed by Sabrina and now Jake, my Golden Retriever. We have opened programs at several facilities together.

Bear has since crossed Rainbow Bridge. Maureen and I are now best friends, dedicated to enhancing well-being and education with pet assisted therapy. We make a difference. I am very happy that these two wonderful people are my very dear friends.

I encourage you to take a deep breath, relax and enjoy all of Maureen's publications, and Awareness Centered Training, a long awaited for follow-up to Train Your Dog, Change Your Life."— Kathy DeLong, RN, PP, LTE

MEET MAUREEN

MA—Counseling Psychology—Antioch University, Keene, NH

BS—Organizational Management—Leslie University, Cambridge, MA

Board Certified Counselor, Certified Professional Dog Trainer, Yoga Alliance—Registered Yoga Therapist

Licensed Team Evaluator and Instructor, Pet Partner's Program and R.E.A.D.

Founder: Dog Talk Training and Wellness Sanctuary LLC

New England Pet Partners Inc.

Co-Founder of the Pet Wellness Festival

Author: Canine Training and Survival Guide, Train Your Dog, Change Your Life, Daily Doga Inspirations, publications on canine / human relationships

Maureen has presented workshops on dog behavior, family systems and the dog, workshops on domestic abuse and violence (dogs and children) and pet assisted therapy.

Member: National Board of Certified Counselors, Association of Pet Dog Trainers, Yoga Alliance, American Council on Exercise, International Association of Animal Behavior Consultants, Animals and Society, Pet Partners, Reading Education Assistance Dogs, Latham Foundation, New Hampshire Non Profits and Hudson Chamber of Commerce.

www.dogtalk.com, www.newenglandpetpartners.org, www.dailydoga.com

Pinch me! Am I writing another book about my love for dogs and how they have changed my life? Ow, guess that means yes. Thank you for loving and making the world a better place for dogs.

I have loved and shared my life with dogs since I can remember. I used to study dog breeds in the back of Spiegel's catalog, threatening my mother that "when I grew up, I'd get big dogs." True to my word, I have lived with big, small, three-legged, deaf, blind, crazy, aged, pedigreed and mixed.

Forever grateful for their presence in my life, we created moments in our small, backyard jungle that paved a path for my adult passion and career. Dogs lead me to paths I may never have found on my own. Living and learning with dogs continues to change my life on every level.

Oftentimes as a child my plea was "don't hurt my dog." I can still hear meows, although muted, of the kitten that my father dropped down a sewer, calling it a "feral kitten that we can't keep." Thank goodness even then I knew there were better ways.

I was more sensitive and sensible than other kids at school. I attribute some of that to genetics and the good common sense of my mother and grandmother, for allowing me to have pets. From generation to generation, we have the opportunity to learn from the mistakes of others and our own.

What I have learned as a counselor (human and dog) is that all families have skeletons, secrets and stories that are colored with episodes of drama (tragedy, climax, happiness, sadness). Beliefs and core values, passed on from generation to generation, give us a chance to appreciate our history and create change if it is not suitable to our well being.

We have advantages and access to information to help us make informed choices as adults. We have choices to create different lives as we become wiser.

As Dr. Seuss says in *Places You'll Go,* "we have a brain in our head, feet in our shoes, we can steer our life in whatever direction we choose!" I am grateful that I grew up with *Cat in the Hat,* and that it was not thrown in the sewer like my kitten.

Dogs provided me with a safe place, companionship, love, connection and a career. My teenage years and "escape" marriage at nineteen years old, quickly followed by a divorce, had dogs as my protector, partner, friend and therapist. This is huge job description for a dog, so thank you! Dogs need jobs within the scope of their expertise and ability. Dogs go beyond the call of duty when it comes to human emotion.

Thank you to those who echo stories of the "imperfect" family and close connections to dogs and other pets. I empathize. If it helps, the perfect family is an illusion, like the perfect dog. Perfect is whatever it is at that time in our lives. What we do with the experiences matters.

As with enlightenment, we can strive for perfection. We discover that the journey is the path to enlightenment. It is in the mirror, working on goals, eating, playing and loving our dogs.

> What would we have to do with our time
> on Earth if we were perfectly enlightened
> or our dogs perfectly trained?

History repeats itself until someone is brave enough to break the cycle of misunderstanding, violence or ignorance. This includes with pets (or other species) who share our lives. We can hold onto to what is meaningful, let go of what we do not need, and create positive and educated change.

> If we believe in ourselves, change has no
> choice but to positively flow out to others.

Stepping out of the familial box is not easy (homeostasis). I share this because most dogs live and interact with people. Homeostasis simply means we remain status quo even if miserable, scared and unhealthy. We become accustomed to a comfort zone or a stronger status quo. Status quo is okay as long as we are not keeping it that way on purpose or to avoid change.

Many will not trade-up until they experience extreme trauma, danger or hit rock bottom. I have seen dogs in situations of learned helplessness that is directly related to the human's helplessness. Dogs will freeze in fear, not knowing who to trust. It is disheartening and it takes time to build trust again.

Choosing to focus on your positive core values, letting the negative go, and clarifying conflict, is empowering. When we make even a small change in our thinking and behavior, whether it is about family, friends, work or dogs, it can have a positive trickling effect on others—or confuse them.

Change may be met with resistance. Many people spend their lives circling the drain, trying to avoid being flushed. Others realize that they can get out of the sink or take a diver down the drain to see what is on other side.

Survival techniques are learned at an early age for all species in different ways and environments. Conditioning from others happens to all of us, and is unavoidable, especially for infants and puppies. We are born, and someone takes care of and teaches us, with their current knowledge and ways of doing things. This does not mean that it is the only or best way of being for us, or our dogs, as individuals.

I have been with clients who believe they will offend grand-parents or parents, teachers or even neighbors, some who have been deceased for years, if they decide to train their dog in a different way. I encourage them to take a deep breath and take the plunge. A lightning bolt will not strike you dead if you choose to step out of the box, even a little. Most of the time, it is those little steps into the unfamiliar that wake us up and bolster self esteem.

Dogs are excellent at reading body language. If in doubt, become more observant. Dogs have taught me how to listen and observe, scan a room, and read expressions with detail. Growing up, finding hiding places before the storm (dog getting thrown across a room or tied to a door knob and kicked) became a survival (and coping) skill. My little dog and I spent moments inside of an empty cabinet or under an oil truck, waiting for it to be "cleared for safety".

The picture of my life was being painted then. As a counselor and dog behaviorist, I know when to back off from a dog who is fearful, or a person who is angry, all useful instincts. I have a hard time seeing the world in black and white, and was taught that dogs only see in grey, which we know today is not true. Now, I see in vivid colors and the dogs see muted shades of colors. Together, we balance to pleasant mid-tones.

Finding refuge is what we and our dogs do when we are confused, fearful, and oftentimes, wise. Dogs will hide under chairs or beds or back themselves into corners. If dogs perceive a conflict or fearful situation, and this can be someone chasing them to get a toy, they will run, hide or warn.

Being aware of our dog's intrinsic and external body language and vocalizations is not only educational, but bodes well for us when in precarious situations (getting mugged). Dogs send a clear message, in clusters of behavior (body language), that they are scared and confused—"leave me alone, stay back, until you calm down." Stepping aside, backing up, taking a deep breath, and letting angry energy go through a wall is a useful skill in any relationship, career or stressful situation. Head butting only gives us a headache. Step aside and let the "other" put their head (and anger) through a wall.

Dogs have taught me how to listen to my intuition, balance energy, observe thresholds (enough is enough), boundaries and tough love. I have lived with dogs all of my life, so have made mistakes. If I didn't, this book would be boring. I wouldn't have anything significant to offer that is unique, or know that training dogs must start with awareness of our self, then the dog.

The only time I have been bitten was when I was not paying attention to the cues the dogs were giving me and stressed out. It was traumatic for me and the dogs. It took months for me to feel confident again.

The gift was a heightened sense of awareness. Even experienced dog trainers and behaviorists can lose control and get bit in stressful situations with multiple dogs. *It hurts!*

Dogs share our drives like fight or flight, freeze, appease, react or faint from holding our breath too long. Dogs suffer sensory overload, in high intensity, with senses (sight, sound, smell) that are keener than ours.

Almost everything that happens in my relationships with dogs is like living in a house of mirrors. They reflect our experiences and commitment to daily living, learning, understanding and training.

When we are stressed, overwhelmed, overtired or angry, we cannot make sensible decisions. A dog cannot effectively and pleasurably learn in fearful situations, except for how to defend themselves. Too little exercise and too much stress manifests into destructive behavior (chewing, biting, lunging, anxiety, fear), and poor health.

Healthy nutrition and body awareness, and taking several brain breaks through-out the day, with nose-to-navel breathing, gives us clarity and an opportunity to make better decisions that makes living more enjoyable. It is easier to be empathetic and effective when we are calm and present.

A breathing break gives our body and brain a chance to re-energize—putting sensory overload into perspective. Dogs are like sponges, soaking in emotions and stress. Like us, they need time to chill-out after stressful events like pet assisted therapy visits or transitions in life (re-homed, new baby or pet, job change, illness or death).

Dogs are accepting companions, teachers and therapists (in their own way). Remember, they are dogs and a different species. They deserve responsible and mindful advocates for their well-being. In return, they willingly give us even more.

Take a deep breath now. I do not believe in the rosy notion that dogs are unconditional and non-judgmental. They love us more unconditionally and non-judgmentally than humans. We can create drama and stories out of a twig falling to the ground around a relative's foot. Why did that twig fall on her foot instead of mine? I have heard stories that have lasted for generations, including my own, keeping family members estranged and labeled, long after that family member, friend, person or dog is deceased. Does anyone really know what happened? Fact recall gets more skewed and vague as time goes on. If is that important, clarify, then let it go.

Dogs live in the present moment. Wolves or dogs do not hang on to lifelong grudges or revenge. To survive in the wild or a home, dogs use species specific coping and survival skills that work (Pawt 2, Behaviors and Drives and Pawt 4, Body Language and Stress).

Dogs associate in context, (Appendix A, Big Confusing Word Dictionary), remembering situations through associations, but not always in the way that we humans perceive. It benefits us to take a breath and a step back to observe our dogs when they behave in particularly annoying ways like lunging, barking too much and at anything, or digging ridiculously large holes in places we wish they wouldn't. When dogs do something we do not want, in places we prefer they didn't, what happens next in the relationship between human and dog could last a lifetime.

Dogs do something and move on. Whether it's right or wrong in our eyes, our reaction or response should be meaningful and relatable to the volume of the situation. If we are exhausted and our dog digs a little hole, and we erupt, is this in context to the situation?

Empathy is a beautiful world that we should all embrace. The world would be a more peaceful place. I consider myself privileged to be invited into a dog or wolf pack with caution. Amazingly, I am calm. I get to view the world from another's perspective. People who embrace other species as part of the Universe are less self-centered and have more empathy.

Anyway you chew the bone, dogs teach us about ourselves. When whining about our dog's behavior, we become aware of what needs to change. Without trying very hard, we turn out to be more compassionate and patient because we live with dogs. We want them to be healthy, reliable, well trained, listen intently without judgment, keep us company.

Effectively teaching and communicating in an understanding way to our dogs is a lesson that we can transition into other relationships (work, career, family and friends). If we aren't getting something that we want from our dogs or others, then it is back to the house of mirrors, to explore what we are not doing for ourselves to get what we want from them.

Intrinsically, and with insatiable curiosity, I am honored and content when I am in the company of others who enjoy dogs. Genuinely I want to know about their relationships. Often, not a word has to be spoken between beings that live with dogs. It is an "aha—I get it moment." Watching our dogs respond to others can tell us a lot. Dogs are authentic. If the dogs do not like someone or act suspiciously (stay away), I pay attention. If the dog is immediately attracted to someone they meet, in a friendly way, I feel comfortable.

My friend Stella, who passed away at 93 and loved dogs, shared, "it is a knowing that needs no words." So simple, so true.

Dr. Jane Goodall, who I glowingly met, shares in *Reason for Hope*, "if I had one wish it would be to see the world through their eyes (her beloved chimpanzees) if only for a moment. If we do not recognize what is happening when other species are becoming extinct, then we do not recognize our possibility of extinction." When I asked Dr. Goodall where I should "be" during a photo-op, she replied, "Look me in the eyes." I did, and felt an instant connection, without words.

The late Cindy Fischer, M.Ed., TTouch Practitioner, founder of the Pet Wellness Festival, and author of *Pets have a Story to Tell* shared, "animals make me aware of my connectedness with others. In the big picture, we want the same thing, understanding, acceptance and love."

I no longer care what anyone thinks about my passion for dogs. If you love dogs, you know; we may be of different cultures, with diverse causes but we share a common bond—our strong connection to dogs. Living and learning with dogs makes us better people.

Awareness centered training (ACT) is my continuing legacy that I can share with those who want some. Not all of us like the same dessert. To me, dogs are juicy and delicious, metaphorically (I don't eat them)!

Forever connected, forever changed, genuinely embrace each treasured moment with dogs. For dogs, I will do whatever I can to lessen their burden by raising awareness about education, relationship and well-being.

When Pablo Casals reached ninety-five, a young reporter asked him a question: "Mr. Casals, you are ninety-five and the greatest cellist who ever lived. Why do you still practice every day?" Casals replied, "Because I think I'm making progress."

PRELUDE

Welcome to a joyful, easy way of thinking about dog training and well-being. I love dogs and I am not shy about sharing that living and learning with dogs has changed my life. How About You?

Whether you are getting your first puppy, adopting a dog or have been enjoying dogs all of your life (like me), let's take a journey together to share, laugh and create loving, respectful relationships with our dogs, ourselves and others.

An evolved sequel to *Train Your Dog, Change Your Life*, which barked about positive training and relationship, and how we can't change our dog's behavior until we change our own, Awareness Centered Training (ACT) takes this concept and training, *beyond the positive.*

Living and learning with dogs can be a powerful vehicle for change. Cultivating awareness is an opportunity to get to know yourself and your dogs. On a practical level, it helps us to make conscious choices.

We live in a "hurry-up" world. Dogs are large target audience earning billions of dollars in marketing (food, equipment, knowledge, and social media). It can have positive and/or negative effects on our dogs and us!

Along with technology and extreme choices is sensory overload, a new (pseudo) diagnosis popping up at veterinary and mental health clinics. First time puppy parents are excited and confused at the same time with the many choices on how to creatively train, when to train, where to train, what to use, how often, how hard or soft, how loud or quiet, and in what color, size or shape. I know, a long sentence, so imagine what it feels like for a puppy.

When is enough, enough? How many roles are our dogs suppose to fill for us? What do they need to be happy, healthy and confident? How can we help ourselves and our dogs calm the chaos?

Let's explore this together and discover how to reduce anxiety and stress, and bring back the simple joy of living and learning with our dogs, less expensively and effectively.

If you are feeling overwhelmed, ask (notice) your dogs if they are too. Imagine the relief when instead of being adorned with a muzzle collar that makes them go cock-eyed, or a harness that leaves welts in their armpits; they are praised for walking calmly on or off leash.

Imagine when you call them; they gleefully come because they know something good it going happen. Imagine working with your dog in harmony; a smooth flow of asking for something, they respond, and as a team you accomplish the task. Imagine relaxing with a "relaxed" dog.

Are you ready for a positive change that can help you shift energy in any direction you want with your dogs and others? Clearing the clutter and calming the chaos will help create space in our minds. Discovering what our dogs truly need to be their best creates a pathway for a healthy relationship.

Change is not easy, but with awareness centered training, it can be easier! Look at your dog right now. This is your best friend. I don't know about you, but I cherish my best friends. I want them, dog or human, to enjoy being with me.

Do I allow them to walk all over me? No. A respectable balance can be achieved in any relationship with clarity, compassion and confidence. Sometimes we lead and sometimes we follow.

While living with our dogs, we learn about ourselves too. We begin to realize that it doesn't matter how much we spend on something, or how important it is to us, the dog may chew it up or pee on it anyway. Does this sound familiar?

Dogs are authentic. Whether being carried in a fancy tote, or working on a rescue boat with a lifejacket on, what you give is what you get (genetics, nature, nurture and training). Usually, there is no ulterior motive for dogs than to please use and get their needs met. Dogs enjoy working and playing the same way we do if we have a job description and training, and enjoy and qualify for the position.

The exception is humanly and/or culturally controlled like being born and conditioned for a specific purpose or job (working, hearing, seeing, service and therapy). Can we really know if what these dogs do is enjoyable? If they don't know any other life, how do we know? Balance comes to mind. We work all week or at projects and like to enjoy time off to relax and not make decisions. Dogs need this relief for total well-being too. They need a chance to be dogs.

With social media, visuals and instant guides to everything from "training our dogs with a guru" to "seven days to a flat belly", the notion of spending some "real" time socially interacting with a living being is inviting. Dogs can help ground us in reality or they can drive us nuts.

Dogs appreciate the clarity of clear communication, rather than vague notions of what we expect. We can visualize behaviors we want to change, be as positive and happy as clam, but if we don't communicate what we expect of them clearly, it is like taking an 1800 mile trip without any directions.

Awareness centered training is clarity and relief for the dog, and cognitive for us. Even if you are a first time dog parent, simply pretending you know what you are doing, will make a difference to a dog. Our minds guide our words and body. Eventually, with guidance we can teach what we want our dogs to do.

Learn as you go to get the timing, skill and direction—spot on. This takes practice. In the mean time, dogs will appreciate your confidence of clear communication, teaching them what to do, when, where and for how long. Think of it as networking. One behavior connects to another.

Many great leaders have shared that although they had a vision, skill and determination, what made them successful was planning, flexibility and confidence in themselves and others. Dogs respect confidence in our voices and body language, not bullying. Bullies eventually get decked, put in prison or live alone.

As a business leader, one has to be prepared for a variety of challenges, cultures, and differences in learning ability and skill. Employee's strengths and limitations are ferreted out, and hopefully a good match is made to benefit the organization and the employee. Dogs are as varied as employees and a different culture entirely. Viewing it this way helps to put it into perspective.

Consider this for a moment. How often have you been misunderstood (relative, friend, store clerk, health care professional, employee)? Have you ever been on automatic control while driving your car, cooking dinner, listening to someone or training your dog? You arrive at a destination but can't remember how you got there. It can be dangerous driving a car; we can burn ourselves cooking dinner and ruin a well-planned meal. We can be ignored by the other person when we want them to listen.

Highlight this with a neon yellow Sharpie when it comes to training our dogs. They begin learning the moment they are born. They live in the present moment and have keen senses (hearing, sight, smell) that enable them to be aware of what is going on (peripherally) around them, like a panoramic x-ray.

When they join our family life, we are not just teaching them, they are teaching us. The bonus is that we can transition what we learn with our dogs into other areas of our lives (career, friends, family, work and play).

Dog training approaches have evolved, for the better, over the last decade. Positive training is, without a doubt, one of the most gratifying and popular approaches. Most training classes, books and online media has evolved, using gentle and positive approaches like clicker training, food lure training, and motivational training.

Awareness centered training has evolved my training classes and with private clients. Still positive and gentle in approach, it focuses on being present in the moment, breathing, teaching manners and respecting differences (dog and human). It is a guided approach similar life coaching for humans. We can have all the goals in the world, but if we are not aware of our skills or how to put out plan into action, nothing happens! We remain stagnant, become complacent and sometimes depressed.

Nothing fuels the creative process and training our dogs, like a spacious and observant mind, and the freedom to express ourselves without retribution or judgment. Amazingly, dogs and people learn quicker. Many leave with the same feeling you get after an exercise or yoga class or whatever gives you a feeling of relaxation.

Positive is relative depending on the individual's perception, their skill set, goals, culture, environment, and most importantly, the dog. What I have found interviewing families and their dogs, trainers and other behaviorists is that oftentimes we get so hung up on the positives and the equipment that we lose sight of what we truly expect and need from our dogs. If we are not aware of what our dogs are doing, or what we want them to do and why, how can we meaningfully and effectively teach it?

We can't change what we are not aware of. We can't change what we are aware of without action, regardless of how positive we feel. Let's explore. Training is seldom just about the dog or what the dog is doing to us. Dogs are not doing anything we are not allowing them to do. We teach others, and our dogs, how to treat us.

First, we need to be clear and confident about what we want, and how we will get it (planning). We cannot do that if we are stressed out, glued to a cell phone, or doing the banshee dance because our dog ate the shoes we left out of the closet. If someone left something I enjoy right in front on me, I would grab it.

ACT is integrated into daily living and learning with dogs. That's where we live most of the time with our dogs, not in a classroom. All you need are your dog's natural behaviors, skills, and essentials for well-being. The rest is real meat on the dog bone and choice.

The bonus is enhanced well-being and a balanced relationship with your dog, yourself and others. Give yourself permission to unleash (or not) your dog, practice creating a space in your mind, and manage stress for a healthier (and longer) life.

ACT can be used indoors or outdoors, in class, at play groups or when visiting a friend or family member. There is no timeline. You decide how fast or slow you want to go. Be mindful that teaching puppies earlier makes life easier later on (for you). Puppies are sponges that soak in everything they see, hear and smell. This does not mean that our dogs, or we, can't continue learning. I hope you do because that is what rejuvenates our brain cells. Dogs who are bored become lethargic, depressed and destructive. Keeping our brains and bodies active, and modifying when necessary, improves our quality of life.

ACT is non-competitive and uncomplicated. Isn't that a relief? Think inside or outside of the box—or both. No guru or special training equipment needed, but indulge if you choose. There are times when dogs are safer enclosed, on a leash, and supervised. All dogs should be wearing their identification tag, just in case they slip away. Micro-chipping is an alternative (small rice size implant).

ACT encourages joyful easy training (JET) techniques that are used every day like eating, playing and exercising. JET is the "skills" that you will practice with your dog. We will cover housetraining, crate training, and important dog savvy, good manners behaviors and lots more.

Learn about every day must haves to create a happy, healthy and confident dog, while getting healthy (Pawt 6, Dogs, Balls and Balance).

Does your dog have balls? Embrace a sense of humor, because it lightens attitude. When we breathe and smile, our internal body responds in kind. You will notice in photos throughout the book that I am using fitness balls. We train and evaluate pet therapy teams. This helps us "get fit" while getting dogs use to things that roll and bounce.

We benefit from being in different positions with the dogs stretching and balancing. Training from a variety of positions, as you will learn with the *Networking Grid,* (Pawt 5), creates dependable dogs that are familiar to sights, sounds and smells, in a variety of environmental situations, whether by your side or from a distance.

Socially enhancing behaviors like gentle, forward, back-up, wait, take-it, leave-it and enough, take a few minutes to teach and can save you a lifetime of grief.

Focused training (FT) teaches us to wake-up and save time to smell the lilies. The core of FT is capturing and shaping behaviors that we desire in the present moment. Stress and boredom decrease because we are not repeating—we are relieving. When we are present, centered and focused, the dogs learn much quicker.

Socialization and manners (SAM, Pawt 3), must be on every responsible dog parent's agenda. SAM creates reliable, confident dogs that enjoy life with other people and dogs. A few times a week will harvest enormous benefits. How much, where and for how long, is as individual as the dog.

Relaxation Training (RT) teaches our dogs "self-control" and how to relax on cue. Even when we are lazy, our dogs can be great and learning. RT is an integral part of ACT before, during and after a training session. Teaching our dogs to rely on us in any situation is empowering for us and less stressful for the dog.

Rather than "me Alpha, you Dog", we are a team
and can yield to each other with respect?

Being aware and present, balancing energy, focusing and relaxing helps people and dogs learn how to be alert but unfazed in the midst of madness. Dogs get into trouble when they are not trained in an understanding way, left alone when they shouldn't be or are bored. They are not getting enough exercise.

The Positively Essentials, (Pawt 3) is all you need to raise a puppy into a healthy, contented and trustworthy adult dog, regardless of lifelong goals. Training should be flexible, fair and forgiving. Consider how you would like to be taught when learning something new. If we remind ourselves of how it feels to not have a clue, while trying very hard to figure it out, then we can empathize with how a dog feels in unfamiliar situations.

Discover what turns you and your dog on. How do dogs use breathing and body language to relax themselves and others? Easily get centered, in the a few seconds, and maintain an inner sense of peace, through-out the day.

Develop increased communication, listening and "brain power" skills that will reflect in all of your relationships.

Feel the rhythm when you connect with your dog; like dancing with a partner you've practiced with for years, or dance with yourself, that's okay too.

Rather than regimented coursework, enjoy a flow, training from Level 1, to 2 and 3. Move as quickly as you like or take an easy-going approach. The natural and necessary tasks that you do every day for your dog will become "teaching tools". With practice, it is as easy as brushing your teeth.

Automatically learn how to sense energy shifts and redirect behaviors (barking, jumping, lunging and growling) into more suitable pathways.

Yes, we can yield to our dogs, and they to us, without fear of losing leadership or alpha status. Become aware of the training tempo, like dancing with a partner or driving a car. You need to know where are going, and put on a signal, then turn.

Reap the benefits of healthy living and well being because of the enduring friendship with your dog that is created out of kindness and respect, not fear or myths.

In relationship and as a team, you have choices and freedom of expression to make mistakes, learn and create change. Take a dive and meet a challenge.

You are always on a path to somewhere. Where is it taking you and your dog?

INTRODUCTION
Living and Learning with Dogs

We have been living and learning with dogs (Canis Lupus Familiaris) since the dawn of man. Thousands of years ago, in the mists of prehistory, humankind made friends with the wolf. For the first time, humans encountered another being they neither ate nor got eaten by. The friendship formed in that far-away time and continues to flourish today to the tune of billions of dollars and over 400 breeds globally.

The relationship between humans and canines has always been seductive and distinctive. No two species have formed such a close and mutually necessary bond. Fortunately today, we are more educated, and most treat dogs with respect, as a different species, NOT a lower ranking one on the food chain. Even bottom feeders in the deepest depths of the ocean or earth are balancing our eco-system.

When we pocket our egos and take off our blinders, we recognize that humans are animals too. If we are higher ranking, than along with that comes wisdom, empathy, mindfulness and compassion. We should know better.

According to tradition, a dog saved by Noah discovered a leak in the ark. The loyal dog plugged the leak (and saved the ark) by sticking his nose into the hole. *It reminds me of the Aflac Duck who plugs the hole in the boat so his people don't drown.* This selfless act has chilled the dog's nose forever. We all would like to believe that our dogs would save us or at least try.

We like to think that dogs are unconditional. I believe that they are conditional within the hierarchical pack. Dogs are not judgmental but they have strong imprints, associations and preferences. I have observed time and again, a dog's preference of one person to another, this toy or that food.

Mythical stories give humans the privilege of capturing the essence of our relationship with dogs. From the earliest days of human history, dogs have been our helpers and friends. The first dogs to be domesticated were probably wolves trained by prehistoric hunters to help them track game. More likely it was survival so they tolerated each other's company, in much the same way we do today except that our dogs tolerate our quirks more.

We know that the DNA of a wolf and a dog are the same. After meeting Dr. Jane Goodall, she convinced me that my ancestor is the ape. Like Dr. Goodall, but with dogs, I feel naked in the streets when I am not around dogs for long periods.

Thousands of generations of selective breeding and engineering by humans led to the development of the dog breeds we recognize today, some good and not so good for dogs. The Chihuahua is as much an ancestor of the wolf as an Irish Wolfhound.

It is believed the Athenian general Xenophon wrote the first book on dogs more than 2,300 years ago. Later, a Greek historian Arrian wrote a guidebook on the care of hunting dogs. He advised, "Always pat your Greyhound's head after he catches a hare and say, "well done, Cirrus! Well done, Bonnas! Bravo, my Horme . . . for like men of generous spirit they love to be praised."

This echoes true today with social media, books, movies and reality TV about dogs and their relationships with humans. We see a dog in a movie and want THAT dog. We view a whisperer or guru and want to train that way. Magical thinking and unrealistic goals get humans and dogs into trouble. TV can be educational, but keep it in context. These shows employ teams of people and actors to assist in making that "perfect" 1-hour show.

In ancient Egypt, dogs were venerated as symbols of fidelity and watchfulness. It is believed that the Egyptians first called Sirius the "Dog Star," since that star's appearance on the horizon coincided with the annual floods that made life bloom along the Nile.

Ancient Ethiopians selected a dog as their king. The royal canine signaled his approval or disapproval of ministers and officers *with licks or growls*. The dog's will was followed by all. Has it changed? Consider dogs wearing million dollar diamond collars, tutus and living in their own Beverly Hills mansion. When our dog's lick us don't we feel loved? When they growl are we not scared?

The Greek mathematician Pythagoras, a firm believer in reincarnation, was a dog worshiper, not whisperer. When his followers were on their deathbeds, Pythagoras would hold a dog at their mouths, hoping to capture the escaping soul in the animal's body. I saw that recently on Game of Thrones.

We have many requests for registered therapy dog teams to assist in home, health and hospice settings, to ease the passing of humans. We aren't holding our dogs up to catch souls, but intuitively know that dogs instinctively comfort people in transition. Their keen senses smell sickness and know when death is near.

Dogs fight beside our soldiers in wars. Today, dogs are heroes rather than expendables at the end of the journey. We recognize and honor their noble efforts.

Dogs have a profound influence as catalysts that break barriers of communication. Dr. Temple Grandin shares in *Animals make us*

Human, "Dogs do more than that. They impact our lives so much that when they are sick or die, we grieve more than we do for human relatives and friends." What a powerful message.

Dogs drive target markets making corporations extremely wealthy (food, toys, equipment). It is a more than a little scary for new puppy owners to be faced with 70/30 rather than 30/70 (30 percent marketing and 70 percent education, relationship and well-being).

Dogs enhance well-being and education in healthcare facilities, schools and libraries reading education assistance dogs. Several teams were asked to come to the University of New Hampshire during senior exams to help calm students. Turns out, we calmed the staff too. Management thought there was a fire drill because the offices were empty. Dogs are magnets, attracting people to them for diversion and connection. Relaxed dogs can calm people.

Dogs detect drugs, seizures, see and hear for us and protect. They make the world a safer place to discover. They lead us on adventures that I personally would not venture on my own.

> *When we find ourselves at a crossroads, we don't*
> *know what's ahead. That's living. When we are at*
> *an impasse, someone is angry, or our dogs don't*
> *do what we expect, we can use this opportunity to*
> *wake up, moving from ambiguity into awareness.*

For dogs, I join hands in connection with anyone who is aware that dogs change our lives for the better. We are responsible, as their advocates, to ensure their shorts lives are lived humanely and with the best possible well-being. Whether working dogs or lap dogs, dogs deserve a chance to be healthy dogs.

PAWT 1

Awareness Centered Training (ACT)

Let's begin by exploring what dogs mean to us, and how interdependent our relationship with dogs has become, since the dawn of man. Allow yourself to breathe into this with an open mind. Free your mind of anxiety. Explore new paradigms and create new patterns, with your dog's help, side-by-side.

We will review "pertinent" behavior history, but not to the point of nausea or boredom. Why bother? You can find it on Wikipedia, and the Internet Explorer, colored with many stories, opinions and research. Some make sense, and others are mythical or wishful thinking.

I have summarized what has made a difference to me, while living and learning with a variety of dogs and assorted people. Visit the "Big Confusing Behavior Terms Dictionary" in Appendix A, when you feel like it. No rush! It isn't going anywhere. If you download the E-version of ACT, please don't read, text and drive. Your dog will miss you. Do like us on Facebook—please!

Allow me to offer you freedom of expression, and an opportunity to think inside or outside of the box. Use what speaks to you, placing the rest in a safe place for later use. You may decide like I did several years ago, that enough is enough. I watch, listen, participate, try a few new ideas or pieces of equipment out, then decide what works best for me and the dogs!

It is of little relevance to the dogs, or me, if a whisperer, guru or duly noted distributor of dog training and equipment products, says it works. I have to clarify, see, use and experience it for myself, and then get the dog's opinion.

How dogs enjoy learning and how I feel when I am teaching is important to me. I am not interested in results if it means damaging my relationship with the dogs.

Doing what matters most, for you and your dog, is as individual as dog breeds, shapes, colors and cultures. If I inspire one person to change their life while training, living and learning with dogs, my goal is accomplished. I have made a difference.

Honestly, I am happy to get up close and personal, within reason, to share a range of emotions and love that we have for dogs.

I am one hundred percent sure that dogs shift energy when they walk into a room (pet assisted therapy). Dogs are catalysts for breaking barriers of communication.

I am honored to be a voice, and interpreter, for dogs who help change lives. We can do the same for them with awareness, education, relationship and well-being. I love dogs. How about you?

Intervention for Recovering Dog Junkies
Said with a Deep Breath and a Smile!

Evolution is amazing and mine has been walking a path with dogs from childhood on. A collection of learning experiences has been harvested from the interaction, contribution and feedback of students, colleagues, friends and, ultimately, the dogs!

I am a self-confessed recovering dog junkie. I would have too many if I was not aware of quality of life. Over the years, I have made mistakes and turned them into learning opportunities, but not without pain and agony.

Dogs have taught me to think outside of the box and that is okay to remain in the box too. I have learned from four legged, three legged, deaf and blind dogs. They have graciously suffered with disease and died in my arms with pure forgiveness.

I empathize with the heart-squeeze of loss (Pawt 8, Celebrating Life). It may not be that "extreme" for everyone, but most multiple dog (or pet) owners and trainers, will relate to those "what was I thinking" or "how can I go on" moments or years.

When it comes to dogs, we defer to the heart, losing all ability to make sensible decisions. We see that dog, puppy or kitten and just know that we are the one who can change their lives. *The truth is—they change ours.*

When we first began the Dog Training and Wellness Sanctuary, we thought about changing the name to *Woof-Poof, Instant Dog Training*. There is still magical thinking today. Society can present a fantasyland for the express purpose of getting us to love, buy or adopt dogs. Don't be fooled. A lot of hard work and effort goes into TV dog stars and most live ideal lifestyles. Adoption, in my opinion, is the same as buying. We are adding a living being to the family. We have had many adopted dogs, and it is just as costly if they need medical and psychological attention. Revolving door adoption is out of the question because it doesn't work and the dog suffers, although I would rather see a dog returned to a shelter or foster care than remain in "bad match" situations.

I bow down to people like Sue Sternberg and others, who are working diligently to educate and create better adoption programs and holistic environments. Dogs are stressed when in transition. True colors generally do not present themselves until the dog is settled into a new home. We need to be vigilant with assessment, being sure that a dog is appropriately matched with a family or someone more experienced. Otherwise, it is not win–win, which is the goal. It is lose—lose and generally the dog dies.

*Be sure the heart string is connected to the brain
stem before buying or adopting a puppy / dog.
The dog may be adorable. Be sure that energy,
ability, education and finances are available
before adding a living being to your life.*

I have lived with many dogs, large, small, adopted and bought specifically because I loved the breed and wanted to challenge myself in competition. At any one time, we had five dogs. This is mild in comparison to some. We have been through thousands of dollars for treatments for cancer, grieved until our eyes bled, and been caught (YES I ADMIT THIS) in the middle of a dog fight brought on by stress mine and the dogs.

Dogs can and will fight if not compatible and managed. People can get hurt, especially children and smaller dogs. I have been dragged down the road on my face by an adopted Newfie (fifteen years ago). The good news is I refused to let go and had a free facial (exfoliation). Jon-Luc ended up in commercials like Timberland, American Express and Bruce Weber's, Gentle Giants, a book about Newfoundlands. He was my "becomes a behaviorist" teacher.

My heart-smart message to recovering dog junkies like me is that unless you are financially comfortable, have help, and can afford unexpected treatment or other things life may toss your way, then take a deep breath before adding multiple dogs (or pets) to your house and family. Explore your lifestyle and what the dog's lifestyle will be like first (Pawt 3, Multiple Pets).

Having a gaggle of dogs at once gave me experience. Having a peaceable pack is bliss. Before considering adding a dog, there are considerations to explore:

1. Are you financially and emotionally in a place where you can make a positive difference for this dog? Do you have a nest egg put aside for unknowns?
2. Are your other pets in a healthy place?
3. Are you sure they will accept this dog or cat? There are no guarantees.

The blunt reality is that you can't be positively sure that dogs or cats will get along. Be mindful that when you add a pet, it changes the life of your current ones. You will need to manage their interactions until you are sure that it is safe. If it turns out that they will never accept one another (like a divorce), then you may have tough decisions to make on lifetime management or re-homing a pet.

When the heart tugs, connect it to the brain. Visualize it if it helps. The more you know yourself and your dogs, the wiser the choices. If all the dots connect, and you have time, money and conveniences to share with many pets, than from one recovering dog junkie to another, go for it!

Now, let's take in a deep breath and enjoy the journey . . .

Using this Book with Visuals and Websites

There is no right or wrong way to learn, just different ways. Once upon a time they use to tell us not to teach our dogs to sit if we going to show them in competition. They use to say that we need to teach puppies by six months, and only one behavior at a time. Look, puppies and dogs are learning all the time anyway, so if you can multi-task and teach a puppy to flow from stand, to sit, to down, to relax on your side, then this is four behaviors, and bravo! Do it again with music playing, holding a delicious treat, while sitting on a big ball making funny faces and WOW. Now they are use to you looking goofy on a ball, with music playing and getting a treat. What a positive association. To get clarity and strong behaviors, yes, you will have to focus on that behavior. More later . . .

Some of us enjoy audio, others visual, and most do well with blended learning. Start at the beginning, where you will discover the basics of Awareness Centered Training (ACT). Flow into Levels 1, 2 and 3 (detailed in Pawt 5).

Know that you can back stroke to Level 1 or 2 anytime. The journey will likely be three steps forward, two steps back, but you are always one step ahead if you are focused, committed and relaxed.

Embark on this adventure with an open mind. Explore the integrative alternatives that are included in all levels to use daily doing what comes naturally, like eating, playing and living. Create your own dynamic sequences focusing on what you want your dog to do, not what you want them not to do. If you don't know, find out.

Listen to your intuition and the dog's instinct. If something does not speak to you or your dog, try a different approach that feels good, but try.

I invite you to my websites and you tube channels listed at the back of the book. Vignettes are being added to collaborate with ACT, like *Doggy Diner* (Pawt 3) and *Dogs, Balls and Balance* (Pawt 6) training. Be mindful that a sense of careful humor (do not laugh when your dog knocks someone over), and a deep breath, can lighten almost any tense situation.

Whenever your training relationship with your dog meets an impasse, stop, pause, breathe, and return to the last successful place. If that happens to be sitting on the floor, eyes closed, with your dog lying on his or her back, then that is where you need to be at this moment. If it is rolling in the dirt or playing catch to expend energy, then honor it.

Moving forward from one training posture / goal to the next will only be as successful as you and your dog are focused, present and meaningful. Ask yourself, "How am I feeling today?" Ask your dog, "How are you today? Is this a good time to learn something new?" Ask how meaningful or necessary this is for me and my dog.

I encourage you to laugh, explore, and use your imagination while living and learning with dogs. As shared, humor is the most effective survival mechanism. Like breathing, when we giggle, the body releases "feel-good" endorphins. If something does not feel right, practice intuition (your gut feeling) and intention (objective). It is okay to say, "This isn't working for me and my dogs today." Even taking a 5-minute brain break and time-out can reinvigorate you.

You are the driver of the bus. You can think in or out of the box. You can go as slow or as fast as you like. There is no timeline for learning. However, as I have shared, puppies are sponges that soak up information quickly. If you are not teaching them, the environment or someone else will. May as well drive the bus or be the navigator.

Earlier is easier, but does not mean that older or adopted dogs can't learn. That would be like saying that the predominate population of baby boomers are inept. We know that this is not true medically or intellectually. Dogs and humans have different levels of resiliency, health, quality of life, and attitude that determine how well they adapt to learning and change.

Truthfully, I want ACT to be a positive book for your tool box that teaches awareness. I do not expect that anyone will read right through the book or e-book, like a juicy novel. I feel strongly that this will be a "go-to" resource through-out your dog's life and into the next.

To be aware, we have to be awake to the statistics from the American Society for the Prevention of Cruelty to Animals (United States). Nationwide, we have on average (2011) 78.5 million dogs. 5-7 million are in shelters. 3-4 million are euthanized every year, a reduction from 8-10 million, but still far too many. This is not counting cats and other species. The largest majority of dogs relinquished to shelters are three years old and under. The reason is not aggression or bad genes. It is a lack of education and responsible dog care. Wearing blinders won't help. Being responsible, making sensible, informed decisions and training our dogs will help.

Joyful Easy Training (Pawt 5) is the core of ACT. Being aware of when the dog is doing what we want, and quickly snap shooting the behavior with praise, is joyful and easy. You can train anywhere you are with your dog (bathroom, kitchen, bedroom, family room, or car), at any time, using this simple, effective approach.

Level 1—Beginning, Level 2—Moderate, and Level 3—Challenging are guidelines, at varying levels of intensity. Notice that there are *integrative alternatives* at each level. These give you a combination of *focused training* to learn specific behaviors, and *relaxed training* that is included daily while caring for their needs.

When we are aware, focused and relaxed, training
and learning becomes natural, easier and enjoyable.
We become less stressed and healthier.

Puppies begin learning the moment they are born. We do not teach them how to sit, stand, yawn, lie down, or pee and poop. We teach them when, where, for how long, and because we need them to live in harmony with us and our lifestyle. We do not teach everything they need to know, for a lifetime, with a six or eight week training class. Classes are a good place to learn foundational skills—with a good teacher.

You can be your dogs "good teacher". Joyfully shaping behaviors we desire, in the moment, and while doing what comes naturally, like eating, playing and pooping makes sense. Creating a reliable and respectful relationship with our dogs is, I hope, why you are reading this. It is all about teamwork.

Be creative, take a deep breath, and please turn off the electronics for awhile. If I can do it, you can do it! Dogs, and most humans, learn quicker when centered and calm.

We all have strengths and limitations. Some of us are better at finance and engineering, while others are more prolific at being creative (arts, theater, and writing). Dogs have differences in capabilities too; mainly in the way they use their senses that are keen beyond human comprehension. Did you know that a dog's olfactory (sniffing) is 75 times greater than ours? This can put the environment into perspective. It is like sniffing in techni-color.

Honoring these senses and putting dogs to work by having them sniff out and find something of significance, channels energy into positive outlets. Be the director of your training episodes every day.

Living in a House of Mirrors

Sage advice comes in many forms, sometimes when we least expect it. Consider it a surprise gift, like getting an unexpected check in the mail from an anonymous donor. It may drive you nuts wanting to know who sent it. Simply enjoy it when it pops up. As we become more aware, we notice "awakening" messages more frequently. The soft messages, like little whispers, float by us frequently. Sometimes we hear the swish, like a soft breeze. Harder messages come in loud bangs (accidents, illness, death and other transitions).

When our dogs do things that bother us behaviorally, it is like living in a house of mirrors. Try not to take it personally or judge your dog or self. Instead, notice when the same behavior happens repeatedly and what is going on when it does.

Sometimes we are afraid to upset the apple cart or too tired. Other times, we are wearing blinders so we pretend not to see when our dog is doing something obnoxious like growling at people while we are petting or holding them.

Our lives can become a status quo, and that's okay, as long as we aren't keeping it that way on purpose, like to control someone or a situation or live in bliss ignorance.

With crystal clear clarity, the progress you are making with your dog will reflect back to you. It is like living in a house of mirrors

Socialization and Manners) (SAM), in Pawt 3 should be on every puppies "awareness" calendar. We will teach behaviors like stand-stay, sit-stay, down-stay, come, take-it, leave-it and relax, as well as more creative ones, like how to be instantly *Calm in Chaos*, one of many publications that you are welcome to at my website, www. dogtalk.com. There you will find other articles that may be helpful like *Housetraining at a Glance* to post on your refrigerator. In addition, ACT will be available online from Amazon and Barnes & Noble for your e-readers.

If you have any questions, you can email me (Maureen) at maureenr@dogtalk.com. Be mindful that I need to earn a living, so there is a charge for online or in-person private coaching beyond generalized questions. I have an initial lifestyle intake that is nonthreatening, informative, and gives you an opportunity to explore your concerns and dog's behaviors. Private coaching time is used for an individualized behavioral modification plan.

Online dog behavior coaching is limited to general concerns. For deep seated behaviors, I strongly encourage cultivating a relationship with a good trainer or behaviorist in your area.

Please note that ACT will help you prevent, manage and resolve most of your dog related behavioral concerns. Refer to *Behavior Problems and Uncomplicated Solutions in Pawt 8*. All solutions are win–win, non–aversive and require practice and commitment to change.

If there is a boulder blocking your path, go around. If there is a dog peeing on your carpet, pulling on a leash, chewing unmentionables, stressed out, unhealthy or not getting along with children or other pets, enjoy this path to awareness, joyful training and positive change!

My intention is to empower you and your dogs to make sage choices for your health and well-being. Come on give it a try. You have nothing to lose and a lot to gain. Where is your dog? Gleefully call like you are going on a good adventure. Let's go and grow!

Training Your Dog Can Change Your Life!

Training styles, reading materials, and tools make life easier with dogs in some ways. In other ways, it can be overwhelming and stressful. When is enough, enough? Fortunately, in the last ten years, teaching methods have improved when it comes to dogs and children. We know that every species is unique and individual. Therefore, learning has to be distinctive too.

When I wrote *Train Your Dog, Change Your Life* people looked at me like I was crazy, thinking, "Oh no, a Tony Robbins for the dog world". People and trainers loved dogs, but weren't exactly training in a way that related to the "real world living". Most were not convinced that by training their dogs, their life could change. Instead, they wanted an "obedient" dog. My question back then was and still is, "what does that mean for you and how are you going to achieve it, especially in a one hour class each week?"

Today, we know that dogs do, in fact, and with resounding heroism as times, change our lives! There is no way dogs can't change our lives unless we are unconscious. The tide has turned, so let's ride the wave.

We form strong and emotional connections with our dogs that bring us happiness, sadness, fear and love. To form any relationship requires an awareness, education, relationship, well being and empathy. Dogs teach us that no matter what we do, they will still love us, most of the time. What other species does this?

My intention with ACT is to offer possibilities that are not traditionally laid out, aside from the fact that dogs are happier when they know what their place (and job) is in the pack.

With an insatiable curiosity, I have tried a variety of training techniques and equipment. Some work well with one dog and not with another, one person and not another. Is this a surprise? Our society has been discovering this in our school systems for decades. For example, does a child have attention deficit disorder or bored because the curriculum isn't stimulating?

> *"Dogs are my favorite role models. I want to work like a dog, doing what I was born to do with joy and purpose. I want to play like a dog, with total, jolly abandon. I want to love like a dog, with unabashed devotion and complete lack of concern about what people do for a living, how much money they have, or how much they weigh. The fact that we still live with dogs, even when we don't have to herd or hunt for our dinner, gives me hope for humans and dogs."*
> *—Oprah Winfrey*

Looking at the "whole picture", the bigger question might be, "Is it relatable to me, my dogs, lifestyle and well being?" I prefer to look at my relationship with the dogs as teamwork. We have boundaries, goals and consequences for "our" behavior, not just "their" behavior.

We get to know each other while rolling in the dirt just as much as in more focused and formal training. We form a mutually respectful and joyful living and working relationship where I yield and they yield. Like any relationship, it has its peaks and valleys.

Well-meaning networks are springing up worldwide to rehome dogs. I use to have inflated goals of saving elephants, wolves, dolphins, horses and dogs. Realistically, I know I can't do this alone. What I can do is make a difference for one dog at a time.

My goal is to meet each dog and owner where they are at, in that moment, whether scary or not, and to help them slow down, but also wake up! We cannot rehabilitate a rehomed dog that has been on the streets for six months, until we balance stress levels and assess its "true colors." This can take months. We can't instantly lose twenty pounds either. It's enchanted thinking. Physically and chemically, neither is possible.

Whether adopted or a puppy, consider not just training but awareness centered training. Rather than going through the motions unconsciously, visualize what you expect, breathe and notice when your puppy / dog is doing exactly what you want anyway. Let them know with praise or the magic of your smile.

> *"I have more in common with animal people. I find myself disappointed with those who are not interested in animals. They lack a certain warmth and tend to be a little self-centered. Animal people have empathy—this isn't just me talking now. Research has shown this to be true."—Betty White*

Living and Learning in the Here and Now
(Where dogs live all the time)

Let me offer some relief with an opportunity to let go of the timeline mentality, especially with dogs. They do not mind. Dogs are masters of authenticity and live in the here and now. In the same way that we become accustomed to living in a structured way, they do too. The issues with dog behaviors begin when "we" lose sight of this. Knowing that what happens even 3-seconds ago does not matter to the dog, paves the way for an opportunity to practice prevention. Then teach. What do you want the dog to do?

As you become more aware of this, learn to take advantage of behaviors offered voluntarily every day, like watching us, walking slowly, and sitting, lying down or bringing our slippers to us in exchange for their toy.

My observation over many years of working in group and private sessions is that many still expect dogs to instantly know what they are suppose to do, or have done, and why. Dog parents repeatedly assume that the dog is "crazy" because they don't know they aren't supposed to chew the stuffing out of the sofa. Humans will remain upset for hours or days and leave the dog lose in the house for episode two. We are creatures of habit, as you will learn (Pawt 8, Separation Anxiety). We can change with awareness.

Dogs show us with sparkling clarity and with their behavior responses what is needed, meaningful or not. Connecting with our dogs is the first step in teaching or resolving issues.

The following case example is a true story with names changed. It is for educational guidance as you begin your journey into ACT.

Case Example: Suzie loves her two dogs. They live an ideal life, not wanting for anything materialistic. The dogs are healthy, happy and reasonably well-behaved. Like many, Suzie watches TV and uses Internet Explorer. She enters a session and rolls the scroll of what she would like her dogs to do. The goals sound like they come directly from a famous training book entitled, *How to have a Positively Obedient Dog in Five Minutes*. I don't know if there is a book like this, but it sounds inviting. Like many, including myself at times, Suzie is vulnerable to TV personalities, some who are cute. They seem to know what they are doing with a script and resolve issues in one episode (not). Whether it applies to real life or long-term results is anybody's guess. If at least one dog or owner is enlightened, then perhaps it is worth it.

After weeks of training classes, including some private coaching, I noticed Suzie's disappointment when one of her dogs would not down-stay. The response was frequently the same. Suzie would request a "down-stay", and Morgan would lie down and get up. Stay was a challenge. We covered every possible opportunity including "spot-on" capturing of the "down-stay" with praise. Suzie knew what to do, her timing was good, but her motivation was questionable. She laughs or says, "Oh well", when her dog gets up and follows her. Although laughing, the stress escalates. It turned into a habitual parody.

The stalemate with Morgan's down-stay, or any behavior we inspire to teach our dogs, may surprise you. This is a valuable learning experience, not only for Suzie, but anyone working with dogs. Dogs live in the here and now. They instinctually sense if the situation is meaningful. Most of the time, we have the intuitive and intrinsic abilities already. We can learn the skills with guidance of a good teacher or approach. There is an even more important aspect to this teaching and learning called "awareness of the situation at hand".

Eventually, I knew that it was time to become more direct. I had Suzie's trust so I asked, "Is it true that you want Morgan to down-stay anywhere, any time? Is it that meaningful to you? Why do you think he doesn't do it here and now?" I asked her to "not answer immediately. Take a moment, breathe, and be honest. How often does Morgan lie down at home? How many other wonderful behaviors does he do that you love?"

Suzie sat for a moment in silence, which six weeks prior would have been a twitchy and major challenge. She feels she needs to be doing something with Morgan, and I suspect others in her life, all the time.

Silence can be uncomfortable, but dogs prefer it. Suzie genuinely shared, "Morgan is a great dog. He does many wonderful things. When my mother was sick, he was by my side with her. When he lies down at home, I praise him all the time. I lost a dog recently and I am still grieving." She continued, "Emotions have been running deep lately. I guess it isn't that meaningful for me that he does it right now. I think it's funny when he doesn't, but I still want him too when I ask."

There are many key phrased that are key like, "praise all the time" and "it's funny". Most importantly, Suzie was beginning to recognize that it was not that meaningful to her whether Morgan lay down for 30 seconds or three hours. She admitted enjoying have the dogs around even when company came over. She said the dogs were polite and usually lay down anyway.

Suzie felt relieved at being able to work this through. She noticed the conflicting messages she gave Morgan by laughing when he got up and walked away after being told to, "down-stay". It was good for a comedy act, but if the goal was to have Morgan lie down at Grandma's or somewhere else, and stay, then Suzie would have to focus this behavior in a meaningful way and with clarity and commitment.

At that time, I asked Suzie to get up, calmly call Morgan and take a walk around the room, while paying attention to her breathing. I asked her to sit on the floor, on a blanket, and ask Morgan to down-stay. I asked her to say, "stay" and to not laugh if he got up, simply ask him again to "down-stay". She didn't have to worry. Suzie got up and Morgan remained in a down-stay. He didn't move for the rest of the session. Morgan can easily offer a down-stay if that is truly what Suzie wants.

The message we give to our dogs needs to be meaningfully conveyed. When we let go of fixation and stress, and decide what is meaningful at this time, and ask our dogs in a genuine way for a realistic and learned behavior, we get it.

The intensity and boredom of repetitive requests for down-stay, without relevance, was hollow. Top this off with the emotional baggage and Morgan discovered that he could *make Suzie laugh with his non-compliant behavior.*

*Non-compliant behavior from our
dogs can be self-reinforcing.
It is a wake-up call, telling us to explore the relationship,
training approach and well being.*

Healthy Relationships—Team Work

We can always use more ways to engage with others in a healthy way. I read recently that there are only three true job interview questions for prospective employees:

1. Can you do the job?
2. Will you love the job?
3. Can we tolerate working with you?

Sounds like questions we could ask our dogs and they could ask us in return. When we form new relationships at work, with friends, partners and dogs, we may not have relationship building skills yet, but we can learn some.

Successful relationships rely on basic essentials:

1. Communication is open and spontaneous (active listening and empathy).
2. Rules and boundaries are clear and allow for flexibility.
3. Individuality, freedom and personal identity are respected.
4. Each enjoys doing things for themselves and others.
5. Play, humor and having fun together is commonplace.
6. Each does not attempt to fix or control the other.
7. Each accepts themselves and the other's abilities and disabilities, strengths and limitations.
8. Feelings and needs are expressed without fear (assertiveness).

9. Each should be able to let go of the need to be right.
10. Each should have self-confidence, security and acceptance as individuals.
11. Conflict is faced without anger, using a win–win approach and resolved equitably.
12. Each engages in balanced and constructive feedback, (listening, giving and receiving).
13. Each is trustful of the other (or tries to be).
14. Negotiations are fair and democratic (BATNA—Best Alternative to a Negotiated Agreement—a mediator's mantra).
15. Each practices forgiveness of self and others.
16. Mistakes are accepted as opportunities to learn.
17. Each has a willingness to take a challenge out of a familiar zone.
18. Each can enjoy being alone and privacy is respected.
19. Each encourages personal growth, change, and exploration (sniffing is encouraged).
20. Continuity is present in the commitment.
21. Balance of closeness and separation is honored (personal space).
22. Each takes responsibility for their behaviors and happiness.

Healthy relationships are variable and diverse in every species. Mothers say that the bond between them and an infant is instant. However, parents kill their infants in many species including human and chimpanzee. It is shocking, but reality. It is important to know, even if we do not accept it, that it is different for everyone, depending on the situation. There are no absolutes but change, life and death, and that can be disputed too!

More importantly, there are plenty of resources and opportunities available to help us live a quality life, people and take care of our pets. There simply is no excuse not to find better ways of being if we truly want too.

We create our own experience with our dogs and others. Life rewards actions, so making careful decisions about how we live with dogs is of great consequence. We cannot change what we do not acknowledge, thus the *heart of awareness*. If we make up our minds that we will take on a challenge, and pretend we can, than we will. Of course, we need to learn some skills, but it begins with a vision in our minds, determination, and love for our dogs.

Our awareness, as humans, comes from cognition, experience and applying (or not) that experience in everyday living. Even small changes may require long term practice and effort. Good things happen for those who get moving into action. We develop intuition through our experiences.

Awareness for dogs comes from natural instinct, body language, senses, associations and what we offer them while they share our lives. Dogs with good or bad energy can apply it in good or bad ways. It is our choice to help them channel energy into positive outlets. Watching a Border Collie skillfully herd sheep or traverse a hurdle or a Border Terrier blissfully digs to Chipmunk City can teach us how to direct their energy into positive outlets.

We teach people and our dogs how to treat us. When our dogs, or anyone, does something offensive or hurtful, there is power in letting go. Our dogs roll to us or other dogs, out of deference to avoid conflict. Sometimes, they are simply relaxing. Knowing the difference is our quest. When we do not, nutty things happen like yelling at a barking dog (joining in the chorus).

I prefer to teach dogs to relax on their backs because they are STRONG AND SAFE, not afraid and ceding to MIGHTY AND POWERFUL ME. Giving a dog permission to pull or bark on cue is one of their greatest rewards and your relief. Turning lemon behaviors into lemonade makes more sense than getting tangled up in a spider's web of sticky no, no's and blah, blah's that the dog tunes out.

We are often living at a crossroads, not knowing what lies ahead. We often find ourselves in the middles of a dilemma. What should we do if someone is angry at us or we are angry at them? What should we do if our dog doesn't do what we ask or chews an expensive cell phone?

Instead of trying to solve the problem, use it as a question. How can this situation wake up us up rather than lull us into ignorance. We can use a difficult situation to encourage ourselves to take a leap and step out into the ambiguity. Watch a Newfoundland dog leap into an ocean to rescue a person. Imagine if they chose to stay on shore and let the person drown. Some do, but not often, if their abilities are shaped.

I have been involved in pet assisted therapy for twenty years. Dogs have been my therapist, no doubt. Dogs have the ability to shift the energy in a room from sad to positive in an instant. They connect and break barriers of communication (Pawt 10, Dog as Translator).

We pay thousands of dollars to learn how to meditate and improve our relationships. Not only do dogs wake up in the here and now, but they teach us how to navigate in relationships with humans and other dogs, in the here and now. Observing dogs with other dogs is the best way to learn what to do and not to do, if it is a safe interaction.

Dogs are genuine. They do not sit around with a laptop planning on making us miserable or by chewing the chair legs. Humans love stories. I do too but we must try not to project our stories onto our dogs *or anyone else.* When in doubt, clarify!

Dogs do not get mad at us and generally do not want conflict. They do get disappointed, confused and depressed. They have the same serotonin, dopamine and other mood enhancing, or depleting, reuptake inhibitors and hormones that we do.

Many humans confuse dog behavior (growling and playing) for aggression and conflict. Dogs will bite but it is usually out of fear or self defense. Dogs play rough. Most of the time, and without human interference, it is simply playing. Play behavior in dogs and aggression can seem the same (Pawt 2, Thresholds and Drives, Pawt 4, Body Language). Getting to know the difference relieves your anxiety the dogs, and gives them freedom of expression, so that other dogs don't think, "they are weird".

Genetics may load the gun; environment may pull the trigger, But we make choices about well-being . . .

Just Because We can, Doesn't Mean We Have To
Doing What Matters in Unfamiliar Places

The choice between pain and pleasure is an easy one for me and the dogs. We both prefer pleasure to conflict and pain. Realistically, we will experience conflict and pain with others and our dogs. That's life. Unless one is operating out of total ego, or enjoys inflicting emotional or physical pain, why would anyone want to do that to a dog who will come running to us with complete joy?

Just because we can, doesn't mean we have to do a lot of things including training and living with our dogs in ways we are not comfortable.

We are deluged with ways to get ourselves and our dogs smart, skinny, healthy and more attractive. Recently, I was able to watch Dr. Oz for five days in a row. I had to rest because of dental work and writing this book. My eyes (and teeth) were tired. I was intrigued.

Day one was about ways to reduce our belly fat. Day two was about enhancing our faces, followed by disgusting things people want answers too. Why not Google and keep it private? Day three pretty much the same into day four which I think was a repeat.

Day five was the best about his Labrador Retriever, Sally, who was introduced as "the Flabrador". Sally was happy to be with Dr. Oz, the Vet and the audience. She wagged her tail as they talked about how to reduce her weight for a longer and better quality of life. "It's okay Sally, I can lose a few pounds and get called names too." Sally took it in stride while the Vet tried to find her ribs.

With the exception of the Sally episode, I was exhausted from making lists of things to enhance "me". I give sage advice to others so gave some to myself. I scanned the list. "Okay, aside from Sally, the list went into my "save for a few days when the excitement wears off" bin. I have learned that impulsively buying things until I explore them more fully can make me dizzy. A few days later, a quick scan and the list went into the garbage can.

I have a hard time wrapping my brain around, "try this, not that", then the next day, "try that, not this" followed by "try them all", and not said out loud, "to raise sales". Whoops, guess I just said it. I enjoy the enthusiasm, and sense that Dr. Oz genuinely wants to help people and pets. Plus, he's cute. Having women hug, kiss and nearly faint over on a daily basis can't be that hard to swallow.

Splendid, we have choices. We can get aggravated or grab the opportunity to make informed decisions for ourselves and dogs (pets—life).

Just because we can and are told we should (social media) doesn't mean we have too, but thank you for sharing. Inspired by Dr. Oz, I am happy that Sally is benefiting. A dog's health and well being relies on our awareness, action and good choices. Shows like this can help get us moving into action.

Clearly, we love our dogs and vice versa. I am hoping that Sally (all dogs) gets some exercise in moderation, whole healthy and fresh foods (squashed veggies, real meat, fish) and a little fruit to juice up her life while she waits for Dr. Oz to come home. I don't know about you, but I want the dogs to sprint to me, not waddle. I want them to long, quality lives by my side. Personally, I want to be able to bend and embrace them, not fall over (Pawt 3, Healthy Dog, Good Dog, Whole Nutrition).

Awareness Centered Training gives you and your dog the opportunity to explore infinite possibilities. If you are open to the possibility of putting your ego in your pocket for a moment, to be on a more level playing / training field with dogs, you might be pleasantly surprised that the biggest lessons in life do not always come from being human. We can learn from exploring our brain and the dog's brain.

"Being the Best I can be by Using My Whole Brain"

Whole Brain—Whole Dog—Whole Training Approach

Growing up, my mother had a favorite saying for me when I was not focused on my chores or homework, "Use the brain God gave you". Sounds simple, but it has a powerful impact. Medically and psychologically, most of us use about five to ten percent of our brains, give or take a few.

It is exciting to explore how our body and brain (dog and human) have the ability to heal, regenerate and drive our behaviors. We react or respond to any give circumstance depending on genetics, conditioning, and very important, how stressed we are at the time. Given the opportunity to rest for even ten minutes gives our brain a chance to rejuvenate. Often, even minor lifestyle changes for us or our dogs can change behavior.

Let's explore our brain briefly. We know today that we can practice strengthening and balancing our left and right brain to create whole brain ability. What happens in our or our dog's brain affects more than you might imagine, and especially behavior.

According to the paradigm of human left-brain or right-brain dominance, each side of the brain controls different types of thinking. People are said to prefer one type of thinking over the other due to a number of reasons (genetics, conditioning, brain injury).

In psychology, it states that one side of the brain controls specific function (left-brained or right-brained). We know today that the brain is not nearly as dichotomous as once thought. We can exercise our whole brain, teaching one side to work with the other (Team Brain).

The Right Brain and the Left Brain
Together = The Whole Brain

According to the left-brain, right-brain dominance theory, the right side of the brain is best at expressive and creative tasks. Some of the abilities that are popularly associated with the right side of the brain include:

- Recognizing faces
- Expressing and reading emotions
- Music
- Color
- Images
- Intuition
- Creativity

The left-side of the brain is considered adept at tasks that involve logic, language and analytical thinking. The left-brain is often described as being better at:

- Language
- Logic
- Critical thinking
- Numbers
- Reasoning

While we have a natural tendency towards one way of thinking, the two sides of our brain work together in our everyday lives. The **right brain** focuses on the visual, and processes information in an intuitive and simultaneous way, looking first at the whole picture then the details. The focus of the **left brain** is verbal, processing information in an analytical and sequential way, looking first at the pieces then putting them together to get the whole. While often over-generalized by popular psychology and self-help texts, understanding your strengths and weaknesses can help you develop better ways to learn, study, teach dogs and improve our life.

Every day, we face new challenges and opportunities at home, work and with our dogs. A balanced approach to develop creativity, innovation, and to help us train our dogs, is practicing techniques to raise awareness, focus and train the "whole" brain and "the whole" dog.

Regardless of what side of your brain is stronger, whole brain thinking is required to succeed in the twenty first century and beyond whether in corporate, at home, or training dogs:

Goals Driven:	**Vision Driven:**
Analytical	Creative
Intelligence	Intelligence
Results Driven:	**People Driven:**
Operational	Relational
Intelligence	Intelligence

Creativity is a core competency for leaders and managers and a crucial component of balancing work, home, dogs and renewal time for self. Creativity requires whole-brain thinking with right-brain imagination, artistry and intuition, plus left-brain logic and planning. Organizations led by "creative leaders" have a higher success rate in navigating innovation, employee engagement and rapid adjustment to change, *The Work-Life Management System, Getting Things Done, David Allen.*

Generating fresh solutions to problems, and the ability to create new products, processes or services for an expanding market, are what gives a company its competitive edge. The most successful dog training schools and private coaches recognize that this applies to today's dog owners and dogs, most of who live in a fast paced society. Having the ability to offer realistic lifestyle change, in a cost and time effective way can be crucial to saving a dog's life.

Okay, now that we have the "basics" of how human brains navigate, when healthy, on a daily basis, let's look at one of my favorite part of the dog's brain and how it works, the SNIFFER (Olfactory). One of the newer research videos using MRI's to explore "canine cognitive function" and the dog's brain during various activities is at www.emory.edu. It is worth a look to see what areas light up a dog's cognitive brain.

Learning how the dog's brain and sniffing (olfactory) drive behaviors explains why they turn into "deaf, dino dogs", especially in exciting, unfamiliar places or when meeting new dogs. Have you experienced that moment with your beloved dog where you turn invisible? Me too!

The Dog's brain is similar to ours, except
that their senses are heightened. Imagine
sniffing in High Definition or 3D.

The Cerebrum and Limbic System

Billions of cells make up a dog's brain. The cerebrum of a dog's brain is the part that controls emotional, behavioral and learning functions. When people teach a dog to sit, this is the area of the brain that accomplishes the task. When a dog marks its territory, the cerebrum is responsible. The cerebrum influences affection or aggression shown by the creature.

The limbic system is a network of cells in the brain that combines the learning and instincts of a dog. This system controls the five senses, emotions, joy, anger, hunger and even sex.

Cerebellum and the Pituitary Gland

The cerebellum is located at the base of the brain and is responsible for muscle control. The spinal cord extends from the brain down into the spinal column. It is full of nerves carrying signals from the brain to the rest of the body.

The pituitary gland is a small hormone-releasing gland attached to the bottom of the brain. It is a link between the endocrine and nervous system. The pituitary gland plays a large role in growth, milk production, skin color, ovaries and the testes of a dog. When a female dog comes into season and a male dog picks up the scent of estrus, the molecules are sent to the pituitary gland. This gland will help a dog decipher when a female is ready to breed or is coming out of estrus.

Olfactory Bulbs, Vomeronasal Organ (V-Organ), also known as Jacobson's Organ and the Pineal Gland Dogs Sniff in Techni-Color!

Olfaction, the act or process of smelling, is a dog's primary special sense. A dog's sense of smell is said to be a thousand times more sensitive than that of humans. A dog has more than 220 million olfactory receptors in its nose, while humans have about 5 million. That puts "sniffing" into perspective. Purely, dogs light up. They love it, they need it, and we can use it to our benefit as a reward by putting sniffing on "cue". For example, walk calmly with me for 10 minutes, and you can "go sniff to your heart's content".

Because of this keen sense, dogs are able locate everything from dead bodies to forensic cadaver material. They work with humans to detect seizures, cancer, and what about those great drug sniffing dogs at airports and who work in law enforcement?

The vomeronasal organ, also called jacobson's organ, is a round pouch of receptive cells just above the roof of the mouth; it has ducts that open to the nose and the mouth permitting scents to enter it. These scent molecules are sent to areas of the olfactory bulbs to be processed so the dog's brain will know what to do with them. *Note: Allowing dogs to sniff is not only rewarding for them, but expends energy in a positive and very rewarding outlet.*

The pineal gland helps a dog to sense environmental and seasonal lighting as well as affecting breeding. The gland contains melatonin and helps to control metabolism and even sexual development.

A dog's mammalian brain is much like that of a human's. The various sections control different functions (front, mid and hind brain). Natural chemicals send constant messages throughout the dog's system. These signals tell the body when it is in danger (fight or flight instinct), needs food, when to breed and even how to teach good dog manners, (sit, down, stay, come and relax, etc.).

Being aware of this "basic information" gives us an opportunity to recognize when our dogs are best able to learn. Learning happens all the time. When dogs voluntarily offer behaviors like "sit", and we reward them with a "good", learning becomes easier.

When dogs and humans are calm, focused and in the moment there is more of a tendency to respond to us and learning, rather than react haphazardly (barking like a lunatic at squirrels while on a walk).

Under stressful conditions, when the dog (or we) is not focused, shaping (training) becomes difficult or impossible.

Whole Dog Approach

Awareness centered training practices / trains the "the whole brain" and the "the whole dog". If one area is weaker, then we strengthen it.

The dog's brain may be more primitive but is equally adept at learning and balancing, left/right and front/back brain activity, when they learn self-control. We discover how to motivate, shape and re-shape behaviors using techniques that match the way the dog learns.

Begin with you. If you are aware of strengths from the right brain, then develop the left brain, and vice versa. Brush your teeth and write with the opposite hand. To improve balance, stand on one foot while washing dishes or grooming the dog. I get on my knees when brushing out our Newfie, and extend one leg, then the other, getting a good stretch. A sense of humor helps because toothpaste lands on the mirror, the writing looks like I've been drinking, and if the Newfie moves out of a "stand-stay", I may wobble. That's okay because we can "reset" and "try again".

Walk your dog on the other side, then "switch" guiding your dog behind you to the opposite side. Behind is better so you don't trip over the dog. This is a standard walking technique we teach dogs and owners. It is useful especially in high-energy or unfamiliar situations, when walking the dog. If you aren't sure about passing by something or someone, switch, and put the dog on the other side. Your body provides a barrier easing stress for the dog, and possibly preventing the other dog or person from invading the dog's personal spatial bubble. Most importantly, challenge yourself and have fun.

Class or Train on My Own
Integrating ACT training into daily living and learning with our dogs is easy, cost effective, efficient and satisfying

The answer is easy . . . either or both depending on you, your dog, and experience (explores more in Pawt 7). I will emphasize that all dogs need socialization and manners (SAM), even 3 pound lap dogs. It is a frightening world for a dog, whether in a baby carriage, purse or carried, to be exposed, too quickly, to unfamiliar sights, sounds and smells.

A good training class, with a motivating and knowledgeable instructor and excellent handouts can help make training a new puppy or dog easier. Good teachers and counselors will review expectations, lifestyles and offer support and solutions. They are relatable and appreciate differences. They get people and dogs involved, while encouraging accountability for efforts and progress outside of class and at home, where the majority of learning happens, good and bad.

Focused class time is maximized when there is a smooth flow and balance of communication, instruction and practice. It is easy to see whether someone is truly interested in what they are doing or passing time.

> Dogs are not trained in six or eight weeks. It is a life adventure. Dogs and humans journey through stages of development and learning experiences (emotional and physical).

Whether training in class or on your own, requires commitment and respect for the relationship, whatever that means to you. Not every person enjoys exercising at a gym. Not every dog enjoys a dog park or canine fitness boot camp (Pawt 7, Dogs Park v Play Group v Walking the Dog).

Get to know yourself and your dog. Honor uniqueness. Focus on abilities, not flaws, challenges, not limitations.

Dogs who are sitting aren't jumping. Dogs learn self-control, patience, and get rewarded when doing behaviors like watch-me, sit, down and stay.

Have you ever noticed that eight
positive things can happen,
but we endlessly focus on the "one" negative.
Next time, with awareness, ponder the negative,
learn, and then let it go. Focus on the positive!

Imagine for a few moments that we are in the Land of Oz, or choose your blissful sanctuary. People care about their dogs, sometimes more than the humans in their lives and for good reason. Dogs listen, know how to play, and do not intentionally hurt us, unless out of fear or confusion.

Today, people are zooming into class like missiles launching into space. Dogs are latched up to a muzzle collar, being lead like a horse off to the races. Before I continue, let me clarify that we "all" say and do things we regret, mostly at times of stress and anguish.

One evening in training class I watched as a woman blew into the room like a tornado, cell phone glued to her ear and the dog's eyeballs hanging out of their sockets. The dog looked like she was on crack and her owner appeared to need tranquilizers. The dog's nose collar was half on, half off. There wasn't a clue from this person that they were aware of anyone else in the room (self-centered).

She bullied her way to a chair, nearly knocking over a Yellow Labrador puppy's owner. Others began clearing a path for safety and some stayed away all together. The puppy missed some good socialization opportunities.

Seemingly, this woman had not taken even a few moments to de-compress before grabbing the dog and blowing into training class physically, but certainly not mentally. The puppy did not stand a chance to learn a thing besides how to knock the nose collar off and run off to play with the other dogs. The owner retrieved her pup, then scolded, "no, no, bad puppy".

I wish I had my video cam on to show this person how ridiculous and preventable this could have been. I'm human, not perfect, and I can empathize with many, but this was a train wreck waiting to happen.

I asked the class to find a safe space and begin nose-to-navel breathing. It only takes a few seconds and shifts the energy in the room from chaos to calm. At the same time, the woman asked me to take her dog so she could go to the bathroom. "Yes, sure, I am your servant." Can you guess my answer because that wasn't it?

By evenings, I am tired too, but I enjoy teaching, interacting with others, and I bring my "A" game to class. My patience was waning. I advised her to "take herself and the dog to the bathroom, and "while there, take a few deep breaths". I offered to take her cell phone and bag, which she gave to me, and . . . it worked!

Those few moments which seemed like fifteen minutes, from her breezing in like a tornado, to breathing in the bathroom, helped to calm her into her senses. She began to wake up to the fact that she was in a room with other people and dogs, not alone, in an elevator.

This woman and her dog graduated from class with flying colors. She become focused, calmer and insisted that her husband and two children "take turns to help her with the training." Clearly, like many, she was exhausted, stressed to the max, and adding the dog training to her already busy agenda sent her over the edge, free falling with the puppy in tow like a parachute.

This is a not rare occurrence. It is happening too often because we are suffering from sensory overload. So are the dogs! Have you ever been standing in line at a bank or grocery store, and someone, deliberately or not, walks in front of you? What did you do? I suggest taking a breath. In that space between breathing and acting, you may discover that this person needs to be in front or maybe they are just rude.

Some people do not have social skills. You have a choice to say, "Excuse me, but there is a line, thank you" or "Hey, get in the line or I will punch you in face." Which one will make you feel better and, in the long term, have the better outcome? Consider that you could get punched back or start a riot. Behavior begets behavior, and there is good and bad energy.

I hope you are giggling and relating to these common occurrences driven by a need to be first, do more and get it all done. Everyone can benefit from stopping, breathing, and arriving in the present moment, even for a few minutes.

Plan ahead for dog training class like you would any project. Bring a positive attitude and it will radiate right back to you, creating positive associations for your puppy / dog.

When you go to a concert or a movie, you are asked to turn off your cell phone; same for dog training class. Usually, by the end of 1 ½ hours, most dogs and their families are so relaxed, it is as if we slipped a tranquilizer into the water bucket or sprayed anti-anxiety medication in the air. It's all about breathing and attitude.

The ambience where you train your dog matters whether at home or in a training classroom. Energy creates energy. Energy can be good or bad, manageable or uncontrollable. You know the difference by whether "you" can get your dog's attention without going crazy or getting frustrated.

When learning anything new, we (dog and person) need quiet time to focus on the task like "watch-me" and "sit". If the TV is on, music blaring in the background and a child is squealing, how can the dog learn? How can you teach? As I mentioned, they will learn anyway.

Set aside opportune times to teach, for a few minutes, two or three times a day. Integrate teaching into what needs to be accomplished anyway like feeding the dog (Pawt 3, Doggy Diner).

Gradually, we introduce and increase what we teach, in different places and for longer periods, (Pawt 5, The Networking Grid). This includes delivery, distance, distractions, duration, diversity and discrimination. I might add "determination" because giving up isn't an option. The Grid helps increase attention, in a variety of environments. If you have are having communication challenges with your dog, practicing variations of the "Grid's", will help to grow your dog's repertoire of behaviors and alleviate boredom.

From this vantage point, I encourage you to look at dog training and yourself through a wider lens (peripheral like dogs), one that includes developing deeper communication skills that will assist you in every part of your life.

Knowledge is empowering. How we learn is as varied as breeds of dogs. Many of us thrive on a blended learning style, employing a combination of audio, visual and practice. Choosing equipment (tools of the trade) can be complex or easy. There is a lot of hype about clicker training and for good reason. It works! I enjoy it, but it is not for every person or dog. Taking in a deep breath, moving on . . .

Click, Clack, Cluck—Oh My
Clicker Training Clarity and the Magic of Your Smile

What works for you and your dog? You decide! It must be positive and kind, especially with puppies. Kindness is not just a word, but an action; one that that has a positive trickling effect. Positive is relative, depending on the person, dog and what you are teaching. For some dogs, having us leave them alone may be positive. Positive "approaches" in dog training usually means "no aversives" or "physical punishment". The dog learns without fear.

Let me clarify that my dogs do not walk all over me and I have trained with many different approaches. We have a symbiotic relationship that is interdependent, not smothering or consuming.

We can get ticked off at each other, and then we have make-up "play" or share popcorn, when we are calm.

I prefer to remain blissfully ignorant when it comes to any training or modification method that hurts or scares dogs, although I have stomped my foot and banged pans together, as a "quick" intervention, to head off a dog fight.

You can successfully train your dog by blinking your eyes or with food, clickers, clucking, whispering, and my favorite, the magic of your smile or the scowl of your frown.

Awareness centered training with or without clicking works exceptionally well. Let's explore this briefly and then you decide if clicking is the best choice for you and your dog.

Approaches to training are individual,
some working better than others.
One isn't right, the other wrong—just different,
as long as it is fair, and the dog is not damaged,
hurt, or in fear of humans, in any way.

When is enough, enough? Just because we can, doesn't
mean we have too. Equipment is available to help
make training easier, not to confuse us or hurt our
dogs. Choose what works best for you and your dog.

Puppies are learning whether you are teaching them or not, so
you may as well pick an approach and give it a try. As a cross-trainer, I
use different approaches, much in the same way I exercise. It depends
on the situation, the dog, or me, and how I, or the dog, feel that day. I
like to shake it up and try new ways of connecting with and teaching
my dogs. Sometimes it works, and others it does not.

With any approach or equipment used comes the blunt reality
that one has to know how to use them effectively, and practice. Our
body won't become tone if we do the same things all the time. We
need a mix of cardio, strength, flexibility and relaxation. Training
dogs is no exception.

Trying different approaches, at different learning and wellness stages, of a dog's life, is one of the many advantages of awareness centered training. Rules are meant to be challenged. Just because they say we should doesn't mean we have too.

Clickers are a tool that, when used effectively, work remarkably well. Clickers have clarity and the clicker sound marks desired behaviors, like sit, down, sparkle or wag your tail. Focusing on one behavior at a time works best in the beginning stages of learning. Later, you can increase the level of training, clicking when you get two, three or a series of completed sequences.

I use clickers for rehabilitating dogs that are afraid of human voices, but in variable levels of sound, beginning with very soft. Clickers are especially clever to use with blind dogs for obvious reasons. If you get a "sit", you click. I lived with a deaf American Bulldog (not pictured in this Image) for 14 years. She was "unilaterally" deaf meaning she could hear a little in one ear. A loud click worked. My facial expressions and body language worked even better. Visual direction and touch works best with hearing challenged dogs.

If you join a group class where clickers are used, the first step should be learning how to use the clicker. Otherwise, they are confusing for you and especially the dog. Clicking in a family dog training class, where children use the clicker freestyle, confuses the dogs and drives the instructor bats. There needs to be instruction and guidelines prior to clicking.

Clicker timing and skill is required to shape the behavior you want pronto. For example, "watch-me", click, "good" and reward. Competing with environmental stimuli can be a challenge. If someone is uncoordinated and new at clicking, it won't help self esteem and motivation, if by the time they click a "down", the dog has gone off to play with a Wubba (Kong) or the dog across the room.

The clicker needs to be available; the clickee needs to be spot-on with timing for the behavior desired. The dog needs to be present and "aware" that you are clicking for that behavior.

For new "clickerites", I suggest a private coaching session or two before entering a group clicking class, unless the class is "specific" to clicker training only, and the instructor has experience. Time needs to be focused on "clicker skill" first and then integrated into shaping behaviors you desire.

What matters more than the tool is being genuinely in the moment, and focusing on the behavior you want to shape. Your voice and smile, I am guessing, are attached to your face, so are instantly available! Your thumb is useful, pointing up for GOOD and down for NOT SO GOOD. Shaking your hand can be used to cue "shake". Hands on hips, with s scowling face, mean BOMBSHELL (not good, let's try again).

The magic of your smile is as powerful as a clicker. When you get a behavior that you adore—smile. Gauge your reward, whether it is a treat, toy or massage, with the intensity and challenge of the behavior offered.

Asking for a behavior multiple times, when the dog captured it well enough the first time, is like cleaning an already clean toilet with a toothbrush. Siriusly (Sirius = Dog Star), it is a waste of energy. Get the behavior, mark it, and reward. Bravo!

Request ✦ Response ✦ Reward
Gauge your reward to the level of the response . . .

Let's Open our Minds to New Possibilities

Indulge me in sharing that dogs deserve at least the basics of humane shelter, safety, care, nutrition, exercise and training. Be gentle with yourself and your dogs. You can challenge yourself and your dog as much, or as little, as you choose.

Embrace mindfulness and being in the moment because that is where the dog lives. Seeing the world through our dog's point of view, while teaching them the skills to survive in a human world, is as results oriented, as you are a good teacher.

In years of working families and individuals, I have discovered that training our dogs relates to all other areas of my life with clarity, compassion and confidence.

Be *The Little Engine who Could and ACT.* If we think we can, we will!

Where is your dog right now? Is s/he lying down quietly, on a blanket, by your side, across the room or in another room? You can shape that behavior by simply getting up, going to your dog, with a smile and saying, "good relax or good down."

Thinking Inside or Outside of the Box—Your Choice!
What are the Possibilities?

Let's embark on an adventure in teaching our dogs all they need to know to live happy and healthy lives, without pain, and as quickly or slowly, as we like *(precious commodity these days)!*

Oftentimes we are informed that if we want to grow in self-awareness we need to think "outside of the box." An attraction lures us into new ways of doing things, especially if it sounds exciting, easy, or promises wealth and prosperity. Our dogs will be instantly trained if we simply use this collar, that leash or piece of equipment. It's enticing to try out new challenges for ourselves and our dogs, as long as it is safe and works.

Thinking outside the box and thinking beyond the box, (also called "thinking outside the square") is to think differently, unconventionally, or from a new perspective.

This phrase often refers to novel or creative thinking. Embracing this concept, we can teach ourselves and our dogs to not only use the "whole" brain, but think "inside" or "outside" of the box.

The "Youngmen Technique", inspired by a joke from comedienne Henry Youngman, has been taught in victimology training programs, corporate and to thousands of students, in three countries for decades.

Paraphrased, at the United States / Mexican border, a guard sees a man crossing into the United States. The man is riding a bicycle with a box balanced on the handlebars. The guard pulls the man aside, tells him to get off his bicycle and opens the box, but all he finds inside is sand. This goes on every day for two months: the man comes across the border on his bicycle with a box balanced between the handlebars, and every day they open the box but find nothing but sand.

One day, the guard sees the man at a store and says, "Look buddy, you drove us crazy. Every day for two months you came in on your bicycle with that box of sand. What were you smuggling?" The man says, "Bicycles."

The point of the joke, in illustrating parallel thinking in problem solving, is to always consider, "OK, I see the sand. Now, where's the bicycle?" The punch line is 'Learn to think outside the box". Anyway . . . moving on . . .

Depending on the circumstances, there are times when we are focusing solely on one aspect of a behavior, when the answer to our issue with our dog might not be the behavior at all. It could be the teacher or the environment or something else. It may simply be a bad day. We all have them and so do our dogs.

In ACT, you will notice familiar behaviors (sit, down, stay), especially if you have trained dogs before. What is unique is the notion that you can "instantly" learn to stop, breathe, and consider, aha, just maybe, if I change my approach with my dog, even a little, (like sitting on a fitness ball or lying down, or standing backward instead of frontward), then I may get a more enthusiastic response. We are moving around our dogs all the time anyway. ACT suggests moving with "awareness" to see if one small change can make a big difference.

Getting flexible and fit while training our dogs is an
added benefit, while alleviating boredom for them.
It also fulfills the need to teach our dogs in variety of
positions, places and with different communication
techniques (hand / voice / body language). Always
begin up close and personal, and then add distance and
duration. Teach the concept with patience and a smile.

The first time I started training on the floor or a fitness ball
(Pawt 8, Dogs, Balls and Balance), the dogs went excitedly crazy
with interest. Anything away from regimented training is a relief.
The dogs offer me the same behaviors but with a new enthusiasm.
Plus, I get to exercise while training (multi-tasking) with my favorite
partners, the dogs.

2012 5 28

Journey, the Newf, personal exercise coach
to Maureen, helping her do ab crunches while
learning to "sit", "stay", and "high-five". You
can easily choose different positions (standing,
sitting, lying down) to teach your dog to respond
to you in a variety of situations / postures.

Channeling Dr. Seuss
The Places You'll Go
You have a brain in your head,
Feet in your shoes.
You can steer your life in any direction you choose.
You are on your way,
You know what you know.

Dogs are Learning all the Time

We are learning all the time too. Dogs begin learning from the time they are born. They learn quickly. By the time they are six months, they are equivalent to an eight or ten year old. By one year, they are about fifteen. At two, they are about twenty four. At three, they are about thirty depending on nature, nurture, socialization and manners (SAM) and training.

The following is a guideline, not a bible or death sentence, of the stages of puppy—to—adult dog development. Like us, dogs can continue learning until their last breath, in different ways, at different levels. More eloquently, they can teach us how to live and age with acceptance and grace!

Critical Stages of Development

- Neonatal period: Birth to 12 days
- Transition period: 13 days to 20 days
- Awareness period: 21 to 28 days
- Canine socialization period: 21 to 49 days
- Human socialization period: 7 to 12 weeks
- Fear impact period: 8 to 11 weeks
- Seniority classification period: 13 to 16 weeks
- Flight instinct period: 4 to 8 months
- Second fear impact period: 6 to 14 months
- Maturity: 1 to 4 years (most of the time)
- 4 years and beyond (bliss with a trained and socialized dog)

This may sound like a simple concept to absorb, but many still think of one year old dogs as "babies". By the time a dog lands in a human family, most have already experienced more of life than we (humans) do in half a lifetime.

Regardless of challenges (adoption, deaf, blind, deformed, ill-health), dogs are one of the most resilient and adaptive beings (species).

Different theories, paradigms and approaches have been researched, tested and evolve over hundreds of years. Whether a dog is young or old, they can learn new "normals" and "behaviors", just like us, with understanding, patience and awareness centered training.

PAWT 2

Behaviors and Drives—Oh My!

Paradigms, Patterns and Perks (Empowering and Fun)

Places to Sniff—by JJ Bucket
Places to sniff,
Paws and nose on the ground.
I can safely sniff, sniff,
While you are around.

*Sniffing is as important to dogs as inhaling a pleasant
aroma is for us (grass, ocean, rain, flowers blossoming,
meals cooking). Allowing dogs to sniff while on a walk
is a reward that can relieve stress and balance energy.*

A paradigm is a set of evolving patterns or models that give us an opportunity, based on hypothesis and assumptions, to view different insights. Paradigms have different perspectives (positive, interpretive and critical).

Theories are a set of logical propositions that are presented in a systematic way that describe and explain any behavior. They are logically constructed statements, open for research, testing, reviewing, reformulating and modifying. "Why do I need to know this to teach my puppy?" You don't, but it helps to better understand ourselves because we are creatures of conditioned and learned patterns and habits. Have a yawn to relax, and have fun with it.

Patterns are formed, over time, by people and other species, including our dogs (habituation). Patterns can be structured or change due to environment and life transitions.

Change is not easy (addictions, habits, aggression). The longer we wait, the harder it becomes. Does this sound familiar in anyway? Anyone who has struggled with a bad habit (themselves or others), or has adopted a dog with a nasty habitual behavior (see Appendix A, Big Confusing Words Dictionary) knows what I am talking about. Habitual behaviors are not always bad, but we know what the bad ones are (biting, chewing the wrong things, peeing and pooping in the house, or worse, obsessive compulsive disorders). OCD's generally need medication and extensive therapy, whether for human or dog. Medication, accompanied with behavior modification, is the best treatment plan. Think of yoyo dieting. We can try half dozen different motivational plans to lose weight, but without behavior change, it's up and down, up and down . . .

The good news about paradigms and patterns is that they have perks. These perks give us the freedom to change, or adapt to change, through evolution. Sometimes, we have no choice. We aren't apes anymore, so swinging through grocery stores may be alarming to others. We might get arrested. Dogs experience transition and change in similar ways that we do. Dogs quickly learn to adapt to change to get their needs met (survival).

Awareness centered training (ACT) is cognitive in that "If we believe that we can change, we can". Once aware of what we can accomplish, we have to commit to taking action, one baby step at a time. The mantra is three steps forward, two steps back, but always one step ahead.

Our dogs can learn, re-learn, adapt and change if it makes sense. We need to be "aware" of what needs changing and how meaningful is it. If we love our dog and they are biting us or others, that's very meaningful. We want to change this, the sooner the better. If a dog is lounging on the bed and chews the pillow, that may or may not be meaningful enough to some people. They'll start laughing and go buy a new pillow.

Many people talk about wanting to change behaviors, but prefer to remain in a comfort zone. To truly change a dog's behavior, it needs to be realistic and relatable. We need a plan and commitment. That plan needs to be realistic and implemented regularly to be successful.

Stay with me now. Try not to zone out because this applies to us too. How often have you said, "I've had it and I am going to change". Taking in a deep breath, holding, and exhaling—GOOD! Oxygen rejuvenates the brain, and then the brain sends messages to the body that everything will be okay. You and your dog are fine, just the way you are as long as you are not remaining in an unhealthy set of patterns on purpose. More later . . .

On this journey, to best understand how our dogs learn, it is helpful to review the basic history of dogs, behaviors, and what drives (or not) these behaviors. I intend to keep this short, sweet and simple. You may discover that many of the behaviors that drive our dogs—drives us too!

Awareness, by definition, is a combination of consciousness and responsiveness. Color this with mindfulness and you are on your way to awareness centered training and positive change in your life.

Centered is being focused while training or doing anything of significance (driving a car). Dogs that learn self-control, and how to expend energy into positive outlets, and are trained to relax, live longer, healthier lives. They have their paws on the ground, not the ceiling or our chest. They use the brain in their head to think and voluntarily offer behaviors. They are focused on a specific task that we assign and redesign, to make life less boring for them.

Centered for us is when we arrive home and realize it, not on auto-pilot. When I am present (in the moment), I spend far less time correcting, and more time observing, capturing and rewarding (shaping) behaviors I desire.

Evolution, experience, research and history, gives us an opportunity to take advantage of what our visionaries, mentors and historians have learned. We can use what works well and change or discard what no longer works. We gather information so that we can make informed decisions. We make mistakes so we can learn and grow.

Through-out ACT and beyond, I encourage you to form your own opinions and embrace mistakes, because that is how we learn. Use imaginative ways to attain your positive goals.

Self and dog awareness is about becoming the best we can be, as a team. You are unique and perfect as you are too. You are special and so is your dog. ⤚

Ivan Pavlov (Ring them bells for Salivating Dogs) Classical Conditioning

As I shared, seldom do I have puppy clients ask me about classical or operant conditioning. However, it is sage to know a little about why, aside from dying, food is so important to dogs and us. You can form your own opinions and paradigms.

Ivan Pavlov (1849-1936) will ring a bell, as a Russian physiologist who studied digestion in dogs. In Pavlov's studies, he observed that the dogs he was studying would salivate before food was placed in their mouths. He thought the dogs were associating the lab assistants, or the sound of the door, with the food. He tested this theory by ringing a bell just before feeding time. After a number of trials, ringing the bell caused the dogs to salivate. *(Pavlov's work in classical or respondent conditioning explains reflexive behavior, like salivation.)*

Salivation applies to all species. Have you ever begun to salivate while watching a commercial for your favorite mouth watering food?

> "There is a moment during our interactions with
> dogs when a light seems to go on. It is within that
> split second of illumination that we realize that
> training our dogs is more than just where and when
> to pee, equipment, toys, food and vet visits. It is
> about us noticing that moment of awareness."
> —Maureen Ross

B.F. Skinner's Box
Operant Conditioning

Skinner is regarded as the father of Operant Conditioning, but his work was based on Thorndike's law of effect. Skinner introduced a new term into the Law of Effect—Reinforcement. Behavior, which is reinforced, tends to be repeated and strengthened. Behavior, which is not reinforced, tends to die out-or be extinguished and weakened.

Skinner (1948) studied operant conditioning by conducting experiments using animals that he placed in a *"Skinner Box"* which was similar to Thorndike's puzzle box.

B.F. *Skinner (1938)* coined the term **operant conditioning**; it means roughly changing of behavior by the use of reinforcement that is given after the desired response. Skinner identified three types of responses or operant that can follow behavior.

Skinner identified three types of responses or operant that can follow behavior.

- 🐾 **Neutral Operants**: responses from the environment that neither increase nor decrease the probability of a behavior being repeated.
- 🐾 **Reinforcers**: Responses from the environment that increase the probability of a behavior being repeated. Reinforcers can be either positive or negative.

❧ **Punishers**: Response from the environment that decrease the likelihood of a behavior being repeated. Punishment weakens behavior.

Through-out ACT, we'll focus on the natural instincts and necessities that have intrinsic meaning to dogs and humans, with a twist of humor, and meaningful connection. Yes, I'm being a little snarky when I say that, "beyond getting electro-shocked in a box, without nutrition, we will die".

What Skinner brought to light was that through "repeated associations" with things of value to the dog (going out, playing ball, eating) the behavior mores meaningful.

Skinner (1904-1990) was influenced by Watson and Pavlov. A doctoral student at Harvard University, Skinner discovered that he could systematically change the behavior of rats by giving the rats a food reward for pressing a lever. Kind of like us receiving our "pay-check" for a good week's work or a "hug" as a loving gesture. He expanded this work to pigeons at the University of Minnesota. *He ate them afterward, just kidding—adding a little humor to see if you are awake.*

Thorndike's Law of Effect
Responses that Produce Rewards
Tend to Increase in Frequency—*Connection is Instant*

Skinner's view is that a dog learns that chewing furniture is dangerous when the owner is present and safe when the owner is gone; especially if the dog was reprimanded for enjoying a good chew seconds, or minutes, after the enjoyment.

It is kind of like catching your partner in bed with someone else. The act is complete so what do you do? I am a non-violent person, but chances are, depending on my day, this would take me to the edge. Someone would be running fast, without their clothes, and me on their heels videoing.

Humans would understand this vignette. For a dog it is different. You must catch them in the act for any fair training to be accomplished. As difficult as it is to contain your emotional angst when the dog chewed your favorite DVD, you must let it go, and pick up a mirror. Prevention is the best teacher when you are not available to teach.

I am sucker for surveillance and recommend that if you intend to leave your dogs home alone for extended periods, set up a video cam. You will "not" be catching them in the act of doing something wrong, but you can view when it began. This will give you an advantage, knowing how long you can leave your dog, if at all, home alone, outside of a crate or confined, safe area. You can spot exactly when the dog became bored and turned into a lunatic (destructive behavior).

Separation anxiety (Pawt 8) emanates from the dog that becomes slightly anxious when left alone and feels better when he chews. When the owner arrives home, the dog will act submissive, anxious or fearful, in an attempt to avoid punishment. The dog knows he will be punished because it has happened before. He associates it with the owner's homecoming. What the dog does not know is WHY! There is no connection unless the connection is made instantly. He greets his owner with glee and gets bopped for doing something that relieved stress. It can become a vicious cycle.

John Watson's Little Albert (Ahhhh, Another Rat)

John Watson (1878—1958) was an American Psychologist who established the school of behaviorism. Watson earned his PhD from the University of Chicago in 1903. He believed, and turns out he was right, that we are not just biological. Genetics, environments (and choices) shape our behaviors. He studied 100's of infants, including his own, little Albert. While a white rat was present, John made a clanging noise several times. Little Albert became fearful of noises and anything white, not just rats! He concluded that fears are learned—not inherited. He rehabilitated little Albert with counter-conditioning, pairing something positive while looking at a rat, while clanging a loud noise. Tadah! Consider a dog's reaction to noises, sights, sounds and smells? Where are they? What are they looking at? Who are they connecting it with?

ACT and Positive Reinforcement (PR)

Whatever the training task, whether keeping a toddler quiet in public, training a dog, coaching a team or writing a book, it will go faster and better, and be more fun, if you know how to use positive reinforcement. The basic laws of reinforcement are simple, but work better with "awareness and timing". Integrating positive reinforcement into daily living and learning with our dogs makes life easier and pleasurable.

Reinforcements are relative, not absolute. Rain is a positive reinforcement for ducks, a negative one for most cats, and a matter of indifference to horses, cows and Newfie dogs, who love to swim.

Positive Reinforcement is anything, which, occurring in conjunction with a behavior tends to increase the probability that the behavior will occur again. Awareness and positive reinforcement go hand in hand.

Negative Reinforcement (NR)
Empty the Garbage or Cover it Up
(A good metaphor for living too)

Negative Reinforcement is taking away something bad, like glaring at your dog as they are about to stick they head in a garbage can. If you cannot be present to teach "leave-it", please put a lid on the garbage can. This is uncomplicated, and many trainers will be scrunching their faces. The fact is that in today's fast paced life, many people, especially "moms", do not have time to teach "leave-it" at the garbage can. Even if they do, the children will leave the garbage unattended while playing with the puppy.

You traverse into a repetitive cycle of "no, no, no". The dog (or child) learns to get attention, so it is becomes self-reinforcing. Garbage is powerful and fun to explore for dogs. It can also be dangerous if they eat the wrong thing (rotten food, bones, tongue stuck in cans).

I have made significant money on private sessions with multi-tasking parents who say, "My dog is eating the garbage. Then, we end up in a game of chase through the house so I can get the pork chop bone out of her mouth." Take time to supervise children around dogs. Teach the dog to "leave-it" repeatedly. Otherwise, prevention is the best option. Put a lid on the garbage or move it to a secure location.

Whenever our dogs do what we ask, or stop doing what we don't want them to do, when they look at us, we must smile. Otherwise, glaring at the dog and saying "leave-it", and they do, is an example of NR. Follow this up with a reward and "good dog". We want our dogs to love looking at us.

> "Between Stimulus and Response, there is a space. In that space lays our freedom and power to choose our response. In our response lays our growth and our freedom."—Stephen R. Covey

Positive and Negative Punishment (PP and NP)

I kept going back and forth on whether or not to even talk about punishment. I attended another dog training conference and decided why not? Punishment is intricately woven into society and highly misunderstood (drama). I listened to one professional speaker after another share their educational opinion what punishment is or not.

The bottom-line is that it depends on culture, meaning and intensity. Universally, I sense that we agree that reward and consequence should equal behavior, especially if you want to maximize on teaching certain behaviors and eliminating others. Phew!

Examples of punishment in dog training over the years has ranged in intensity, insensitivity and barbaric. Some are pointing fingers, spanking, hitting, spraying lemon juice, duct taping mouths, pepper spray or air horns into the face, shaking by the scruff of the neck, alpha shakes, leash jerking (repeatedly), and the abuse of hi-tech electrical equipment.

These interventions are used and recommended too frequently by inexperienced people that harm dogs. If it does not feel right, listen, clarify, and don't use it.

Punishment is relative, and in degrees, depending on who is doing it and to whom. If you are an independent thinker, like me, a punisher might get punished right back—at—yeah. I simply will not tolerate, in class, when I see a four-month old puppy that weighs twenty pounds (giant breed) with a prong collar. Wake-up, smell the roses and safe the dog noses (and throats). There are better ways.

Researchers and behaviorists have tagged two more definitions Positive Punishment and Negative Punishment. Positive punishment is when you present something bad and the behavior is less likely. It is usually physical punishment. Your dog may think twice before jumping on you again if you smash him in the muzzle.

Consequently, you can break your dog's nose, crack a tooth, or "you" may require a knee replacement. When I hear people talking about doing this, still, I simply ask, "How's that working for you?" "How do you feel afterward?" People ask me if I have tried this. Sure, I tried the knee to chest with my Newfies. Reflecting, it may have worked once. My knee hurt lots, but not as much as looking at my Newf who was trying to connect with me, in her own way. Try using knee-to-chest with a Border Terrier. Silly!

I would rather be "aware" of high energy level opportunities to teach my dog to "sit" or "relax". If a dog unexpectedly launches at me from outer space, I turn around. Alternatively, I may walk away. Instead of clocking me, I teach them to, "go and get their favorite ball or toy". In between, all life rewards like eating require a sit. From the beginning, teach the puppy / dog to sit in front of humans and reinforce this with the "humans" too.

Negative Punishment is when you take away something good; the behavior is less likely (maybe). Let's use jumping again, as an example, because dogs jump to greet each other. It is a natural dog-to-dog, meet-greet ritual. You come home; your dog is excited to see you or a visitor, and gleefully slams you or a visitor, into the wall. You turn around and walk away, taking away a good thing—YOU.

You can do this a 1,000 times but it makes more sense to ACT. You are "aware" of the greeting energy, so teach your dog to go and get a stuffed toy or to "sit". If your dog is not able to control their greeting energy, be sure they are in a safe, confined area, so that you can de-compress, then teach them how to greet. Use a leash if necessary.

A last word on punishment is that it may cause displeasure, but can also be physically or psychologically damaging. It does not eradicate a behavior unless it is brutal enough for the receiver to STOP the behavior. *Example: mace in the face temporarily stops an attacker, but you better run, it won't last forever).*

When you use punishment, you may explode (poof) the dog's whole repertoire of good behaviors too, not to mention squashing his or her spirit. Be careful. Using punishment successfully is a skill. If it does not work the first few times, stop.

A corrective reprimand, in the moment, should
be followed up with teaching the dog what
to do, when, where and for how long.

I love my dogs. We have agreements. If they test me, they have privileges taken away, like "off the bed." I go back to exploring what's going on in my life—any lifestyle transitions? This affects them too. Then, back to baby steps and basic training that includes teamwork and respect.

Regression is a gift when it comes to dogs. If we relax our behaviors for any good reason, it is okay. If the dog starts to act out, then we know we need to ACT training. It is kind of like riding a horse (or a bike). For some reason, you stop or can't for several years, then decide to take it up again. The brain cells and body remember. Keep practicing.

I don't like bullfighting, but I respect cultural diversity. As with punishment, it is a cultural and individual choice. Personally, I could not raise a bull, sell it, and then watch someone spear it to weaken it, then send it into a ring, so that people can yell "Ole'"—while some good looking dude in fancy attire spears the rest of the life out of it. I don't think we should be brutalizing our dogs with painful training devices either.

In the same vein, I am a hypocrite. I eat meat, poultry and fish, but I do not raise it, catch it or pluck it, and if I did, it would be humanely.

Okay, now you know I am a real human . . . back on track . . .

ACT by shaping the behaviors you want, while
preventing and not reinforcing (laughing,
touching) the behaviors you do not want
(win-win / paws-up).

Dogs do What Works—Identify the Payoffs

Dogs are obedient to the "laws of learning and association", not especially to us. I know, disheartening! They do things to get their needs and pleasures met and because it becomes a habit. This habit can be good or bad, just like energy. When a dog does something that we do not like, and we are not present to say, "That's mine, this is yours, or a simple "hey" or "enough", then we need to let it go.

A dog who sits with her chew toy in her mouth, cannot jump, chew, knock grandma over, indiscriminately eliminate, lick themselves in front of company, or chew on us. There is already something good in their mouth. The message is to be "aware", think ahead, and use prevention. What do you want your dog to be doing, with what and where?

Dogs do what works, so identify the pay-offs. If a dog greets you by jumping, and you smile and give him a big hug, then you have shaped the jumping.

The Mantra: You do something for me,
and I'll do something for you.

Reinforcement Schedules
Breathing in . . . this will be painless

Rewarding behavior repeatedly increases the tendency of that behavior. At work, do you do a better job when you are applauded during performance evaluations, or when told that the project you just worked on belongs in the trashcan?

Example: Down becomes a target behavior when a dog is reinforced each time he lies down with a "good down".

The behavior will eventually plateau out in frequency; stop rewarding the behavior each and every time it occurs. You will reward most of the time when it is new, then half of the time when they get it, then spontaneously for the best behaviors. This will facilitate the shaping process, making the behavior more resilient to extinction. WHAT? It goes like this!

If your dog is use to getting rewarded every time, then suddenly isn't, the behavior goes into extinction: No treat, no behavior, the heck with you. A good metaphor is the "lottery". You buy a scratch ticket, hoping to win, but realize you may be struck by lightning first. You take a chance anyway. Conversely, you go to a store and buy a laptop. You get it immediately and use it as soon as you want too.

Do not withhold positive praise from your partner, loved ones or dogs for long periods. Space them out. When

you are getting respect, reciprocate. If you are not,
withhold, and see what happens. If the light does not
flicker with signs of hope, then it's time for "a discussion".

Jackpot the Juiciest Behaviors
What is your Dog's Forte?

Reward the behaviors that knock your socks off! You are thrilled that your dog brought you your slippers. You have been teaching her this for weeks. This deserves a delicious treat, praise, and a game with her favorite toy. Savor the moment, and reward the sweet behaviors you truly desire (jackpot), like a good wine or food.

Journey (my Newfoundland) helps me carry bags upstairs. In the beginning, if I was not careful which bag I gave to her, what a mess. Eggs dripping over everything else in canvas bags are gooey (my dumb). She nearly took the handle off my purse. To her my Sony camera is the same as carrying my grocery bag. An entire bag of fruits and vegetables flew in eight directions, but the glory of her tail wagging, at a job well done, was worth every gooey, grateful moment. She no longer carries my Sony camera.

Variable (Random) Intervals—
Spontaneity—Get This for That!

There are many types of reinforcement schedules. I welcome you to Appendix A to explore them. Variable and/or, I call it "random", is more stimulating, and in my opinion, the most effective. Once a behavior is learned, start reinforcing it occasionally, rather than constantly. This is the root of the "shaping" process. Random reinforcing increases the duration of behaviors and reduces boredom.

Shape the BEST behaviors. Making it enticing, and getting the dog to anticipate, creates a quicker learning experience. The dog perks up. Adding spontaneity is the liver flavor on the bone.

Enrichment activity and training is being used in the best zoos in the United States and for our dogs. Puzzle games enable you to hide treats. Create a fun training environment by having your dog "watch", "sit", "stay", "down", then release them to their puzzle game to find a ½ dozen treats.

Differential Schedules are Cool

As soon as a behavior is put on schedule, select examples of the best behavior for reinforcement (cuter, faster, slower, and calmer). How stringent the criterion of a behavior depends entirely on you. Timing is necessary for sharper training and shaping, but a timeline is not, unless it is important to you. Yes, it works better when you are quick, but you won't "go to hell" if you are not. Your dog is not doomed. What matters most are your goals and the well-being of the dog.

Stimulus Control (Stop, You are Driving me Crazy)

Anything that causes some kind of behavioral response is a stimulus. Some stimuli can cause responses without any learning or training: we blink at bright lights, jump at loud noises, and hold our noses at offensive smells. We sneeze. So does my parrot who imitates me. Other stimuli are learned through associations. They become recognizable signals for behavior:

If your partner comes home in a bad mood, don't tell him or her right now you just spent $400 on new vacuum, adopted another dog without discussing it first, or booked a vacation in Tahiti. As with training our dogs, timing is a vital. Some goals need planning and respect for those involved.

Traffic lights make us stop and go; we leap to answer phones, buzzers and whistles, and close our eyes when a squirrel gets run over. These are called conditioned or secondary stimuli.

Conditioned Reinforcer—Primary Reinforcer

A primary reinforcer is a reinforcer that a dog is born needing such as food, water, shelter. Secondary or conditioned reinforcers are stimuli, objects or events that become reinforcing based on their association with a primary reinforcer.

A dog isn't born wanting to play with a squeaky toy, but when that toy is paired with primary reinforcers such as fun and social interaction, it becomes a conditioned reinforcer. The toy can then be used to reinforce behaviors you like, just like you would use a food treat as a reward.

Unconditioned Reinforcer (UR)
An Association of What is to Come

The dog doesn't learn to like and work for food. In the wild, it is a matter of survival. Living with people s/he learns to live and work for the praise, play or click that happens to mean food. We must feed our dogs healthily. That is why food is an empowering training tool. What we shouldn't do is "food-dump" (Pawt Pawt 3, Doggy Diner). It is a waste of good connecting and training time.

An unconditioned reinforcer is something that the dog finds inherently rewarding (food, attention, a toy, or anything of high value) and can be used as a reward. An UR leaves a dog wiggly with anticipation of what is to come. I get excited just thinking about a night out, delicious dinner and one day to not have to make decisions.

A "reward marker" can be a smile, click or the tone of your voice when you say "yes" to a good and desired behavior.

A "bridging stimulus"—bridges the time gap between the behavior you liked and the actual reinforcement. It is like a performance review with a salary increase. You wait six months; get a good review and a raise for a job well done. The difference for dogs is they will not understand waiting for six months, so we have to be clever by keeping them motivated.

Habituation

Habituation happens to all of us. Consider that you brush your teeth with the same hand every day. Now think about other things you do daily. If nothing earth-shattering happens, like someone ramming your bumper or a piano falls on your head, it pretty much stays the same, doesn't it?

Habituation is a decrease in response to a repeated behavior (familiarity), until something changes it. After you become accustomed to a sound or happening, you pay less attention to it. Dogs do too. That is why socialization and manners (SAM), and desensitization to sights, sounds and smells are so relevant. The more dogs are exposed to the stimuli in the environment, the less likely they are to be spooked or reactive to it.

Conversely, habituation can be behaviors we want to change, increase or decrease, like taming adolescent energy. Behaviors will not change, increase or decrease, unless we change our own behavior response, and effectively teach our dogs what we want, and how we want it, in different situations.

Dogs live in context. It takes time, patience, and repeated exposures to desensitize a dog to unusual and unknown stimuli, and it needs to be in each room and environment (indoors, outdoors).

Depending on the dog, age and previous exposure, we need to be vigilant about taking the changing and teaching process, one step at a time, gradually increasing the stimuli at a successful and calm distance.

Generalization
Does your dog sit at home but not in the park?
Here's why!

Generalization is a simple concept but important for dogs. Again, dogs live in context. There you have it. We need to teach our dogs to do behaviors in each room and in a broad variety of environments. I realize I sound like a parrot, but this important. Otherwise, the behavior you teach, in that room, is the behavior you are NOT likely to get outside in a different or more stimulating (exciting) environment. Essentially, we become invisible.

Whenever your puppy or dog follows you into a room, have them do something for you like "sit", "down", or "sit—stay", even for a few seconds. Practice this in every room, upstairs and down, and wherever you go with them. When you go for a ride and arrive at your destination, ask for a "sit", then say, "thank you" before walking on.

The environment can change the equation because it is pure entertainment for dogs. Think about gearing up that Saturday night movie and popcorn. After walking for ten minutes to release some energy, have the dog "sit", and especially if someone is rollerblading by.

Randomly ask your dog to "down–stay" on a walk or wherever you exercise.

Learned Irrelevance (tune you out)

Anyone who has a husband, teenage or mother-in-law knows learned irrelevance. I stopped listening to my in-laws quiz me on the color of my hair about 20 years ago. My partner tunes me out unless I make myself big like the cat. Teenagers zone out and then tune us out. A dog will stop paying attention to a request if it has no intrinsic meaning to them. What that means for your dog is your quest!

We have to make it more valuable, and sometimes, they have to do what we want just because "we said so." That's a fact of life while living and working with other beings.

The dog tunes out insignificant (to them) blah, blah, blah. Repetitively asking them to do a behavior like "sit", and they do not, is a sign to "stop". It is like asking our partners to clean the litter box, even though he agreed to do it three times a week. Spice it up with the dog. You have to take a few steps backs, breathe, and get more exciting. I am still working on the litter box because that needs cleaning to keep the cat healthy and using it. Instead, I stopped cooking dinner for a few days, and informed him, "I didn't have time, I had to clean the litter box".

Consider varying the tone of your voice. Whisper training is a favorite for me and many of my training colleagues and the dogs enjoy it. Whispering intrigues dogs who can hear. It could be that it is a relief from boring tones and inflections, and more like how dogs would communicate with each other. Listen to the inflection of your voice. Record yourself. Would you come to you if you were a dog?

Orienting Response (Reflex)

The orienting response, also called *orienting reflex*, is an organism's immediate response to a change in its environment, when that change is not sudden enough to elicit the startle reflex. The phenomenon was first described by Russian physiologist *Ivan Sechenov in his 1863 book Reflexes of the Brain*. The orienting response is a reaction to novelty.

In the 1950s the orienting response was studied systematically by the Russian scientist *Eugene Sokolov,* who documented the phenomenon called "habituation", referring to a gradual "familiarity effect" and reduction of the orienting response with repeated stimulus presentations.

If someone walks into the room, you would probably look, or pretend not to, while at the same time using your super duper peripheral vision to catch a fleeting glance. Dogs will do this every time a new dog enters the training room, park, house or pack. If it occurs multiple times, chances are the dog will begin to ignore it. If you ring the doorbell 25 times in a row, a dog will eventually stop barking, or fall asleep.

Systematic Desensitization and Counter-Conditioning
The Ideal Combination

Systematic desensitization is the same technique used by counselors for people with phobias who are excessively afraid of spiders, dogs or flying in airplanes. The person is taught to relax with breathing techniques. They are then introduced to the fearful stimulus (like spiders), at whatever level he or she can tolerate (without anxiety) while continuing to practice a relaxation exercise. The stimulus (spiders) is gradually intensified, at whatever rate the subject can handle, always building on successive approximation.

The real-life necessity of having to leave dogs alone requires that owners slowly build on desensitizing a dog that is experiencing separation anxiety (an over-diagnosed disorder). Slowly build toleration, not "flood" the dog with long periods of being alone. Flooding would be filling a room with spiders, then opening the door and giving that spider-phobic person a shove.

Begin with small "home alone" sessions with the dog confined in an area where no damage can be done. Then increase the time left alone *(Pawt 8, Uncomplicated Solutions to Common Behavioral Problems)*.

Counter-Conditioning (the extinction of an undesirable response to a stimulus, through the introduction of a desirable, more compatible response: Phew! Don't worry about it. Breathe in and exhale saying "so calm." If your dog is spooked by a tree and starts barking, slowly walk near the tree while hand-feeding healthy treats. Don't say much because your voice will inflect your emotion. If you are calm, fine. If you are angry because that jerk on a bike just flew by at warp speed, nearly knocking you over, don't talk. Just give treats. Dogs can't bark and eat or hold a stuffy in their mouth, at the same time. It is an incompatible behavior. You are beginning to create a positive association to the tree, managing the barking and learning to ignore people without manners.

Give me a Job (I have credentials)

Even lap dogs like Japanese Chin need a job. If their job is keep you company and your lap warm, so be it. All dogs, regardless of size, should be granted the privilege of socialization and manners to make the world a less scary place. Suppose your dog needed to be left with someone for an extended period. We don't want our dogs to be so attached to us that they feel as if their world will crumble if we needed to go away, become ill or they do and need to stay at a hospital. Trusting others is for their well being.

Dogs with high energy drives need an appropriate and positive outlet to channel this energy. You can sense energy swirling around a Border Collie who needs to herd something, dead or alive. If you don't have sheep, then create games where s/he can find something to herd (Pawt 6, Creative Games, Dogs, Balls and Balance).

Balancing energy while teaching behaviors like touch
the target (on fitness ball) sit, down, stay, wait,
leave-it and take-it teaches a dog to respond in a
variety of environmental situations and we get some
exercise too! These exercises should be taught in a
variety of positions (standing, sitting, lying down).

Thresholds and Drives (Dog-O-Meter of Awareness)

The term "threshold" has a variety of meanings depending on the situation. A threshold is described as that point, which can happen quickly, when a dog's behavior changes from desirable to undesirable. Dogs can be playing and then it detonates into atomic warfare. Dogs can become overly reactive (barking incessantly). Conversely, they can become fearful and submissive (rolling over and urinating). What we do before, during and after makes a difference.

Thresholds refer to energy levels that may begin normally, but escalate to stressful levels that get out of control. Observation of body language and vocalization (if any), gives us a "warning" that something is going to change.

Going over threshold (out of control) causes the dog's fight or flight reflex to activate in the brain. Overloading the stress circuits diverts energy to survival, rather than listening to us.

Since teaching or modifying a behavior, particularly in highly reactive and energetic dogs, involves learning, being "aware" of our dog's thresholds in a variety of situations, helps us keep them in sub-threshold. For example, the dog is excited but not going to grab, shake and toss a small dog because we have recognized it and redirected the dog to a calmer behavior, like down or "here's your stuffed toy".

Depending on how well we handle stressful situations ourselves is similar to how dogs react when they about to cross over to the dark side. Like going through an airport security check, it is obvious that we are moving from one point to another. If something buzzes, we can be sent back a few times or retained. This can raise our stress levels knowing that we might miss our flight. We may get angry or yell at security personnel and then get detained even longer.

It makes more sense to take a deep breath and cooperate. We can write a complaint later or call appropriate authorities. At that moment, our goal is to get through security and get on the plane or have a drink, especially if it was something silly, like a wired bra or forgotten Swiss army knife in our bag.

The tricky thing about thresholds is that they are fluid and depend on context. They can change from hour to hour. Many factors can influence a threshold level of intensity like location, number or types of people or dogs present, physical considerations, events that happened previously (associations), hormones and other variables. Even keeping our dogs ten feet away, while we assess a situation, may not work on this particular day. On this day, our dog may be more comfortable at twenty feet or not interacting at all.

If we have practiced socialization and manners (SAM), in a variety of environments, with sights, sounds and smells, the success factor rises. It is infinitely impossible to control every nuance of what happens between human and dog or dog-to-dog. As "Bullwinkle" said to "Rocky", "Are they friendly spirits Rocky?" We might say, "Is it friendly energy Rover"?

Being "aware" of our dog's thresholds with other dogs, people, and children, and in different environments, gives us an opportunity to prevent behaviors and manage the energy driving it. Watch your dog meeting and greeting other dogs. How did it go most of the time? Noticing the interactions between your dog and other dogs can tell you a lot. Did your dog back up? How about the other dog? Were their hackles (fur on back) up? What is the energy like around you? Is it noisy or quiet? If the dog is having a calm meet / greet, then a bully enters the pack, it can change everything.

It is a case-by-case assessment, being mindful that even if your dog is 98% "savvy and safe", other dogs may not be, *(Pawt 4, Spatial Bubble and Body Language)*. If your dog is interacting already and you notice the body language, vocalization and energy level increasing to unfamiliar levels, then take a deep breath and "calmly" intervene by calling the dog. They may not come unless they are fearful. If they do not come, serenely walk over. Take the collar and hook up your leash. Walk away to a place where you and the dog can get grounded.

Similarly, we can be our dog's best advocate by being aware of our surroundings before unhooking the leash or venturing into unknown territory. I suggest having your dog sit or at least stand still before releasing the leash, and only if the environment is conducive to the dog enjoying it.

On a scale of one to ten, how energetic are you? How about your dog? Are you matched well? Even if you don't have as much energy as your dog, knowing ahead of time that a normally high energy dog, like a Labrador Retriever, will need alternative ways to channel energy, into constructive and creative enrichment games, is awareness, prevention and management.

Knowing your dog's threshold and energy levels can help reduce destructive behavior, especially from boredom or misdirected energy. Planning and organizing enrichment activities for your dog, while you are away, can focus energy into positive outlets, (Pawt 6, Games).

Regarding children, dogs and tug-o-war games, relax. Many veterinarians and some trainers advise against these games. I do on a case-by-case basis. Parents with children and dogs need supervision and game rules. The dog can grab the tug and run off, or worse, knock the child down, grab the tug and child's toy, and run off. Unraveling and reshaping behaviors will take more time and patience than simply teaching them from the get-go (mine, yours, ours, take-it, leave-it and drop-it). Supervise games with children and dogs, as well as dogs with new – addition – dogs.

The following is an example of an avoidable "train wreck":

Case: A women called frantic that her Miniature Schnauzer, Beckham, bit her. She did not require stitches. She had been through a 6-week training class and took a break. Admittedly, she relaxed her training. The dog was now 7-months old (adolescent). She had a 3-year old toddler. The dog grabbed the child's doll and ran off with Mom in hot pursuit. What began as a giddy game, with Mom and toddler laughing, turned into a game of chase and increasing emotions. After 5-minutes, the scene turned into a now screaming toddler who wanted her doll back and a Mom on the edge who started yelling.

The dog ran under the sofa. Mom reached in and "bam", the dog bit her. Beckham stayed under the sofa for a half hour, until he was clear of present danger. Mom called for a private coaching session. "Good job".

This is a common scenario. In a few sessions that began with a review of basic manners, including doggy diner training, Beckham was easy to manage with boundaries, focused games, and supervision especially when with the toddler.

If it had been the child chasing the dog, what then? This was a combination of chase, prey, juvenile dog behavior and a lot of fun until Beckham got scared. Human emotions affect our dogs until they get use to us. Games should be supervised, played fair, with start and stop times.

What are the Dog's Drives?
Same as Ours, and Not Black and White!
Fight, Flight, Freeze, Faint and/or Appease
Orient, Eye Stalk, Chase, Prey, Grab,
Shake, Dissect and Consume

What drives a dog's behavior? What drives our behavior? We come in all shapes, sizes and personalities. Some of our drives are inherent and others conditioned. Conditioning (how they are taught) plays a big role in how a dog, regardless of their drives, learns how to control their drives and live with us in harmony.

Some dogs may have higher levels of intensity or what some behaviorists call hard or soft wired drives. Understanding how we can shape the drives is even more central than analyzing whether the dog was born hard or soft wired. Having the information is helpful. Adding boundaries, guidance and enrichment can shape and manage the behaviors before they escalate to uncontrollable levels.

Different dogs (breeds and mixes) have drives at varying intensities, similar to our different personalities, needs, and energy levels. Genetics may load the gun, environment may pull the trigger, and then we make choices for a quality life and well being.

Before a drive that is powered by instinct goes nuts, it is wise for us to be "aware" of and "focus" these drives into positive outlets and enrichment games in a variety of situations. This keeps dogs out of trouble and us sane!

We share built-in survival and coping mechanisms with our dogs like fight or flight. Let's explore.

Insight about chase, prey, grab and shake drives can prevent unnecessary incidents between children and dogs, dogs with dogs, dogs with toys, and dogs with live animals in the environment. It gives us an exciting opportunity to better direct the drives into practical activities.

It will not prevent a dog with high prey drive to never touch a chipmunk when given the opportunity. We can teach an emergency "stop", "leave-it" and "come". Even then, I'll be honest; it doesn't work with our Border Terrier. If she sees a chipmunk and is loose in the yard, I have to throw a hissy fit and ring a bell (that indicates dinner) to get her to come. Even then, it is questionable. She needs "to think" I'm going to die. Eventually she comes because "I think" she is embarrassed, especially if other people are around, to see her human companion rolling on the ground crying, or running in the opposite direction, jumping up and down like a pogo stick.

In human relationships, opposites may attract. The attraction is to be with someone whose qualities we admire and may be lacking ourselves. What are your dog's qualities, strengths, tendencies and energy level? What do you admire? What would you prefer to be more subdued? This helps us explore relationships with others too.

As a multi-tasking person with a high, but balanced, energy drive that comes from living with three very different breeds of dog, I believe that dogs can help us shape and balance our behaviors. Parents have shared about the diversities of their multiple children. Being accepting of their differences and proactive, helping them discover and develop their strengths, creates confident dogs and/or children.

As an example, the Newfoundland dog tends to move through life with a watchful eye, has spurts of energy and a nana personality. Newfies calm me down and they are excellent with children. Some view Newfies as couch potatoes, sloppy and needing too much grooming. I see them as a great dog, working in pet assisted therapy, which can calm overactive energy. I carry a drool towel and make sure to keep them cool.

Conversely, a Border Terrier's (and similar terriers) well-being is goal driven to rid the earth of vermin (rats, moles, chipmunks or anything that resemble them). Terriers have energy levels, ranging from stand and stare into a hole for an hour, to accelerating into fifth gear in one second. They can be can be stubborn and bark (a lot) when excited. Knowing this gives me the ability to create an environment that can channel her energy into safe games. If you have a fenced back yard, you may get a wiggly delivery. Folks, this is part of the "Border Terrier Acceptance and Agreement Package".

Our Greyhound is grateful, whimsical and playful. Greyhounds are bred and conditioned to use their keen sight and speed to race after a lure. When retired from racing or breeding, most Greyounds make delightful companions, who stay velcroed to your side, and use their wide-eyed expression of innocence to get to sleep on beds.

Greyhounds are conditioned from living in kennels and crates, and being leashed almost all of the time, except when muzzled and let out to exercise and for bathroom relief. They learn from an early age that walking beside their caretaker is a safe place to be. Our Greyhound enjoys the pleasure of a fenced yard, fluffy bed, good nutrition and love. She will prance around, then run for 30 seconds and happily collapse. Greyhounds are not marathoners. They are short distance sprinters. Salukis are marathon runners who accelerate to 45 mph in a matter of seconds. Good to know if you fancy one. Keep them on leash!

Attraction to a dog that is opposite may enhance your personality or not. Be proactive, explore the breed or mixed breed, and determine if they are compatible with your lifestyle.

1.   What are your intentions with this dog?
2.   Are your intentions in the best interest of the dog's needs too?
3.   Do you have other pets and will they be compatible?
4.   Can this dog enhance your life and you theirs?

Maybe, like me, you love dogs and the ability to be flexible. I enjoy working with a variety of energy levels and drives. It balances mine out.

Dogs are predators. Therefore "prey" is an important drive to be mindful of, especially if living with children, smaller dogs, cats and other furry delights. For example, a Greyhound is tested as children and/or cat safe or tolerant before being adopted. Regardless, supervision is essential until you assess the range of intensity and level of the drive.

Drives present themselves at varying levels of intensity, depending on the environment and how the dog (or we) is feeling. In "thresholds" we talked about them being fluid and in context. If you were getting mugged or worse, what would you do? One person may defend themselves, punching the intruder in the jugular, while another may pretend to throw up, faint or beg for mercy. If you got mugged twice in a year, once in a mall parking lot, and another in your car, with someone sitting in the back seat, holding a gun to your head, you might react very differently.

Drives are instinctive behaviors accompanied by rising and falling of adrenaline (a hormone produced in high stress situations). Constant activation of this stress response can deplete the body, and create fatigue or non-response.

Focusing strong drives (chase, grab, shake) into supervised games with boundaries is similar to human sports. It requires boundaries and coaches or all hell can break loose. The adrenaline junkie may go overboard and start punching someone out. Hockey comes to mind, but pushing, shoving, hollering, and over the top behavior happens in other sports too.

Observing dogs interacting, you can pick out the bully (no social skills), the woos (extreme conflict avoidance—please, don't hurt me), and the equalizer, who will go between two dogs (splitting) calming the escalating energy.

Exploring these drives is knowledge. Knowledge is empowering, helping you direct your dog in safe and fun interactions. Visualize a dog chasing and grabbing a stuffed toy and then shaking the stuffing out of it. As long as it is their stuffed toy and it is a safe milieu (children or others won't be hurt), then it is fine to give them this outlet. Otherwise, a live animal (bunny, squirrel) would be dead. It puts the power of our canine jaw into perspective.

People will giggle at a dog that is shaking the stuffing out of toy. In this scene, the dog is being reinforced for de-stuffing a toy, which gives permission to pulverize other items too, including children and their toys *(Pawt 3, Mine, Yours, Ours)*.

Prey drive is the instinctive inclination of a carnivore to pursue and capture prey. In dog training, prey drive can be used as an advantage when directed well like retrieving items. Dogs can be taught to find and carry objects for us like keys, bags and cell phones.

In predators the prey drive follows a sequence: orient, eye-stalk, chase, grab-bite and kill-bite. In wolves, the prey drive is complete and balanced for survival. In different breeds of dog it can be skewed due to amplified or reduced human-controlled selective breeding for various purposes.

I assess a dog for prey drive by using moving objects like stuffed toys, balls and a robotic dog. Gradually increasing the range of intensity, while observing body language, assesses what the dog's capabilities are from low to mid to high ranges of tolerance. I would much rather see a dog try to kill a robotic "Pluto" than a living being. This is imperative before a dog is placed into family situations especially with children and cats.

Managed prey drives can be beneficial for teaching games such as fly ball, fetch and tug-o-war. Working dog skills (Schutzhund for example) uses motivators that a dog strongly enjoys doing (chase, catch and shake).The difference with a well, positively trained Schutzhund dog is that they know, with a specific cue, when to let go.

The search aspect of the prey drive is valuable in detection dogs such as Bloodhounds and Beagles. The eye-stalk is a strong component of the behaviors used by herding dogs, like the Border Collie, Maremma and Australian Shepherd. Herding is the reward.

In many dogs, prey drives are so strong that the chance to satisfy the drive is self-reinforcing. The reward comes in the chase. Extrinsic reinforcers are not required to compel the dog to perform the behavior. Training is required to guide and manage it.

The prey drive can be a disadvantage if sporting dogs like a Labrador Retriever who must have a strongly inhibited grab-bite to prevent wounding the stock (pheasant, duck).

Bully breeds like the Staffordshire, Pit Bull and Old English Bull Dog have an amplified grab-bite. They were originally bred to "bait bulls" (restrain bulls by hanging onto their noses).

Narcotics detection, and search and rescue dogs, must have enough prey drive to keep them searching for hours in the hope of finding quarry or drugs.

Fight or Flight is the instinctive behavior to flee or evade capture by a predator. This fight or flight Instinct is a feeling of anxiety, fear or terror, when a perceived predator is approaching. The Fight or Flight instinct tells the prey animal to defend itself or run away. If these instincts are warped in human or dog, havoc can break loose, and balance needs to be restored with training, and/or medication.

An example of a prey animal is not always small. It can be a horse or cow, regardless of their size. When a prey animal smells, hears, sees or senses a predator in the vicinity, the prey animal will immediately react. The first reaction takes only a split second and may include an alert to other prey animals in the area. The alert may be a sound, a sudden rising of the head and neck, sudden pricking of the ears, a stomping or striking of the ground with a front foot, a flick of a tail (flagging) or a bounding leap away from the predator in pursuit. These gestures are a means of alerting and even protecting other prey animals in the group or area.

These fight or flight instincts may have been passed down from generation to generation and can be a learned skill. Prey animals teach their young about predators, evading predators, hiding from predators, and even physically defending themselves from predators.

Dogs are predators. Having a leader makes their lives easier, so they can understand their place in the "human" pack, and learn the difference between friend and foe. Dogs are happiest and most balanced in overall behavior when there "drives" are well recognized, stimulated and satisfied, through directed play and activity.

Being "aware" of our dog's' drives gives us the advantage of creating simulated, guided games with boundaries, like gathering up all of the items you have placed ahead of time, in the back yard or in the house.

We take turns yielding. Sometimes the
dogs pull, sometimes I do! It is okay as long
as long as we respect each other.

Who Wants to Be Obedient Anyway?
Rolling of the Scroll (Metaphor)

Not me! I don't expect my dogs to be "obedient" either. I want a mutually respectful relationship where we learn, play and work together as a team.

Obedience is defined as the state or quality of being obedient, compliant with, or submissive to authority. When dogs are submissive, they are cleverly doing what they should, like rolling over to an older dog, or rolling in the dirt for pleasure. If they are submissive to us, we should be grateful, as long as they aren't urinating too. Rolling and peeing is a sign of extreme deference and not necessary in any relationship. A dose of self esteem training, rewarding good behaviors and creating positive and safe associations is required.

When a puppy or dog rolls and pees, this is the ultimate sign of appeasement. Try to be neutral and not overly emotional. This is as low as they can go to show you that they do not want a conflict.

Historically, the connotation and meaning of obedience training came from the World Wars. We were taught to be the "alpha" and "pack leader". The myth was that dogs needed a prong collar and leash and regimented, repetitive training with firm language or worse, physical restraint. Then the dog was forced into submission by being toss on its back and stared at, like a "wolf" would do.

Clarification: Wolves and dogs know we aren't, well, wolves and dogs. Fortunately, most dog trainers and behaviorists are evolving too. We no longer put women or autistic children into sanitariums. We are wiser and know that we no longer need to beat up dogs to submit to us or "alpha".

Can you think of a more submissive and compliant creature than a puppy? In most cases, they are willing to do practically anything we ask (within reason) just for the heck of it.

Awareness centered training (ACT) and the following joyful, easy training (JET) techniques will help you train your puppy or adult dog by shaping behaviors doing what comes naturally every day.

Throughout the journey, you will learn about yourself too, and how to creative positive change in your life, all thanks to the dog. Are you ready? Let's go!

The different people, who are crazy enough
to think that they can change the world, are
the ones who usually do . . . ~Steve Jobs

A. B. C.

The A.B.C.'s of behavior shaping are universal and simple. By the way (BTW), you are not seeing double. I will repeat several areas through-out ACT, as reminders like socialization and manners (SAM). All you need to remember regarding any behavior, dog or us, is that

A. There is an antecedent (something happens)
B. There is a behavior (good or bad) and
C. There is a consequence (at varying levels and should equal the behavior to make a effective change in behavior)

R. R. R.'s (give a little growl)

This has not changed over the years. Whether for dogs or humans, the equation is simple, rab, gab, rab:

A. Request a behavior (RAB)
B. Get a behavior (GAB)
C. Reward a behavior (RAB) (the one you want)

1.2.3. Guidelines for Shaping and Re-Shaping Behaviors

Whether a behavior is desirable or not, heinous or simple, you can shape or re-shape with this easy equation, followed up with practice and commitment. *Know that behaviors that are in place for long periods may take 100—1000 repetitions to change. The change has to be achievable and the training relatable.*

1. Be aware of the behaviors you want, *especially if desirable*, like "walk on loose leash", "sit", "down", "stay", and "come"
2. Reinforce and/or reward the behavior you want as quickly as you can and as often as possible
3. Plan on teaching these behavior in a variety of locations

Guidelines for Re-Shaping Behaviors that You Don't Want

1. Be aware of the behavior, *especially if undesirable*, like— jumping
2. Prevent the behavior from happening by teaching an incompatible, better one, like "sit" instead of "jump"
3. Be careful not to unconsciously and continually reinforce the undesirable by paying more attention to it or touching, smiling or giggling.

PAWT 3

Positively Essential for Dogs who Live with Humans

What Really Matters Mantra

Joyful, easy training (JET) can happen every single moment we spend with our dogs. Opportunities to spot a behavior and shape it are plentiful if we are "aware" of what we want, and pay attention to rewarding them.

How Old Am I—Really?

Let's de-mystify beginning with a dog's age. Behaviorally (developmentally), not chronologically (one, two, three), your dog is about fifteen years old at one year. At two they are about twenty-four. At three—about thirty.

*Genetics loads the gun, environment pulls the
trigger, after that we make sage choices*

It is helpful and necessary to consider history, genetics, breed specifics, environment, nature and nurture, for each dog (or person). Save energy stewing over whether the rehomed dog may have been abused or the puppy may have been "only". The basic information is helpful to plan for the best well being and training approach. I was the "only" child of a second marriage. I am okay, and so are my dogs, because that was then and this is now.

Beyond the basic information to make informed decisions, what matters is what is happening and where we are trying to go. Reflect, learn, let go, and move forward. Begin where you are with your dog.

Unsure of where your dog is at behaviorally? I empathize; I have adopted and work with many adoptees (clients). Begin at the beginning with the basics of healthy nutrition, reduced stress, and slow and easy training. Exposure to the environment should be gradual and safe. Soon enough, you will learn about the dog's challenges and "true colors". Most adopted dogs need an adjustment period to transition, find a place in the pack, and all need foundational training. Often when an adoptive dog settles in, they begin using the same coping mechanism they did before whether on the street, in a kennel or a not so understanding home environment.

Respect all stages and ages of you and your dog's life and transitional stages. When we are 88, how will we want to be treated? As we or our dog's age, we need to modify our lifestyle, health and nutrition, but we do not need to become complacent.

Dogs teach us valuable lessons on aging gracefully. They teach children how to respect other species. Together, we can learn something new every day. We are valuable, appreciated, and can still get attention without setting our hair ablaze at any age. Dogs can too, without acting out or peeing in the wrong place, as long as we are considerate to their changing needs.

FOUR E, E, E, E'S—Sparkle
Engaging, Embracing, Energizing and Encouraging

Engage with your dog in a genuine and understanding way, in the moment, because they sense when you do not. With sparkling clarity, dogs tune in and out of our moods. If we are boring, they will respond in kind.

Embrace dogs as a different species. The moment you do, communication challenges become opportunities to learn.

Focusing energy into positive outlets is healthy for us too. Dogs encourage us to exercise and take care of ourselves. This does not have to be a marathon. It can be a 10-minute walk. We feel good when we feel needed, and dogs need us.

While meditating with our dogs, dream of a sanctuary or beach in Tahiti. Using nose-to-navel breathing and teaching them to "relax" benefits us. When dogs learn self-control, they use it in more excitable and stressful situations.

Encourage them to be the best they can be, while honoring uniqueness. Be their friend and the person your dog thinks you are. It is magic!

If our dogs are not learning and start acting out, turn-it-around and inquire, am I present and aware? Could I have prevented this or done it differently? Is what I expect realistic, relatable and communicated in an understanding way?

Pack Leaders Yield Too!

Dogs need a pack leader, but even pack leaders yield. Like team sports, there are boundaries. Pack leaders (wolves or dogs) do not go around tasering each other. The pack leader expends very little energy getting his or her point across. In the wild, wolves usually hunt at dawn and dusk. There are anomalies (strange, unique and unusual) in nature and life. It is not black or white, but usually nature maintains balance. Oftentimes, this means that survival of the pack means survival of the fittest and fastest.

Dogs know they we are not dogs. It is a respectful
relationship between two species living in
harmony, accepting each other's differences.

To survive, they have an established hierarchy with an alpha, beta, blustery middle-rankers and omega. Alpha and betas may hunt together and with the pack. The female may be wiser and faster or vice versa. The goal is harmony in the pack and survival.

Domesticated dogs do not hunt for their food, but as you will discover in Pawt 3, *Whole Nutrition, Good Dog, Healthy Dog*, they have preferences. Most species, if of sound mind and body, know what they need to be well. Most dogs pick meat, not grains.

To explore more about wolves consider *Jim and Jaime Dutcher's Living with Wolves* or visit *National Geographic*.

Dogs are domesticated and part of the family, but still a different species, more relating to Wolf (spelled backwards, Flow). Even though dogs will imitate humans like our Newfie, Journey, who will sit in a chair, with front legs hanging down, as if imitating humans sitting, she knows that she is a Newf; pretending to be human, probably because it feels good to let her legs hang low.

Do I think she really wants to be a human? No, she is pleasing her human and imitating behavior, to be close, because it is a good place to be. This is part of "our" time together. It is my choice to allow it. When I ask the dogs to "go lie down" or say, "this is my time", they know what to do, back up, lie down or go away.

We bow to each other every morning in gratitude for each other's company, however short. I am happy to take good care of them with healthy nutrition, wellness vet checks and moderate exercise and games they like. We enjoy goofing off. What I have discovered is that when we are "goofing off" is when we learn the most.

The following can be integrated into day-to-day training for puppies and adult dogs. For those of you, who have trained and lived with dogs before, consider an open-mind. Explore new possibilities and especially awareness, focusing and centering. If you are not taking at least one deep breath before you begin training with your dog, try it.

Being a passionate woman who wants to make a difference, I empathize with muti-taskers. Staying grounded as we flow (or zoom) through the day's activities helps to keep us centered. If you have the desire to seek new challenges, be in different places, and do many projects, breathe in deeply, nose-to-navel. We can meet obligations and arrive at many destinations in relaxing and graceful ways, without knocking others over.

Positively essential for puppies and dogs paves a path to good beginnings that flow gently into Level 1 with mild intensity and challenge. You remain close to your puppy or dog, most of the time, except when calling them. Call your puppy to you several times a day in the house or outside (safely).

Level 2 offers a moderate increase in the level of intensity and challenge and the "Grid", gradually increasing activity, and rewarding better and quicker behaviors.

Level 3 is more challenging, but still gradually (not flooding) increases strength of behavior, reliability and confidence for you and the dog. The more confident we become as teachers, the more confident the student. Dogs need to be sure that we at least "think" we know what we are doing, so practice and pretend.

Video vignettes are being added on a regular basis to assist in visual demonstrations, as most of us are visual / audio learners—You Tube Channel (www.youtube.com/dogtalkmedia).

Creating a Safe Place for Dogs and Children
Opium Helps

Organize, plan, implement the plan, understand the need for flexibility and change and make the change (OPIUM).

Dogs deserve the same patience, compassion and understanding that we would want if we were learning something new. Teaching your puppy, and children, to be confident and respectful towards each other, will create a healthy and safe relationship that will last a life time. There are rules and boundaries in any game of sport or relationship, and this includes dogs with humans.

Be aware that for puppies and many rehomed dogs, stepping into a human family environment is like us being parachuted into a foreign country where we do not know the language, customs or culture. What would you do to survive? You would likely figure out basic survival *Abraham Maslow's Hierarchy.*

Each of us is motivated by needs. Our most basic are inborn, having evolved over tens of thousands of years. We must satisfy each need in turn, starting with the first and most obvious, survival.

Only when the lower order needs of physical and emotional well-being are satisfied should we be concerned with the higher order needs of influence and personal development. If the things that satisfy our lower order needs (food, clothing and shelter) are swept away, we are no longer focused on getting a flashier car, ten more pairs of jeans, or a dozen more dog toys.

We plan for events, jobs and vacations. Save yourself, and the puppy, heartache and stress by planning before you bring the puppy home. Keep it simple and sweet (KISS).

Whether you buy from a reputable breeder, online or open your heart to a rehomed dog, the basics of prevention, management and safety will be the same.

Before you get your puppy / dog, meet, greet and interview Wellness Veterinarians and Groomers. Cultivating this relationship ahead of time will create an easier transition and reduce stressful decision making. Choose professionals who you feel comfortable with. If you are not comfortable in their presence or with their approach to pet care, then your puppy or dog won't be either. They will sense your stress.

Healthcare professionals should be willing to meet and greet before the actual visit. Desensitization and positive association to sights, sounds, places, peoples and smells must be gradual and as positive as possible. Life is unpredictable, but we can be grounded (emotionally) if something unusual happens while with our dogs.

Are all family members prepared (children, other pets)?

> *Beforehand, create a puppy safe house with a crate or comfortable confined area, where your puppy can relax when he or she arrives at their new and unfamiliar home. Give them time everyday to rest, renew and take in the newness.*

Puppy proofing is cost effective. Puppies and dogs are curious by nature. They seek and find anything that will amuse them, including electrical cords. Learning new behaviors and discovering new "things" must be supervised. Our Newfie is nicknamed Agent J. J. Bucket for a good reason. Whenever she was missing for a few seconds, we knew she was exploring baskets. At three, she still does.

Prevent, Manage and Teach (PMT)

Create boundaries and safe havens like crates and baby gates. Get down on your hands and knees and crawl around to get a puppy's eye view of the house. Dogs have peripheral vision (surround). They see THINGS in STRANGE places.

From the kitchen, to the bathroom, family room to the bedroom and trolling into the garage and down to the basement—be sure that clothing, chemicals and anything that might be harmful is contained. This may be a good time to organize, or discard of, the last several years of expired items, and those you need to find right away.

This includes children's toys, paint, sporting equipment and tools of any kind. My partner is a hockey goalie. Need I say more? Pucks can be lethal if swallowed. Tripping over a hockey stick hurts. Chewing a hockey stick, that resembles any stick to a dog, is sacrilege. Antifreeze has a sweet smell. Even a few drops could kill a puppy.

Trashcans need secure covers. Food, bones, onions, chocolate, aluminum foil and cell phones can be fatal. Bundle wires and cords with twist ties and move them out of reach until you teach—"leave-it". Even then, if your dog has freedom to explore the house, play freely with children, or we get busy and forget they are explorers by nature, it can be dangerous.

Listen to your intuition and allow your dog's natural instincts to teach you how to teach them.

It does not take long for puppies and dogs to learn what is *Mine, Yours, Ours* (to follow). Dogs generalize, so when they first join our family homes, they do not know what the difference is between a child's doll or their stuffed teddy or bone. A white comforter is the same shade of navy blue. There are fifty shades of every color to dogs, and dogs do see color.

Set the precedent now. If you want to snuggle with your dog on the bed, teach the off first. If you get annoyed when a peach comforter gets designer mud paws, but you still want to cuddle on the bed with your dog (I do), then be proactive and close the door until you wipe their paws.

Crawl into the bathroom and bedroom (dog's eye view). What do you see? Any laundry around? Do they have your underwear? Take it away, saying "mine", and give them their own toy while saying, "yours."

Yard and Garden areas are pure entertainment. Be sure that dangerous debris (glass, lawn and yard tools) and children's toys are picked up and secured, unless you are present to supervise.

Have a dog house or kennel? Be sure it is secured and in a place away from the fence. When dogs are free exercising, or if it snows, they can climb on the house and out of the yard. True story. This happened to a client. Their dog hopped the fence and killed the neighbor's cat, which was tethered. The cat could not escape.

Create safe areas for your dog to spend time outside with fresh, clean water and plenty of protection from the cold or heat.

Puppy Safe Check List At-a-Glance

Cupboards, Lamps, Tables, Clothing, Shoes and Slippers, Trashcans, Cords and Wires,| Furniture, Toiletries, Power Tools, Pesticides and Chemicals, Secure, Safe and Comfortable Fencing or Confinement

For a complete list of plants and chemicals

that could harm your pet

visit www.aspca.org

Emergency Hotline: 1-888-426-4435

or get to your local Emergency Veterinarian.

Dogs with Children

Dogs and children live in the land of discovery and can learn from each other. To create a respectful bond, children under 12 must be supervised around dogs, at all times, and especially near food bowls or coveted toys. They can participate in care and play, in short sessions. Puppies and children have high energy levels. Knowing the thresholds (when enough is enough), and managing them will save your painful and heartbreaking experiences.

Puppies consider young children littermates, not moms, dads, or teachers. They will grab, bite, growl and knock them down in the same manner they would their canine siblings. Children will giggle, wiggle, squirm and scream. Dogs will react as dogs, mouthing, jumping and pawing. Dogs will grab each other while growling, and this is normal behavior. When they do this to a young child, someone may get hurt.

Dogs are not play toys or baby sitters. I say this gently, but strongly. A nurturing dog may react in the same way as they would if a pup whined. They would pick the pup up by the scruff of the neck and walk off. A puppy will comfortably dangle, but an infant or toddler could choke to death. Being "aware" of this sets the stage for a positively growing and respectful relationship between child and dog.

There is a two-page hand-out of the following available at www. dogtalk.com/dogtalkmedia. Please follow these guidelines and share them with others. I can only have a positive trickling effect.

When greeting dogs, wait and ask before
touching. When possible, approach dogs from
the side, especially with strange dogs.

S.A.F.E.R.

1. Supervise interactions between children and dogs.

2. Anticipate risky situations (visitors, unfamiliar dogs)

3. Follow through by teaching children and puppies how to gently and safely interact with each other. If you do not have the time, then separate them until you do.

4. Educate—Dogs are good at being dogs. Children are good at being children. If you want dogs to accept children, have them help feed the dog, one kibble at a time if it is safe.

5. Respect and Role Model: Whenever you are going through transitions, and we all do, this will affect the dog too. Preparing them now, by teaching basic manners, paves the way for safer interactions and a respectful relationship between children and dogs.

Multiple Dogs and Other Species
Dogs with Cats (Meow)

Dogs and cats enjoy and/or tolerate each other's company very well most of the time. Every situation and relationship with any species will be different.

Cats need an escape route or private, gated area. Dogs will eat cat food and poop (yuck). First meet / greets should be supervised. It is beneficial if where you acquire your kitten or adult cat has dog interactions already. If not, ask a friend with a cat safe dog to join you for a cup of coffee. Keep the cat and dog at a safe distance.

Initial meet / greets (dog-to-dog, dog-to-cat or dog-to-human) should be calm, at a distance and until you assess the situation. What is the energy level like? How about the body language? Does one or the other appear stressed or backing away? Until both are moderately grounded and calm, err on the side of caution. It only takes a few minutes to breathe, calm down and make a wise choice. A bite can happen instantly.

Certain breeds of dogs have strong prey drives (Pawt 2, Thresholds and Drives). Puppies may perceive an older cat as a play toy. Some cats are simply not interested in interacting with anyone. Some, like our Maine Coon Cat, sleeps on the dog bed with the dog one day, then acts like being near the dog is an insult the next day. Cats are generally independent and fickle.

Consider these things before you bring a dog or cat home, or force an interaction between them. A little precaution and common sense (proactive) goes a long way to preventing an incident (reactive) and possible injury.

Dogs with Dogs, No Guarantee
Connecting our Heart to our Brain Stem

I love dogs, so I have to be realistic and sensible for their sake and mine. Like many, who find themselves in the position of adding another dog to an existing family dog pack, it can be a challenge. It is not a decision to be taken lightly.

Some dogs have great people skills, but lack dog skills. You can help by guiding them to calmer distances and areas. Choose dog-friendly-dogs who are used to playing and interacting with other dogs. If your dog is stressed, growling or whining excessively, this is an indication that they have no desire to interact at this time.

There is no guarantee of positively good and safe interactions between dog and dog. It increases dramatically when dogs have been socialized and taught even basic manners, dog-to-dog and dog-to-human. There is the possibility of good human management—dog-to-dog. It is not always easy. Sometimes, you need to feed, walk and keep dogs in separate areas for safety.

So many variables in the home and environment can change interactions, dog parks (Pawt 7) come to mine. Transitions in a home or existing lifestyle can change interactions between dogs due to stress of owners and dogs. Illness and aging changes the way an older dog may respond to a new bouncing puppy.

Dogs can live together in harmony when they are a good match, find a comfortable place in the pack and with good human leadership. Providing guidance when introducing any two dogs, from a distance, improves the probability of a peaceful interaction.

While a desire to enjoy twice the companionship has the potential to yield interspecies bliss, it is not without complications. Transitioning from a one dog family to a two or multiple dog household requires careful planning, common sense and a reality check. Are you emotionally, financially comfortable? Can you provide commitment to training and well being? The safety of family members, including other family pets, is essential.

Let's explore some of the motives when we are considering adding another dog (or pet). It helps to connect our heart to our brain stem.

The best possible scenario for another dog or dogs is to bring us pleasure and companionship. It may be a first puppy. Congratulations for reading ACT. Dogs make us laugh and can lower our blood pressure. They provide companionship, acceptance and motivate us to exercise (usually). They can teach children relatable responsibility and about other species.

On the other hand, without training, socialization and manners (SAM), and good health care, they can cause damage, become ill, and require a commitment of time, scheduling, money and patience.

Filling the Void

A common and heart-centered reason for wanting another dog, presented by clients, is the anticipation of the death of an aging dog.

An emotional concern is that the pup will be expected to fill the void of loss, a big job for a little pup. Plus, this pup is an individual and may turn out to be entirely different than the current dog.

Like having three different children, each dog is an individual. Trying to duplicate the first dog (unless you plan to clone) or making unfair comparisons, simply is unfair. Intuitively and emotionally, realizing that this new dog may or may not be thrilled with other pets, or they him or her, is reality.

The Buddy System

Another common reason for add-on dog is to provide companionship for the current dog resident. There are several obvious benefits of creating a two-dog pack, kind of like "Noah's Ark". Busy lifestyles require most owners to be away for eight or more hours. Another pet can make the isolation more interesting provided both dogs get along or have a private space.

Having someone come in during the day for exercise and potty breaks is essential. Doggy daycare is an option, but is not preferable or appropriate for all dogs, and particularly adopted dogs, until after an assessment.

Here's a consideration: the addition of a puppy can benefit or undermine the mental and physical health of an aging dog. Do you really know for sure that your older will benefit? The normal and playful activity of a pup may be annoying or injurious to an older dog. Crate training the puppy and supervising time together, in short sessions, is preferable.

If the older dog has not spent enjoyable time socializing with other dogs, in their lifetime, consider this decision carefully. Your current, older dog should not have to be set aside or get its tail chewed on by a puppy, while children giggle. The older dog's schedule and routine should be kept as it was before the new pup arrived.

On the bright side, a healthy, well adapted older dog that in the past enjoyed interacting with other dogs, safely and without injury, may enjoy the opportunity to teach a puppy the ropes of good doggy manners. Another dog can bring the spark back into an older dog's life, making them feel "alive" again.

Children

It is normal for children to be excited about a new addition, whether a baby brother, sister or pet. It's a good idea to have a family paw-wow explaining what the situation will be like. Everyone can be involved, at appropriate age-levels, in caring for the aging dog and the new pup. There will be emotions, and with multiple siblings, boundaries need to set (schedules, interactions and caring the dogs).

Better Luck Next Time

These cases give me a pilo-erection (hair standing on ends from neck to tail). I won't spend a lot of time on this aside from live and learn, but don't do not do it again. The only species that tends to ruminate and make the same mistakes repeatedly is humans. This message comes directly from those dedicated to working in shelters and educating people on responsible dog guardianship.

Some people select a second dog because the first dog "didn't work out". Okay, make a mistake, but be accountable, and learn from it. With good intentions, people will visit a shelter, then decide to adopt or buy a cute dog breed. Please plan and know that it is a lifetime commitment. The United States has more than 8,000,000 dogs in shelters, many that are euthanized every year.

We research before buying a house, car, groceries, having a baby, a washer and dryer, even bottled water! When it comes to adding a living being to a family pack, we need to do the same research, planning and choosing about long term care and well being.

Do your homework before adding a living being to the family pack. If it is a dog, integrate awareness centered training into daily living and learning with them.

Try Again, Maybe We Can Fix It

Another motive is the "try it again" dog to fix the first dog. If Cisco is digging holes and barks constantly, a second dog will learn through role modeling how to dig bigger holes and bark louder in harmony with the first dog. You will likely amplify your already existing dilemma.

Dogs relinquished to the backyard, downstairs, crate or kennel, to avoid uncontrollable behaviors, can't learn how to behave. Adding another dog to fix this dog will only aggravate the problem if the "current" dog resident doesn't have any manners. If they are good dogs who enjoy interacting, and listen to you, then it might work.

The solution may be to spend time training your current dog, then think about an addition.

Humanitarian

In some cases, the reasons for acquiring a second dog are primarily humanitarian. I do events at shelters, so I know the feeling. There are always dogs that I could easily pick up and take home. However, I pause, take a deep breath and do a reality check.

We humans are altruistic and want to make a difference. Many dog lovers rescue strays, abused and abandoned animals. This is a noble cause if done carefully and the dog's quality of life is improved. That depends on the quality of life now. Will it be better?

Safety

The easiest and most dangerous thing to do is to immediately allow the new adoptee the same freedoms accorded the current pet(s). Withhold introduction until you know that the new dog is free of contagious disease. Observe behaviors. Concentrate on integrating the new dog SLOWLY and on NEUTRAL territory.

Socialization—Worth Revisiting

A top on any puppy or dog's agenda for successful integration in the world of humans is socialization and manners (SAM).

We want dogs to be people-friendly. As shared, there is absolutely no guarantee that dogs will be dog-friendly. Do you like everyone? Dogs don't either. Not all dogs enjoy dog parks, day care or other dogs. They will learn to tolerate situations with your guidance and management.

Some dogs have great people skills, but lack dog skills. If you have a pup, seize the opportunity and socialize. I am positive that you will have, at the least, a reasonably reliable, predictable and manageable adult dog. Your dog may not embrace every other dog with a big sloppy kiss, but as a team, you will enjoy a trusting and enjoyable relationship based on awareness, education and respect.

A well-socialized dog is more resilient and likely to adjust to living in a pack, human or canine. A well-socialized dog is less fearful of new situations and relies on you for cues before making the next move (bark, bark, lunge, lunge, jump, bark).

Every dog-to-dog interaction is different depending on the signals that the dogs give to each other and the environmental cues. Most often, we humans have missed them until something happens. Be aware; keep your eyes on your dogs and other people's dogs.

Puppies need to learn how to navigate their way with other pups. They pay close attention to body language cues. This needs to happen with as little human intervention as possible, as long as the dogs are SAFE. Growling and vocalizations (whines) are normal while playing as long as the result is not blood and stitches. To learn more see (*Pawt 3, Biting Awareness*), thank you.

Emotions

What happens when a feather drops or a car explodes?
Emotions should equal the event. If a dropping
feather sends you or your dog into a state of panic, it
is time to regress, breathe and balance emotions.

If the dog is socialized and desensitized to a variety of sights, sounds and smells, AND, relies on you for cues, then whether a feather drops or a car explodes, it does not matter. When a loud noise happens and your dog looks at you, smile and say, "Wow, wonder what that is?" rather than, "OMG, HELP, a loud noise, I think I'm gonna die?"

Taking in a deep breath and exhaling, let's continue. During interactions with other dogs, the message that we humans give when we pull on leashes, or express too much emotion, affects the way they respond in similar situations. We can teach them how to respond calmly, playfully or confidently, by being calm, curious, playful, neutral and confident.

Gradually socializing our dogs to sights, sounds and smells in a broad variety of situations, while remaining grounded and sensible, will help create calm dogs who look to us before lunging, barking or conversely, falling into a shivering heap.

Finding a Place in the Pack

In a multiple dog household, dogs need to find their place in two packs simultaneously, one in the human pack and one in the dog pack. They need a leader who sets clear boundaries in both packs.

As shared, families have distinct and different value systems. Dog packs do too. Well-socialized dogs generally survive and thrive in the pack instinctively. They have canine pack savvy.

Here's an example: Wild canines (wolves) live in close family units for survival just like we humans. Even with this close relationship, the affiliation between individual dogs can break down.

Serious conflicts can arise that can cause the death or banishment of a pack member. Each member must learn how to co-exist peacefully. It makes sense for the pack's survival. The "alpha" is not loud or boisterous. The alpha savors their energy, along with the beta, so they can hunt and provide for the pack. All wolves have an important role for survival of the pack whether they are the Alpha, Beta or Omega (considered the lower end of the hierarchy).

Domesticated dogs spend the first 7 or 8 weeks of life with their canine Mom, the Dam. The human family helps with care, food & shelter. In essence, they begin like a wild dog pack, naturally, but are simultaneously introduced to an alien species . . . humans! At 8 weeks, a puppy is removed and placed in the alien, human home. There is no guarantee that a dog in this environment will learn how to relate to other dogs, but if you allow them to interact normally, as early as possible, your chances of multiple dogs' cohabiting peacefully are increased. Prepare to intervene, calmly, if energy in unbalanced. Redirect to a peaceful place and activity.

Should I get Another Dog and What Kind?

Good questions! As a behavioral counselor, I've always believed that people have the answers within. Again, connect the heart to the brain stem. Acting impulsively is easy, in the beginning. The ride home is joyous until the other disagrees that this is a good idea.

I believe that most people know intuitively what to do if they take time to quiet the chatter in their minds. Then, the answer will present itself.

Where are you (and the family) emotionally, financially and stress-wise? Have you recently lost a beloved pet? What is your intention in adding a dog to your current lifestyle? Adding dogs to a peaceful situation adds pleasure. It will also add more work and can upset the apple cart. Are all family members on board and willing to participate in schedules, feeding, exercise and training?

Matchmaker: Male or Female?

Through experience and in my opinion, I've concluded that gender doesn't make a difference unless you are a breeder or the dogs are kept intact (not spayed or neutered). Adding multiple females that can go into heat, and having more than one stud dog hormonally salivating can cause atomic warfare. Responsible breeders are aware of this and do a good job!

A sensible approach is to look at your current dog(s), living situation, goals, and then decide what a good match would be based on assessment. If you are lucky enough to have a litter to observe and pick from, this may make the decision for you.

A common assumption that females are more passive than males is a myth. I have lived with multiple dogs for as long as I can remember. Females can fight as much as males if not managed. It truly depends on the situation, the dogs, the goals and the environment.

Matching the dog to the activity level, purpose and size of the dog(s) living together helps. A Yorkie can dominate a Rottie, but the size differential, even in play, needs to be considered. One heavy paw pounce and squash.

Problems can arise from owning pets of dissimilar sizes and behavioral tendencies. If you own a Newfie and a Corgi, there is no obvious difference in their physical capabilities except shorter Corgi legs. However, if you bring the dogs to a lake, Newfies, being strong swimmers, will poop a Corgi out fast. Conversely, a Corgi will out herd a Newfie. They were once bred to herd cows by nipping at their heels.

I share my life with different breeds including mutts. With careful integration, socialization, positive training, compassion and courage, colored with common sense and awareness, dogs of any gender can make wonderful companions. Make adjustments that are appropriate for each individual dog's strengths and abilities.

Screening Devices—Be a Sucker for Surveillance

Use screening devices when adopting (shelter, rescue, breeder or pet store). Most rescue organizations and breeders do an important job up front gathering information about potential dog parents. Finding a good match is important for dog and owner for all of the reasons we have shared in ACT.

For any dog you are considering, *they are all living beings*, whether buying from a reputable breeder, pet store or adopting. Be skeptical, but listen open mindedly to what you hear. If it sounds too good to be true or vague, it is. Even though the dog is cute and cuddled on the foster caretaker's couch, ask yourself, is it a good "match" for you and your lifestyle?

Observe behaviors and how dogs behave around volunteers. Most breeder and shelters will invite you to spend time with the puppies or dogs.

Look for idiosyncrasies and drives, as well as good stuff. Does the dog sit upon request? Do they enjoy human company? Does he enjoy chasing balls, playing Frisbee, walking calmly? Is she jumping or barking? Does the dog nip at your legs or hands? Does the dog cringe at human contact, especially when trying to offer a touch?

For some dogs, these behaviors may be re-shaped, but you will need to make a commitment with an experienced trainer / behaviorist.

Adopted dogs need adaption time when transitioning to an unfamiliar environment. Turid Rugaas, author of *Calming Signals, Body Language of Dogs (book and DVD)* suggests that dogs be given equal amounts of time to integrate. For example, if a dog has been in a shelter for 6-months, then give them that amount of time to adjust to living in new surroundings.

I have Multiple Dogs, Will they Fight?

Good question with no clear answers. Fighting is a nebulous term and seldom just happens. Cues are visible. We don't pick up on them or we deny them because we so badly want our dogs to love each other and get along. Most dogs have already made eye contact and given several body language cues, especially from the "eye".

It can be as simple as a quick squabble between an adolescent and older dog that is a valuable learning experience. Conversely, it can escalate to a blood bath over resources (food, toys, and humans) for a dog who is a resource guarder *(Pawt 8)*.

Observe your dog's interactions with other dogs including body language, changes in routine, places in the pack, and your contribution, or place in their pack, as their human leader. Watch for displacement and stress signals *(Pawt 4—Body Language)*.

Puppy Breath—Sweet and Juicy

I wish we could bottle puppy breath. We could take it for walks, and when an unfamiliar dog approaches, pop the top off and present it to both dogs, avoiding negative interactions.

Imagine this: An adult intact, male Great Dane
and an intact Pit Bull approach each other tails
up, staring. We pop open a bottle of "puppy
breath" and voila, they start kissing each other's
flews (lips). Okay, back to reality. If you patent
this, remember who gave you the idea.

Puppies and adult dogs usually get along. Puppies acquiesce to adult dogs, looking to them for guidance or role-modeling. Adult dogs smell the same sweet puppy breath that we smell. Well balanced adult dogs will allow a puppy to get away with a lot until the pup turns into a rambunctious adolescent (6-months and up).

An adolescent (a one year old dog is equivalent to a 15 year old teenager) may challenge the older dog. Most are blustery middle ranking leader wanabees, who, when put in their place quickly, by a "true" leader, will adapt. True leaders do not need to expend much energy. A look or movement suffices.

Guidelines for Introducing a New Addition

1. Simulate an association by gradually and safely introducing your dog to other dogs. Use a stuffed dog or puppet! Observe reactions.
2. Introduce your dogs to several dogs before considering an addition, unless your intention is a lap dog.
3. Use neutral territory. Many dogs are naturally protective of their territory, toys and food.

4. If there is a significant difference in age, plan ahead of time for stage of life changes that will occur. Anticipate changes at sexual maturity (approximately 7 to 9 months) and again at social maturity (18 months to 3-years).

5. Have a game plan in advance. Where will s/he eat, sleep and play?

6. Will you feed all dogs at once and where (see Doggy Diner)?

7. Is your first dog possessive of toys, food or you? Then control the toys, food and your affection.

8. Disrupting your current pet's lifestyle may add stress to the relationship. Plan to spend some extra time with him or her.

9. Ask your veterinarian to refer you to a professional who can help guide you through the process.

10. Enroll in an awareness centered training class to bond with your dog. Integrate ACT into daily living with your dog.

Life Rewards and High Ranking Motivators
Eat, Play, Love

Life Rewards Relationship Mantra
You do something for me and I'll do something for you

Life Rewards (LR) are empowering because your dog needs (and desires) them to survive (food, play, toys, attention (us) and quiet time).

Food is not a positive reinforcement if you eat for eight hours straight! Imagine you ate pizza seven days a week, it's your anniversary, and your partner says, "Let's go to Famous Pizza and get anything you want". Not only is this confusing, but boring.

To be reinforcing, the item needs to make sense and be of high value and/or needed to sustain life. If your dog loves being with you, then you are a life reward. This can get tricky so tune into your "awareness channel".

We all work for food.
You can diminish the value of any life reward (LR)
or positive reinforcement (PR) by overusing it.
The training vantage point is in the moment.

If you know what your dog's life rewards are, you can teach anything. Your underwear may be adored, but these are a" leave-it" item. Be proactive and focus on the desired behavior, rather than reactively hissing after your puppy chews your favorite DVD.

Mirror, mirror on the wall,
where was I when the pup chewed my soccer ball?

High ranking motivators (HRM) are what turn us on. What motivates you to get up in the morning, go to work, pay the bills (never mind that one) or clean the house? Whether striving for competition, pet assisted therapy, service dogs or companionship, figure out what motivates your dog and your dog will be eager to learn.

Reserve the top three to five, high ranking favorites, for juicy teaching opportunities. Is it a good game of fetch or a special toy? Is it a walk with you or a hug? Sparingly offer these, reserving them for when you have time to ask for a behavior like "sit".

Do you want your favorite dish 14 times a week? Maybe you do and that is okay. What excites you? I enjoy dark chocolate and good glass of wine on a Saturday night, but I don't want it 7 days a week. It is something I look forward to like a vacation. My dog loves (fill in the blanks).

At various ages and stages of puppy / dog development, nutritional needs, and adding some zip to the training, may be necessary. We have physicals, dental cleanings and do well being check-ins. Dogs need the same relationship and lifestyle assessment during various stages of life *(Pawt 10, Bone Journals)*.

As you get to your know your dog, discover what turns them on. It will empower you and motivate your dog to eagerly learn how to be an amazing companion.

Effort with a Light Touch
"Mindfulness tethers the mind to the present. Initially this
takes effort, but this effort is applied with a very light

touch. It's like brushing your teeth: you brush, you get
distracted, and you just naturally come back. No big deal.
By gently returning to the present, our mind calms down,
and everything seems workable."
—Pema Chodron

Housetraining—*Not Breaking*

We do not break puppies or dogs because they are not things. We teach them how to live in human households, where to eliminate, what to play with, and how they should meet and greet people. Enjoy this gentle and effective hand-out Housetraining-at-a-Glance for gentle to post on your refrigerator at <ins>www.dogtalk.com</ins>.

Crate Haven—*Not Prison*

Crate training and/or some kind of safe confinement (baby gates) is essential if you have a puppy and small children. If you want to create some personal space between you and your dog during private times, doors work well.

If you are attached to your dog, and vice versa, consider teaching them how to enjoy themselves on their own time with self-fulfilling activities like playing with a stuffed Kong, or Wobbler (Kong). These can be filled with their breakfast or dinner (kibble).

Enrichment toys are puzzles your dog can safely interact with, figuring out ways to find treats. It will help you both reduce stress and avoid separation anxiety *(Pawt 8, Prevention, Management and Solutions to the most common Behavioral Issues).*

Instinctively, puppies desire to eliminate after being confined, eating, drinking, playing, resting or sleeping. At about 6 months, they have better control of their bodily functions for about 4—6 hours (strong bladders).

Crates are not cruel if you don't use them for punishment. They are a safe haven for a puppy or dog to hang out with a few comforts (toys and blanket). Many dogs, like our Greyhound, will retreat to their crate for peace of mind. Greyhounds usually live in crates while racing, so it's common sense to give them this freedom of choice and familiarity.

Prevention, and keeping your puppy on a schedule, is the path to successful house training. Supervise your puppy and children (especially under 12) at all times. Puppy play time should be short, about 10—15 minutes per session.

When the puppy sniffs and circles, take him to a designated elimination area outside. When they wake up, take them out. After they run around and play, take them out.

Clean up after your puppy in the house and outdoors. This will prevent playing with, and eating of, poop (yuck). In the house, a safe enzymatic cleaner like Nature's Miracle works well and without odor. Clean up after your dog wherever you go (poop bags). We set the example for future generations and to take care of planet Earth.

Do you have cats? Where is the litter box? For the cat and dog's sake it should be in a peaceful place, and out of reach of the dog. Keeping the litter box clean is helpful.

Be aware that puppies and dogs cannot learn while distracted or extremely stressed. The younger the dog, the more you need to focus on ONE BEHAVIOR AT A TIME.

Do not confuse energy with stress. A dog with good energy needs an appropriate outlet to channel the energy. A dog exposed to stress for long periods, or a fearful dog, need to learn how to relax.

Many dogs I meet are bored and this is confused with bad behavior. Stressed dogs will lie down, zone out, repeatedly make mistakes, hide in corners, and can be destructive, growl or snap *(Pawt 4, Body Language)*.

Exercise your dog every day. Quality time is a matter of choice, but ten minutes, several times a day, for most puppies is adequate.

Dogs who are allowed unsupervised play, for long periods, get tired, but not trained *(Pawt 7, Dog Parks v Play Groups v Walking)*.

When Does Training Begin—Now!

Training begins for puppies when they are born just like infants. There are stages of development and learning, as previously mentioned. Puppies know how to sit at two weeks old. It is a myth that we humans are teaching them how to do postures. We are teaching them with a signal, when and for how long. We just like to think we know everything.

Whether a dog is watching us, or not, training is happening. When they greet us, jump on us, bite us, and we laugh, the event is trained. Being aware can start you and your pup on the right track. Integrate training in everyday living and learning.

The Doggy Diner
Gods and Goddesses of Food

Visit us <u>www.youtube.com/dogtalkmedia</u>

When someone says they do not want to use food as a bribe to train their dog, I am puzzled, but realize it is because of a lack of awareness. I ask a few questions to see if they actually know why and how they are using food.

Food is a powerful training tool if used wisely. Dogs have to eat or the consequence is death. Why work harder than we need too. We need to work to pay our bills and buy our groceries and clothes.

> If we feed our dogs 2X a day, oftentimes puppies are fed 3X a day; this gives us 14 to 21 training opportunities a week to teach behaviors doing something natural, eating. I like this advantage!

How long does it take to feed a dog or multiple dogs? I have 3 dogs. I train in about 3-5 minutes, twice a day. Simply, I want the dogs to do something for me like sit, wait, down, stand, leave-it, back-up, give me a high-five, or chill-out for "2 more seconds", "okay", "5 seconds more".

Rather than throwing their dishes down for a food gobble, I empower myself using something they love and need anyway, food, to teach behaviors to make my life easier. It safely adds in a little healthy competition between the dogs to see which one will make it to their diners first. They are expending mental energy while working for their meals and see me as the food goddess. What's not to like about that?

A bribe comes before a behavior or to tease your dog.
A food reward comes after the
behavior to teach your dog.

Rewards are modified for the challenge, intensity and speed of the behavior. With the exception of puppies and novel (new) behaviors, prepare to up the ante, praising and offering healthy treats often. Over time, food is leveled off to random or variable reinforcement *(Pawt 2, Reinforcement Schedules or Appendix A—Big Words)*. It prevents food co-dependency.

Awareness Note: This is not a behavior modification plan for resource guarding dogs that see their dinner bowl, toys, space or the entire neighborhood as their possessions. It is one of the most empowering ways to prevent and shape good manners around people, food and objects. You become giver of coveted resources while eating, playing, training and loving.

Doggy Diner Training Opportunities (DDTO)

*Having our dogs sit for a few seconds before giving
them their food teaches self-control. This will range in
levels of intensity and energy. If you have multiple dogs,
begin with one, adding in the other. It must be safe.
Puppies, older or challenged dogs should not have to
compete with "Butch the Bully" for dinner. Common
sense is to give them a place to eat that is safe.*

I cannot emphasize enough how important and easy it is to use feeding time, or cleverly dispensed healthy treats, for training opportunities. Keep some in your pocket.

Whether it is welcoming a new puppy, adopted dog or changing behaviors of present dogs, using DDTO is empowering for you as the one who supplies what dogs need and want. Most dogs find great pleasure in FOOD, unless they are ill or conditioned not too.

Plus, it makes sense that we want our puppies / dogs to tolerate human presence around food dishes. We want them to enjoy us hanging around while they eat and know that a hand near a bowl means good things. **Mouthing puppies** quickly learn how to take a kibble "gently" from you. Begin slowly and with compassion. They are learning something new.

Whether with a new puppy or multiple dogs, DDTO works like magic. Food is a primary life reward for dogs. They have to eat to survive.

Dinner bowls are a primary distinction for us and dogs. If it were not for their dinner bowls, dogs would still be wolves or wild packs of dogs. Our domesticated dog, still DNA wolf, is the same when it comes to survival skills AND their digestive system, with the exception that most of their food is now roasted, broiled, baked or processed in vats by big buck companies. We can prepare our own healthy meals for our pets too *(Pawt 3, Healthy Dog, Good Dog, Whole Nutrition)*.

Using feeding time as an integrated part of daily living with our dogs builds a trusting relationship that can be shared with most members of the family—with supervision. Dinner bowls and feeding are a daily occurrence, just as supplying wholesome nutrition for our energy and activities. It is an easy way to begin training with puppies or *reshaping behaviors with any dog.* It helps to build a trusting relationship while teaching the dog how to watch-me, sit, wait and gentle, and especially with supervised children.

Clients will say that the dog jumps on them, driving them nuts. If the dog jumps, put the dinner bowl back on the counter and repeat the sequence. Jump too much, walk away for a few seconds and observe. This takes approximately 10 seconds. Dogs eat their food in about 30 seconds, more if they are older, recovering from illness, fearful or introspective. They learn very quickly that when they are "sitting" and "calm", they get food.

Multiple dogs or if integrating a new dog into the household, requires separate dining areas, especially if one is a puppy, an older adult who may eat slower or an adopted dog with unpredictable behavior.

True colors usually don't present themselves until dogs are settled in. Familiar **survival coping mechanisms** may kick in, perfectly normal for the dog, but may be shocking to us humans. For example, growling or snapping at hands near food bowls. Being mindful of these transitions can help you prevent incidents like biting or resource guarding *(Pawt 8, Dino Dog)*.

The easiest, safest and most successful way of feeding multiple dogs, especially those with a predictable "spatial bubble" is DDT. As long as the dogs are not aggressive, each dog is taught where their dog diner is and asked to sit. A healthy competition develops with dogs dashing to the diner and sitting.

Obviously, you need to be aware of the dog's tendencies or quirks first, so proceed slowly, erring on the side of caution. When in doubt, space them out as far as you need or feed the questionable dog in another room.

If a dog can't sit, (we had a three legged Leonberger), then we look for whatever they can do successfully. If they can't eat comfortably, for example an older dog, fearful dog, or one recovering from injury, modifications are made for their safety and comfort.

Again, and this is important, there are exceptions, at various life stages of life and learning. If a dog is older, slower or sick, they deserve preferences. Puppies need quality (and quiet) time and one-on-one focused training too.

If you are stressed or in a hurry, a stuffed Kong or Wobbler in a crate will help a pup expend some energy foraging for food and stay out of trouble.

> Trouble is anything a dog does because
> we are not supervising or teaching.

Biting Awareness, Soft Mouthing—Begin Immediately

In the real world, hands will be near our dog's mouth. Puppies naturally mouth. Teaching them that they can't is counter-intuitive. Teaching them biting awareness (how hard or soft) is essential!

Dogs learn the difference between a chew toy, human skin, and how hard or soft (biting awareness). Teaching them gently while touching, feeding and playing begins as soon as you bring your puppy / dog home.

Touch your pup, calmly, from head to toe often. This will desensitize them for future interactions with people (wellness visits, grooming, visitors, and interactions with children). When they don't resist or squirm, praise or give a healthy treat (kibble if you prefer). Be patient and do not give up. Saying, "oh, okay, you can go", because they are chewing on your arm, is not acceptable. Reward them when they are "sitting" and "calm".

Doggy diner is excellent for this because you are hand-feeding food while teaching them to "sit", "wait a second" and "gentle".

Observe dogs in play with other dogs. Watching dogs rumble and mouth each other may seem rough. Dogs play differently than we do. However, a dog who knows how to interact with other dogs doesn't get hurt or inflict injury *(see visual of pups interacting at www. dogtalk.com/dogtalkmedia)*. Puppies have sweet puppy breath that we like to swim in.

Older dogs recognize puppy breath so this gives the pup temporary freedom of expression. At about 4 months, puppies start losing puppy breath and baby teeth. They become more independent. Adolescence is not the time to relax your training. Imagine behavior between human teenagers *(Pawt 7, Taming Energy with Benefits)*.

Redirect puppies to appropriate, indestructible chew toys like Gumabones or Kongs. Redirect teenage dogs to positive energy outlets like sport, Frisbee and walking. Walking is one of the best ways to train your dog. When they walk calmly, it is meditative for you. Dogs get to visit the environment and you get to teach them how to control themselves.

Rewards for walking nicely for even 30 seconds may get the dog "sniffing" time, a toss of the ball (safe area) or treat.

> Redirecting is a valuable tool that changes the dog's mind/action from something they shouldn't be doing to something they should. You can redirect a dog that is pulling on a leash by simply turning around. Circle benches, bushes and trees. Walk for three steps and stop. Follow this sequence several times. If you are satisfied with the results, then gradually increase the steps, like dancing with your dog.

Biting Awareness—Integrative Plan

1. Encourage gentle mouthing only.
2. Reaction to hard bites = "OUCH" + sulk / frown.
3. Give the pup what they can chew (safe toy).
4. Hand feed kibble—it is a joyful, easy way to get attention and teach manners like "watch-me", "sit" and "gently".
5. Supervise children and the games they play with dogs (rules, boundaries).
6. Too energetic? Calmly take the pup outside to pee, then to the crate for a time-out *(nap—not punishment)*.
7. In five to ten minutes the puppy usually falls asleep or amuses themselves with a toy.
8. Remember to take them out after they wake up to eliminate (view this and praise), sniff and explore for a few minutes.

Mine, Yours, Ours—*for puppies and adult dogs*

What do we really own forever? We are attached to a lot of possessions that may or may not make us, or our dogs, feel good temporarily. Our dogs will be with us for as long as they can be. Given shorter lives, it is wise to be their best advocate, friend and teacher.

I enjoy spending time in a mutually respectful relationship with the dogs, where we take turns yielding to each other. Sometimes, it is fun to simply hang-out without rules.

Look around. There is an overabundance of toys, equipment, food and clothing for our dogs. Is it true that it benefits the dog's well-being? Or is it to amuse and entertain the human? People love their dogs and the market-place knows it. It is a billion dollar industry. Turn-it-around and ask, "Is it true and necessary for you and your dog"?

I am as vulnerable as anyone else. Like a giddy kid, I have bought, tried and been given every leash, collar, cure-all and piece of equipment on the market. The photo earlier on in ACT of Gary, with a confused look on his face, is meaningful. He isn't alone. We have pointers, clickers, toys, collars and leashes in varying lengths and harnesses that promise to cure jumping and pulling. Some work, some do not. It depends!

Most of us enjoy playing with new gadgets. It gives us a choice. A toolbox needs tools. Dog training is no exception. When is enough, enough? Only we can decide. Like clearing the clutter from my closet, it is a relief when I clear the dog clutter from their closet too.

In "object exchange" I determine what the dogs love by asking, "do you like this or that?" Most of the times, they choose food over a toy, and one toy over another. No-one will ever convince me that dogs do not have favorite toys or enjoy opening new ones (novelty). Like a child who is given too many toys, all at once, they lose interest quickly too.

If this is case for you, do an inventory of all their toys, and play object exchange. Which are the favorites? Choose three, throw the others out, or put them in a toy box. Better yet, create a game by having your dog learn to put their own toys in the toy box. You can rotate them later on, "look, new toy!"

Oftentimes, their favorite toy ends up being something they've dragged in or a cut-off sweatshirt sleeve tied in knots. I swear they know when they have won something at a raffle, like that giant Alligator (Ally) that smells awful. Journey, our Newfie, won't let us toss it away. I have to "sneak" clean it. It is her special pacifier.

What I discovered that is fun for me and the dogs is a little game we play from puppy-hood into senior citizenship called **Mine, Yours, Ours.** The benefit of this game is that it can be as simple or as challenging as you desire. It can be equally effective interacting in human relationships too. It is easy to teach children how to play, "this is mine, this is yours, and we can play with this toy together".

Mine means —"it is mine and leave-it." When our Newfie joined our family at 8 weeks old, we immediately began teaching her what was "mine" (meals, eating a yogurt, having a glass of wine or watching a movie in peace).

Yours is her toy, blanket, dog napper, healthy treats, yogurt (or meal) in the bowl. I have the dogs sit while I dole out carrots saying, "mine", and I eat one, "yours", and I give them one if they are sitting and "ours", we all get one. Yippee—carrot party.

Remember habituation and generalization. Dogs get use to ways of being, doing and the environment. We all do. If we are consistent "enough" with mine, yours and ours, they will be too. They quickly learn what the incentives are of "popcorn night".

Ours is shared time and this is your choice. Shared time might be a game, walk, playing or again, popcorn night. Will it get competitive with multiple dogs? Possibly, but it is no surprise that you must spend quality time alone and in groups, whether with dogs or multiple children. If you have six children, you aren't going to spend all of your time with every one of them, every second, of every day. You arrange quality time to spend with each dog, puppy or child, even for five or ten minutes.

Quality time amounts to what you can give without guilt. Moments are as important as longer, boring training sessions. One minute is "good enough" for one mine, yours, and ours moment, teaching this slipper is "mine", that stuffed toy is "yours", and this ball is "ours", "let's go play".

Instinctively (will it enhance your dog's natural behavior in a beneficial way), and intuitively (does it feel right for you) integrate it as you interact with your dogs during daily living and learning. Be sure to pass this on to other family members and friends too. It is less confusing for dogs (and children) if adults are on the same page with boundaries, guidelines and good social behavior. Games, and life, have rules that need to be honored to learn, grow and interact successfully.

Dogs are habitual creatures and learn through repetition, conditioning and practice, just like us!

What is your "our" time like with your dog? On a Friday or Saturday night, we enjoy a movie and tossing popcorn. That is the "our" night. They know where to go—age appropriate. Once they are settled on their blankets, popcorn is tossed or placed (if necessary). I say, "placed" because if you have an older dog and a younger dog, who might eat and dash to the older dog, you may want to have the older dog near to you, so you can "place" the treat and supervise the younger pooch. For a printed version of "Mine, Yours, Ours" visit www.dogtalk.com/dogtalkmedia.

Five minutes of in the moment

successfully training your dog,

is as valuable as 1 hour of boring, inattentive training.

Therapeutic Chewing: Chew This, Not That, Not Me Gentle Please!

Chewing is therapy for dogs, just like doing something that relieves stress is for us (meditating, exercising, reading, resting). If a dog is chewing illegal items (furniture, clothing, lampshades, laptops), it is a crystal clear sign that they should not be left alone unsupervised.

Prevention and management is safer and more proactive (anticipating), rather than reactive (reprimanding after the behavior).

Even 3-seconds, after a dog has chewed the sofa, is too late to start teaching "leave-it". Teach "leave-it" before and practice each day.

Confine the dog in a safe place with their favorite two or three safe and indestructible toys (Kongs, hard rubber, strong stuffed toys). Test toys out while you are available to supervise, ensuring that it is safe.

The Art of Stuffing (and de-stuffing)—Chew Toys A Doggone Right!

Just like some of us enjoy a good snack, glass of wine, a movie, cup of tea, computer games, sports, or relaxing in a Jacuzzi to relieve stress, almost all dogs and puppies like a good chew. Whether you want to allow them to destuff a toy is your choice. It can be dangerous without supervision. Swallowing stuffing is not healthy. That said, dogs enjoy shaking and destuffing. You can create games where you offer a toy and let them shake, but before any damage is done, object exchange to another. They can release "shaking" energy without damaging themselves or others.

There is nothing inherently wrong with this natural behavior as long as "you" supervise the activity, particularly with children. Young children, under 12, do not have the ability to safely teach the art of "shaking" games. They giggle and the dog can transfer the "shaking" of a cheap teddy to de-stuffing the family room sofa—not a good path.

Your job is to make sure your puppy develops a safe chew-toy habit, with safe toys, before s/he selects other, unacceptable artifacts in your home.

One way to get dogs interested in toys is to make them appealing. Stuff them! Get a Kong or Wobbler and stuff it with kibble. Smear a little almond or peanut butter on the end. Some dogs will expend energy for an hour trying to extract the kibble.

Be mindful of calorie intake and puppy elimination. If they eat in the morning, they will have to go out to eliminate. Most dogs do not like to soil their crates or beds. Some have no choice (kenneled for long periods). If you are offering toys with food, cut back at dinner time (calorie intake).

Enrichment games are boxes and puzzles that dogs (and cats) can enjoy. You place their kibble or treat into the holes and cover it. Spend some time teaching them the concept of sliding the blocks back and forth to "find it". They expend energy in a positive way. Some of our dog's (and cats) favorites are at <u>www.nina-ottoson.com</u>.

Object Exchange—Let's Swap!

Discover what your dog loves and empower yourself. You have heard me talk about this before but it is worth revisiting. I encourage object exchange for all puppies and adult dogs. That is—you choose two or more highly motivating and valued objects (something your dog loves like food or toy).

Begin with having them "sit" or "down". Hold the toy and the treat. Give them an opportunity to choose. Then you exchange. Do this several times. You can have a third or fourth favorite item (toy, healthy treat) and add to that for excitement. Eventually, you extend this game by placing items further away, and begin teaching discrimination (get the ball, Frisbee, stuffy).

It may be that they like none of these, but honestly, how many dogs can live without food and touch? Pick opportune times when they are not full of food or energy. De-compress by taking a walk. When we are meaningful, in the moment and focused, all goes well.

Play the game fair, forgiving and with boundaries. Jumping and knocking you over is not fair. Forgive and ask for a "sit" or "down".

Teaching dogs to swap high ranking items (toys, food) creates trust. Teaching "leave-it" and "take-it" can save your dog's life if they try to eat something poisonous. How many things can you think of that you want your dog to leave?

Drop-It—Okay!

After several weeks of object exchanges, transition to drop–it and the valuable "leave–it". Drop–it is excellent to teach—especially for children. They can get a toy without directly taking it from the dog's mouth.

Children under 12 should be supervised by a sober adult. I am not kidding. Alcohol changes us and the dog is aware of it. We don't sound or act normally. Dogs are masters at detecting changes in body language and chemical imbalance. That's' why we use them for cancer and seizure, rescue and therapy work, and many other jobs that require acute senses of sight, sound and smell.

Children under 12 are perceived as littermates. They can be involved with teaching the basic behavior with adult supervision. Young children do not have good timing, so expecting them to be spot-on shaping behaviors like "drop it" does not work. They need specific directions and instructions like "okay, say sit, and now say "stay", and then, "drop-it". All treats should be given from a child (anyone unfamiliar) with an open hand.

It is natural for a puppy to nip and jump until taught differently. If a child gets nipped or falls downs, and begins to cry, the behavior is shaped for the puppy, and the precedent set for the child to be afraid of the pup. Now, you are backpedalling, and will have to re-shape this behavior, and mend the relationship between child and dog.

Our job, as adults, is to raise awareness between children and dogs by teaching them to respect each other. With practice, most dogs comfortably settle into our household routines and enjoy children immensely. Be mindful that when learning, there is no "wrong" way for a puppy or child who isn't use to dogs to do this. They are learning so your guidance is appreciative.

Teach your dog social manners like "sit"
in front of humans. Giving a "high-five" is
like us shaking hands to say "hello".

Socialization and Manners (SAM)

If you don't desensitize and train your dog, the environment will. The environment is a powerful treasure cove of exciting sights, sounds and smells. We pale in comparison to it. For most dogs, it is pure entertainment. For others, it is a scary jungle. For happy go lucky, grounded dogs it is more like, "wow, look at that, the bush is on fire". It's okay, I'll pee on it".

As your dog's advocate, you can help inspire confidence by carefully introducing them to sights, sounds, smells and cultures in a broad variety of situations. Managed introductions with family and friends will prevent behaviors that can cause stress later on like frantic energy, chewing, nipping and jumping.

Puppies should be slowly socialized outside too. Ten minute walks, several times a day, are enough. Gradually bring them to parking lots and play grounds, allowing them to observe from afar. After a few weeks, increase the amount of stimulation and introductions, a little closer while smiling and saying calmly, "Look at this or that". When meeting unfamiliar people, an introduction like, "look let's meet a new friend", with no alarm reflecting from you voice tone, will let them know that all is well.

Your best approach when meeting others is to move slowly on or off leash. Off leash puppies and dogs should never be forced to interact with anyone or thing that scares them. Let them take the initiative to greet the human or approach the giant garbage can, bikes or wheelchairs.

Make it a good habit to have others ask for a "sit". A sitting dog can't knock anyone over.

Polite approaches to any dog are off to the side, not frontal, slowly and gently. Eventually, most dogs become use to frontal, face-to-face greetings from humans.

Dog-to-dog introductions on leash are questionable. The calmer you are, the better the experience. Dog meet dog, as mentioned in Multiple Dogs, is circle, circle, sniff and sniff some more. This is their business card. Dogs meeting dogs generally works best in larger areas, not boxed into corners, off leash and on neutral territory (not their home). Let's celebrate!

Puppy Pawty

Dr. Ian Dunbar (www.siriuspup.com) is a visionary and mentor. I am proud to call him a friend. He has introduced many valuable concepts that changed my life with dogs, like family dog training. Makes sense that if dogs are living with families we offer "family dog training".

Dr. Dunbar introduced puppy parties long before the start of the Association of Pet Dog Trainers, which is he is the founder. Even if you choose to use online or TV training, socialization and manners is for real world dogs.

Puppy Pawties are supervised invitations to have others gently and effectively socialize and train your dog to enjoy being around people. I share this from the heart because I have adopted dogs who would melt at a puppy pawty early on. Until they are inspired with confidence, I modify meet—greets to successful approximations (may be across the street) to avoid increasing fear or anxiety.

Invite a few people over by email or snail mail. Give healthy treats to the guests, family and friends who visit. Have them ask your puppy for a sit before snuggling and ga-gaing.

The dog should never be forced to interact. This seldom happens with puppies who readily launching into laps. This is a training opportunity with benefits. Have guests put the puppy down and ask for or wait for a "sit".

Upon getting calmer behavior, then indulge with huggy-huggy, kissy-kissy. I love puppy breath too and puppies are irresistible. Take advantage of this opportunity, while they are young, to shape the behavior you want the adult dog to portray.

If you have a 3lb Miki, that is carried everywhere, it may not matter. Most dogs, 10lbs and up, are capable of knocking people over. "Sit" in front of humans is a favorite "good manner" for every dog.

As mentioned, be aware that alcohol changes everything. During celebrations, when family, friends and children are excitedly running around, paves the way for mistakes with a dog. If you know your dog, than you can arrange a safe place for them to relax, then play "tour guide" offering short meet and greets.

Taking into consideration what the situation will be like ahead of time, will prevent accidents from happening. If someone is plowed and suddenly turns into *Super Dog Trainer,* thank them politely for their insights and put your puppy in a safe place. If they won't listen, toss them (the human) out on their rear.

Play Doctor—Touch me, I love it!

Practice handling your puppy every day touching them from head to toe. If more couples did this, there would be fewer divorces. Gently explore the mouth, gums, ears and between the toes. Massage gently (not pound the head), beginning at the tip of the nose journeying all the way down to the tip of the tail.

Make it fun and calm. Teach others how to approach and handle the feet and mouth. Set the boundaries especially around children (no rough stuff). Children and dogs make great play companions, but must to be taught to respect each other.

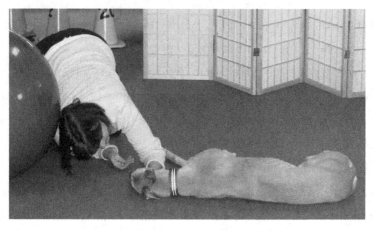

We can teach our dogs to "relax" on cue,
a valuable behavior at the Vet's, Grooming
or settling down when we do.

Jolly Up and Relaxation Training
Learning to Chill-Out

Every few minutes, while playing with your puppy, have a mandatory time-out period. Gently calm her down for about 10 seconds while saying, "relax" or "chill out".

In the back yard, have a leash on and hold the collar, getting them use to hands around the neck. When the dog is calm, unhook the leash and say, "go free" or "go play".

Do this several times to build in anticipation of being allowed to play, but also positively rejoining you with a "come". Call your dogs often, and when they eagerly arrive, ask for a "sit". Reward can be a healthy treat of a toss of their favorite toy.

Relaxation training is as vital as speedy "comes". There are times when we can be silly and times when we need to be quiet. Building in anticipation creates a dog that is eagerly waiting for the next biscuit to drop from the sky.

The best time to teach the actual process and posture of relaxation to a dog is when they are "relaxed". If you practice this on a regular basis, it becomes natural to the dog to hear you say, "Relax please". One way is to guide them into relaxing. When I get down on the floor with the dogs, they automatically enjoy the change of positioning. Within a few minutes, they lie down anyway. This is the opportunity to snap shot, "good relax".

First, take a deep nose-to-navel deep breath. With a treat, guide them nose-to-floor, on their side, or up-side-down. Give it a name, "relax" or "chill-out".

It is especially important with easily
stimulated and high-keyed dogs
to practice "relax" often.

When you catch your dog in the act of relaxing anytime, anywhere, even on their beds, go over and say, "Good relax". Dogs that learn to relax (grounding) have better self-control (walking, visiting).

Sometimes silence is what we need to resolve a perplexing situation. Begin and end each day with a few minutes of meditation (reflection). Before going to sleep, ask, "What should I do or what do I need to do to resolve this?" You may awaken to the answer, or a pathway, to the answer.

Barkeology—Canine Communications
Dogs Bark, We Talk

Dogs bark—we talk, dogs whine—we cry, dogs howl—we sob or yell. When a dog is barking at other dogs or people, yelling at them is like joining in the wolf howl. Redirecting to a distance away from the stimulus will help. Prevent it by blocking the stimulus (close the door or shade) until you have focused time to teach when to bark, at who, and for how long.

As shared, the environment is powerful, especially for dogs who don't get to visit it much. The tendency for most of us is to go for a walk, our dog acts like a lunatic, barking or pulling, and we get stressed, "I don't have time for this crap". Well, consider that this transitions into other areas of our lives. Sometimes, we have to make time for this "crap", or to get rid of excess baggage. Otherwise, it builds up making it nearly impossible to find the shirt we want at the back of the closet (clearing the clutter).

We can make it more manageable and pleasant. It can be easier, as described, by taking it slowly and in less active areas, for shorter periods. Redirect the dog to "you", not at what they are barking at, while taking a deep breath. Eventually, you may want to introduce the dog to other dogs or bring them closer to what is spooking or exciting them, but only when you are focused and calm too. As with any behavior that is driving you crazy, consider how long, where, when and what you are doing during the process.

Barking with the dog, by getting upset and yelling, "no, shut-up or stop" makes it worse. Better approaches are to teach that when you say firmly, but not loudly, "stop", or "enough"—that means, "stop barking". When the barking stops for a half second, praise.

Integrated Alternative

A focused training technique to manage barking is to teach your dog to "whisper" and say "hello". You have to be present and ready to catch a dog getting ready to bark. Just when they open their mouth, click or say "GOOD WHISPER" and give a treat.

The hand signal I use, and you can create your own, is my index finger to thumb. An open hand making shadow puppets indicates "hello". I ask her to say, "Hello". The dog can bark one to three times. Then, I say "thank you" meaning shush.

Bravo, you have become the "barking director" and taught your dog a useful trick that will get a lot of giggles. This gives the dog freedom of expression doing what comes naturally, but in a non-annoying way.

Barking at ringing bells or other environmental stimuli can be managed with focused practice and redirecting. Situational set-ups where several people ring the bell, come in and ask for a "sit", then exit out the door works well if you have the time.

I have learned with three dogs to be present when there is action. They feed off of each other and have different barking styles. Yelling at them is joining in the choir, and possibly indicating that there is danger. I don't want the dogs to think that the UPS person is scary.

Take the time to work on this with and without ringing bells, asking for a "sit" and "quiet". If you are busy and find it impossible at that time, redirect to a quieter environment. I empathize. I am busy, and if in a hurry, it is easier to temporarily redirect the dog into a room or out the back door.

Barking at environmental stimuli is self-reinforcing for dogs. They enjoy it. Some dogs bark at scary (unfamiliar to them) objects. The more we walk our dogs in the environment and calmly introduce them new and novel things, the less they will bark.

Regroup and center, with nose-to-navel breathing, and teach the dog to "sit" and "quiet" in calmer places, then gradually increase to more actives one.

> Desensitization and counter-conditioning work
> well together to create positive associations—
> turning spooky stuff into no-big-deals.
> Begin incrementally (slowly), at a distance (20
> feet away) moving closer to unfamiliar stimuli. If
> your dog becomes anxious, barks or zones out,
> redirect by taking a few steps back, not forward.
> Rushing will only create more anxiety.

Digging Zone—Like us Meditating or Exercising Dogs Dig for Occupational Therapy!

In the wild, wolves dig dens for their pups. Domesticated dogs dig holes to create dens, relieve stress, cool down or find buried treasure. When they relieve stress, they are calmer, better behaved dogs. Sounds like a plan to me.

Chewing and digging is occupational therapy for dogs like exercise, meditation or playing a game of sport is for us. When they are taught to dig in appropriate places, they expend energy in positive ways like burying bones and toys, finding bones and toys, burying them in a different place and finding them again.

The dog's olfactory (sniffer) gives them the ability to dig with gusto to forage out scents, fossils, bones and disgusting, smelly objects. You could say they are scentabetical to our alphabetical. Sniffing and digging are like our laptops and cell phones connecting dogs to the Dognet Explorer.

Digging is meaningful to the dog like finishing a project is for us. However, we can't be glued to the laptop twenty four hours a day. We would become zombies. Digging for dogs can be directed like an episode on *Dogs in the Country*. They can be directed to dig in specific areas.

How would anyone of us like it if every time we eagerly went about preparing a project or presentation for many months only to be told, "That's disgusting, yuck, no, get out of here"?

A dog's request is to give them a place to build their "sandcastles" and "explore". How do we do that?

Shape the digging!

If you are lucky enough to have a puppy at 8 weeks, begin by showing them where to dig. It is as easy as teaching "dig here, not there, "dig for this, not that".

Make it a game of challenge and conquest. Show them their favorite bone or hard rubber toy (Kong®) and bury it in an acceptable and safe excavation spot. Let them find the buried treasure! Praise, "good find".

Take a walk with your dog around the yard and pick out an optimum cooling spot that they can build into a den to relax.

Don't want them in your vegetable or flower garden, and you don't have the time to teach them where to dig? Fence it off!

A *child's plastic swimming pool* can be filled with sand. Make it enticing by burying their favorite toy. Show them how to find it in the pool by pointing the scent out and digging with your hands. They quickly get the idea if the buried treasurer is worth it.

Build a digging zone for the dog. Fence off areas, like your garden, that are off limits. Fill the pool with sand and bury their favorite toys. Like any behavior, you have to teach the concept. They learn quickly. Turn a plastic swimming pool upside down to give them a chance to crawl under and dig. Hide some items under boxes or under paper plates. Make a plate with an X. Your dog will turn into Sherlock Holmes, quickly discovering that under the "X" is a ball or treat.

Give me a Job!

Whether it is catching Frisbees, playing ball, bringing you flowers, poopsicles (frozen winter poop) or fetching the laptop mouse, dogs were bred to work and need to feel useful.

In addition to appropriate digging expeditions, give them a job to do in their daily life plan like carrying bags for you and getting your slippers. You have choices and it is worth the effort.

Don't want your dog chewing the vinyl siding? Then don't tie them near the house. Don't want them digging in the garden?

Then fence an area off where they can dig. Don't want them eating garbage? Then cover it or take the time to teach, "Leave it"!

I have shared that I taught our Newfie to carry bags. Figure out what your dog's strengths are (like retrieving or finding), and teach them to bring items to you. When you arrive home, have them retrieve their toy for you. It pacifies them to have something in their mouth, plus gives you a chance to "arrive".

Tired of the don'ts? Then, teach the dos. Tired of the no, no, no's, then teach the yes, yes, yes you cans.

Jumping for Joy—Jumptown Junction

Jumping is to spring clear off the ground or other support by a sudden muscular effort. The tail acts as a propeller on the way up, ears as a parachute on the way down. Ironically, we teach dogs that jumping is acceptable at a very early age. Puppies naturally rise to the occasion to be near us because that is how they meet-greet other dogs. Most pups are rewarded continuously for pawing at us to say "Hi there", to be caressed or taken outside.

We welcome this gesture of joyful greeting until someone gets slammed into a countertop or has their lap scalded by hot coffee, or worse, knocked down.

A dog's interpretation may sound like this: "Okay, I usually achieve my goals for getting attention, to play, for food, to be picked up or petted, by pawing and/or jumping. Wow, apparently it is not acceptable anymore because I got bonked on the snout. I am confused! What the heck is the matter with this human? How come she is lying on the ground? That never happened before. I think I'm in trouble. Oh oh, she has that mad face. I better run.

Target a behavior like jumping away from the body prevents the dog from knocking us over, while balancing energy and doing something they enjoy.

Sitting Dogs can't Jump Unless they Scoot!

It is a humbling experience to be accosted by a 120 lb Newfie, if they haven't been taught to jump gently and "*on cue*". Putting the jump on cue is *shaping the behavior before it shapes itself*. It is "targeting" in the sense that it gives the dog an opportunity to jump towards a target away from your body, like an outstretched hand.

Create a "jumptown junction" game teaching the puppy / dog to "sit" first. A sitting dog can't jump unless they are scooting. Scooting is teaching a dog, while in sit, to back up, by slowly encroaching upon their space. Have the dog focus on something special like a delicious treat or favorite toy. Here's how —

Cueing the Jump

Begin teaching puppies to sit on cue the moment they enter the human family abode (*a huge transition for a pup*). Shape the voluntary sits, rather than focusing on the involuntary jumping (behavior shaping). When the pup jumps or paws, gently request a sit by bringing a delicious piece of kibble or treat in front of their muzzle, wiggle it, and bring it over the pup's head.

I say delicious because if it doesn't smell or taste good, it will have no value. Set yourself and your puppy up for success. 99.9% of the pups will sit, down or rollover. Probability is on your side here. Work smart, not hard.

Be the Director of the Scene
You had me at "Sit"

Visualize all homecomings and visitations between your dog and friends, family members or strangers on the street (*be streetwise*) before it happens. Pretend that you are the "director" of the scene. Plan, imagine the scene, and ask yourself how do you want this movie to end, a positive interaction or someone getting slammed into a wall?

Factor in unpredictability and be flexible. All scripts get edited. What would be the most optimum scenario? Actors may do some improvising but they have a "*director*" to ensure they give the best performance possible.

Do this for your pup during social encounters. Direct everyone to gently request a sit from your pup before greeting rituals begin. Decide whether you want your dog to jump for a greeting. If so, "sit" must first be grounded in foundational training.

Teach "up" and "off" before requesting a "jump up" from your dog. Dogs can be taught to jump up with their paws on your shoulders, without plunging you through a wall!

Changes in the Script—New Actors

Some actors have a great chemistry that radiates on screen. Conversely, we have all experienced movies that we wished we hadn't paid for. Every interaction between your pup and an individual will be different depending on the environment, and, past and present associations. You can't control every nuance of activity that happens, but as a good director, you can guide the episodes like a "reality show" when family and friends visit.

Your pup may sit for you but not for Aunt Emma, who bends over and in a cheery voice says, "come here, puppy sweetie". If you want this to be a good movie, with a legal rating, direct Auntie Em and others, to request a "sit" with a treat. Trust me; it isn't pretty when someone gets clocked in the nose or knocked down with dress over head.

It is "your choice" whether you want to relax boundaries with visitors or on walks, but my advice is to maintain balance. Ask people to adhere to your puppy training / visiting guidelines. It sets the precedent for future greetings.

Troubleshooting on a daily basis will ensure that your dog learns the difference between what's on and off limits. Behavior shaping should happen before not after the incident. This extends throughout the dog's lifetime in many different scenes including jumping on sofas, beds, tables and countertops.

Choose the pieces of furniture you will allow your dog to jump on. Want to cuddle on the couch to watch, *Jumping on People—Part 8*? Okay, then teach the "up and off" on "*select*" pieces of furniture.

Clever dogs will select their own choice pieces of furniture when you aren't looking, so if you are sure you don't want Tempo on that light mocha sofa, better put Tempo in a safe haven when you go out.

A comforter is a comforter. Although dogs have keen eyesight, they do not discriminate between a peach colored comforter and a navy blue one. If muddy paw prints are going to infuriate you on the peach comforter, better not teach on the bed. An alternate approach (and there are many) would be to put Tempo's own comforter on the bed or teach him to jump on the side of the bed to say good night.

Create a night time ritual like reflecting gratitude for the day's happenings. Hide a biscuit for the dog to find before bed and then say, good night my sweet dog".

The point of teaching power is in the present moment.
Integrate training in the living relationship with your dog,
just as you would with children, family,
friends, on the job or in sports!

PAWT 4

Well-Being—You are the Guru

Sensory Overload

Sensory overload happens to humans and dogs. I work with dogs in pet assisted therapy. Clarity sparkles in Dr. Dawn Marcus's book, *The Power of the Wagging Tail.* They tested levels of the stress response hormone, Cortisol, in humans and dogs following therapy dog visits. The human's decreased, but the dogs did not for many hours, sometimes days. Dogs are sponges of human emotions. We feel good, but have to recognize that our dogs need time to decompress too.

The 4-F's of instinctive behavior, fight, flight, faint and fooling around are shared by humans and dogs. It is accompanied by an increase in adrenaline. Constant activation of adrenaline creates fatigue and eventually muscle atrophy.

Adrenaline is secreted by the sympathetic nerve endings in the adrenal glands. Noradrenaline, a related substance, is secreted by the other sympathetic nerve endings. These are chemical messengers that instantaneously kick organs into gear, causing increased heart rate, blood pressure, and breathing rate to transport nutrients and oxygen at great rates of speed. The body is smart and starts to conserve energy. Continual stress, in clusters, for long periods can inhibit the immune system, in humans and dogs, making us more susceptible to disease.

How can we help ourselves? By recognizing when we need to take a brain break, with our dogs, even for a few minutes. This creates an opportunity for the body and mind to renew, and for us to re-focus our priorities.

Dogs are keen observers of body language and emotional cues. Noticing our dogs' reactions to us, or their lackluster behavior, is a glistening message. When we are drifting into emotional bankruptcy and exhaustion, we can redirect to a calmer place. There is an escape, in the moment, with 468 and/or nose-to-navel breathing. When you breathe, oxygen rejuvenates the body and brain (mind).

Listen, are you breathing just a little and
calling it a life.—Mary Oliver

4.6.8 Breath of Awareness

Inhaling through your nose to the count of 4, holding for about 6, and exhaling for about 8 through your mouth, while imagining "so calm". Even if you simply breathe imagining or saying "one" and exhaling saying, "two", it forces the mind to stop for a moment and renew.

Breathing begins in the nose, inhaling to your abdomen (diaphragm). Breathing in as full as you can, and holding, then releasing even 3X enables the body and brain to rest. A well rested brain, reduces stress in the body, and helps the mind to make better decisions

Case Study with Heart Praise

A private coaching client arrived with a small dog on leash, briefcase and cell phone glued to her ear. The goal was to become a pet assisted therapy team. I was the "doggy trainer." This is a dynamic, multi-tasking business woman. She could not figure out why her dog would not come within 3-feet of her when practicing basic routines like sit, down, walk, come or sit front. The further away the dog got, the more upset she became (counter-intuitive).

After 10-minutes of observation, it was clear that the dog was clever, and in fear of losing her paws. Spikes hurt! It was evident that she had been stepped on before.

After shutting the cell phone, taking off the pumps and breathing, the owner began again with "awareness". She discovered with insight, that big heels hurt small paws and makes her scary. When a dog yelps, pay attention. This dog was less than 10lbs.

They became a registered therapy team, but Yelp was carried during visits. Bravo to this women and that little dog for making a positive change.

There are volumes of information on well-being and nutrition for us and our dogs. Personally, I can't keep up with all the ways that I can improve my health, minimize wrinkles and eliminate fat cells. I could spend a fortune trying. As share, just because we can, doesn't mean we have too.

Being informed is knowledge. Knowledge is powerful and gives us choices that are best for us and our dogs. We are all different. A vegan diet may taste delicious to one person, and like eating ground up cardboard to another. It may be healthy for one and not the other. It is matter of preference and nutritional benefit / need.

The power of intention, guided with intuition and common sense helps us make better choices for our dog's well-being. First question is does it make sense and can we afford it? The following is not intensive or extensive. It is a consideration. Always, consult with your Veterinarian and/or other specialists. There is so much information available, that most professionals can't keep with it. They can offer guidance with the information they have.

What I found to be true is that I am attracted to professionals or experts who have flaws and admit, "they do not know all of the answers." I am apprehensive with any professional who is an expert at everything. This includes doctors, veterinarians and TV personalities. It they are guided by experts, and practice what they preach, including on themselves and their own pets, I may consider it.

Whether it is for our health or our dog's we need to be educated. Information is power and helps us in an emergency, to make better spur-of-moment choices. When it can be put on hold even for a day, then do so. Thank everyone for their enlightening thoughts, gather more information, and then decide if it works for you and your dogs.

Grounding—Getting Ready for Anything

Grounding is the process of bringing awareness into balance with your body and in the present moment. When we spend a few moments being still and focusing on our breathing, we have an opportunity to quiet the mind chatter that is often re-runs.

So much of our daily communication with our dogs is nonverbal, at least for the dog. Keeping our energy balanced helps teach our dogs how to balance their energy too. If we are frenetic, they will be too. If we have grand expectations, but no awareness or plan of how to implement, the dog will be confused.

Depending on how we went to sleep (stress or peaceful) and how we wake (calm and ready) makes a difference on how we connect to our dogs and others.

Dogs make themselves understood with body language, expressions and vocalizations. We can convey better messages to our dogs if we calm our minds by focusing on our breath, letting the thoughts flow.

Set an intention for what you want to accomplish with your dogs or elsewhere. Expect changes because that's life. Visualize these actions in your career, daily chores and training the dog(s).

Remember, you can always take a brain rest during the day, even if it means going to the bathroom—alone to nose-to-navel breathe for 1 minute.

Healthy, Dog, Good Dog, Whole Nutrition

I love information and learning. Like you, I get excited, "wow, really". What is different now, is that I realize not all "sage" advice applies to me or my pets.

Let's begin by debunking the myth that spayed or neutered dogs get fat. They cannot open their own food, and fill their bowls, without our permission. We get fat because we consume too many calories and don't' get enough exercise. Dogs do too. The exception, and this is rare, are dogs or people who are sick and can't move. They are being fed through a tube or straw, so tend to lose weight and muscle tone.

The solution is simple and hard at the same time: eat healthy, move a little more and have a positive attitude. Depression, anxiety (too much stress) can cause weight gain or loss. Some people feel like if they aren't doing something, then something is wrong. Lots of times, we need to do "nothing" before we can do "anything".

Let's de-mystify some of the dog food myths. While we do, 1,000 more will appear on the internet. I am happy to share what I have tried, what I stopped, why, and what I do now. I recommend the Whole-Dog-Journal as a good resource for the top ten whole dog foods and books on whole diets for pets. I say "whole" not "natural" because that is another myth.

Pet-nutrition experts say that the best dog food is made from top-grade ingredients like meat, whole grains and vegetables. Fillers (corn and corncobs, cereal by-products, feathers, soy, cottonseed and peanut hulls, citrus pulp, screening, weeds, and straw) have "no" nutritional value. I suppose they could if the dog hasn't eaten anything for a couple of weeks.

Fillers are added as pet food ingredients to help decrease the overall cost of the food for the pet food manufacturers. Regardless of lowering their costs, we still pay a hefty price, especially if our dog becomes ill.

There are varying schools of thought when it comes to byproducts in dog food. Some say that because a dog in the wild would eat the entire animal after killing prey (skin, organs and bones and stomach contents), that domesticated dogs should get a similar raw diet. I believe it depends on the individual dog and best optimum diet at this stage of health and wellness.

What you don't want in your dog's food (ingredient labels) is unidentified byproducts that you cannot pronounce. Oftentimes, you see "meat byproducts" although less these days due to research and education.

Experts say this can include zoo animals, road kill and what's referred to as 4-D livestock (dead, diseased, disabled, dying). Meat byproducts can include euthanized dogs and cats. Other experts (and we seem to have a lot) that approve of some by-products advise to look for a specific origin such as chicken or lamb byproduct and byproduct meals. I prefer no byproducts.

Preservatives, without a doubt, should be holistic and in vitamin and mineral form, not words you can't pronounce, unless you are an "expert" and positive it is safe. Be mindful that preservatives can be hidden in labels, but unless you have "hidden label x-ray vision", I do not have a solution.

Natural on labels is questionable especially on dog food products (kibble, can, treats). Whole is the operative word. It must say bison, chicken, salmon or meal and whole grains (barley, oats, spelt, quinoa). If there are more ingredients than necessary, or you stop and think "huh", listen and consider moving on.

We have the intelligence and technology to do it better. AAFCO (Association of American Feed Control Officials) is still the "go to" that must be on dog food. This does not mean it is wholly nutritional, but it's a start.

Read your dog food and people food labels. The first few ingredients on the label are supposed to be prevalent in the food. The following ingredients are vitamins or should be. The rest, especially if you can't pronounce it, is questionable. Look it up online. Having vitamins and minerals in balance, is a good thing, but you can supplement.

There are over 350 dog foods on the market. Listen to your Breeder's and Veterinarian's—but be skeptical. Just because they use or suggest it doesn't mean you have too. Your dog, stages of health and age, time, and finances matter. Any changes you make should be gradual unless it is critical (health wise).

If you are planning on switching to a raw food diet, do your homework. With multiple pets, it can be a challenge and takes practice. You need a good resource. With multiple pets it can be expensive and time consuming.

I have used the Raw Food Diet with success. I stopped because I have multiple pets and visit with the dogs in therapeutic environments where people are immune compromised. The concern is pathogens and bacteria spreading form the dog and vice versa.

Infectious disease is two-way. Dogs can catch as much from humans. Preventive measures are essential like washing our hands with warm soap and water before and after contact with anything questionable. Wiping our dogs before and after a visit with someone is essential with grooming or antibacterial wipes. Earthbath Grooming Wipes are gentle and effective. The green tea ones smell fresh and clean. I use them on myself.

Transmitting of infectious diseases is preventable by managing who our dogs encounter, inside and outside. If possible, and this is tough because people want to kiss our dogs, kissing is not allowed when in doubt of passing infectious disease. We can be vigilant, yet while walking out of a hospital (anywhere), someone can sneeze on us. All we can do is the best we can.

Beyond that, it is up to caution and chance. Dogs have about three feet of intestines. We have about 30. Dogs have a stronger acidic ph than we do. It takes us longer to digest food. That's why we tend to get salmonella and they seldom do. Given the rise in MRSA (methicillin-resistant-staphylococcus-aureus) and Clostridium Difficile in hospitals, people working with pets in therapeutic environments need to err on the side of caution.

Rotational Diet with Variety

With multiple dogs, at various ages and levels of health, the best approach for my sanity is Moe's Dog Food. I use rotational feeding with balance and add-ins. The dogs get kibble and can, in balance, with a variety of added squashed veggies, salmon, turkey, chicken or whatever lean meats we have available. Low fat yogurt and a rotation of healthy omega type oils (flaxseed, salmon, extra virgin olive oil) work. Whatever scraps I deem as fresh, healthy and human–grade go into the food processor. I do not apologize or get into peeing contests with people over this. It works.

If you have a membership to a warehouse like Costo's, you can pick quality meats and fish to save money. I splurge on organic eggs and create games to remind myself of what I am feeding on a specific day. For example, Wednesday is egg day and Thursday is fish day.

Rotational feeding is available in the same brands of food. The consumer market (that's us) is driving this, so the distributors are supplying it. This is a good choice because you can serve bison for three months, then switch to salmon, with the same *synergistic variety of vitamins and minerals.*

Whatever brand you choose, look for consistency and a balance in protein, fat and complex carbohydrates (if any). Drastic increases in any level, especially fat, can leave undigested fat in the large intestine, causing diahhrea.

Overdoing and over supplementing a healthy dog or person is a waste of money and could be dangerous. D.E.A.K. is fat soluble vitamins. Too much of Vitamin D, E, A or K can make us sick as they are absorbed into tissues and fat. The excess of antioxidant vitamins and minerals, like C and the B Vitamins, will be excreted by our bodies. That's why our pee turns bright yellow meaning we need to drink more water.

Rotational feeding is a philosophy, not a mandate. Feeding our dogs is emotional. I cannot imagine eating the same thing every day, nor do I believe it is wholly healthy. I don't want my dogs to either.

During an experiment, over several weeks time, I filled two bowls and offered them to each dog. This needed to be controlled or we would have frenzy. Without a doubt, the dogs chose cooked meats and veggies before the kibble. I reduced the amount of kibble so they would not overeat.

What is interesting is that they would eat the kibble too, but I think this is conditioning. They eat kibble, so ate it. The dogs would choose kibble mixed with a can of meat over a plain bowl of kibble. I observed the dog's choices and learned.

Like with the studies done with agriculture animals in the midwest that were tested with various grains in buckets, the animals knew what they needed nutritionally and went directly to the bins with the preferred diets.

I encourage you to experiment, if it is nutritionally safe for your dog, with a rotation diet. Be mindful of gobbling dogs who may try to eat both. Allow puppies and older dogs to eat privately and with supervision.

We are our dog's health advocates. Eating becomes more than simply food gobbling. They brighten up, become eager, and in my strong opinion, get healthier. We are improving their quality of live emotionally, physically and nutritionally.

> Free roaming animals are generally healthier. Dogs are not grazing animals like cows or horses. So, what are they and what is best for optimum nutrition?

Carnivore v Omnivore v What We Condition

All dog and cat families are members of the order Carnivora meaning they evolved as carnivores described as flesh eating predatory members of the animal kingdom.

Has the dog diet changed that much throughout the years? Yes, but because humans change it. Wild dogs prefer to hunt in packs seeking a diet rich in meat sources in the form of small or large animal prey. They eat bones, digest, organs and occasionally are seen eating berries, fruit and some plant parts. This behavior poses some ethical questions—are a few berries and plant parts enough to justify calling our dogs quasi-omnivores and justify the large amount of carbohydrate we find in almost every commercially prepared diet today? I am guessing but . . . probably not.

Anatomically the dog is still a carnivore requiring high protein. Scientists "sometimes" agree that physiologically the dog does not require any carbohydrate at all in its diet, as they are able to sustain normal blood glucose levels by metabolizing fat and protein into energy.

Metabolically, the dog has a few characteristics of omnivores such as the conversion of carotene to Vitamin A, Tryptophan to Niacin, Cysteine to Taurine and Linoleic acid to Arachidonic acid. These are four out of the thousands of metabolic decisions made daily in the dog.

Generally, if you see a lot of carbohydrates in dog food like corn, rice and wheat, it is because it is a low cost (cha-ching) alternative to fresh meat. This may be a good thing for pet food manufacturers but creates health hazards for dogs. Dogs are required to process the extra bulk and fiber that can result in digestive problems such as gas, bloating, increased stool volume and occasionally disease.

When our Leonberger had Osteoporosis at 5-years old, the Oncologist strongly recommended feeding a "no grain and no raw food" diet. This made sense. His immune system was severely compromised.

Eli lived for two more years with treatment and eating a no grain, human grade diet of fresh, cooked meat and veggies. He enjoyed some fruit and loved organic raw eggs, the one exception that was approved. We supplemented, with holistic guidance, anti-cancer fighting supplements.

Choices are many but take a deep breath. Choose a balanced food, preferably one without grain, and consistent within the line (manufacturer) so that you can rotate flavors such as bison, salmon, chicken, turkey, duck and venison every 3 or 4 months.

Whether omnivore, carnivore or comnivore (combo)
wouldn't it be easier if we let the dogs make the decision.
Next time you have a chance, put an ear of corn alongside
a piece of lean steak. See which your dog naturally
selects. If they run off with the corn, I apologize.

Emotional Feeding—Balance and Moderation

I would like to share with you that I am a person who gets up grateful to be alive and sharing my life with dogs. I cannot eat or feed a boring diet. I like variety, and as mentioned, do my own "little" research projects with the dogs to see what they prefer.

Dogs have choices if given a choice just like us. The notion that a one size fits all for nutrition or training is like saying that I can do what Madonna does. I could, but it would be laughable and I would likely land in jail.

One dog may enjoy carrots while another craves celery and the other asparagus. I can add in skim milk and have a dog enjoy it, then try almond or soy milk, and have them look at me like I killed a cow. The core message is it is okay to experiment, as long as it is not harming or upsetting the dog's system. As with living, the goal is balance and moderation.

Loving our dogs doesn't mean overfeeding or indulging them with food. If that is the case, consider exploring your intentions, how you eat and why. When food is love, it is not about nutrition alone. It is about filling voids and seeking love. We aren't loving our "pets" if they are extremely overweight, can't breathe or enjoy activity.

Be mindful to connect the heart string to the brain stem. Dark chocolate is good for us, but the theobromine in large amounts can kill dogs. Grapes may contain mycotoxin, a fungus, when ingested by some dogs can cause renal failure. Raw or rotten garlic and onions can be toxic.

Our dogs do not have the enzyme lactase, therefore are lactose (dairy products) intolerant. They won't die, but they can get diahhrea.

Introduce new diets gradually and pay attention to what your dog is doing, how they look and feel. Stools will tell you a lot but I am seldom concerned by a few loose stools. They can get that from eating something in the yard.

That shared, as long as eyes are bright, coats healthy (unless a hairless dog), dogs are in good shape, getting some exercise and feel well, then I will continue to listen with skepticism, while using my own version of a varietal diet (Moe's Dog Diner).

Supplementing, Should I or Shouldn't I

A healthy, happy dog that is eating a balanced diet may or may not need supplements. When in doubt contact your Veterinarian or wellness practitioner who specializes in pet nutrition.

Older dogs, or dogs with degenerative hip and joint disease, may benefit from a chrondroiton, glucosamine and msm supplements like Cosequin or Glyco-Flex. There are many generic choices too. One may work better than the other. Ask your Veterinarian, preferably an Integrative one, who embraces Allopathic and Holistic well being.

I do not recommend rawhide chews for assuaging biting or other behaviors (barking, chewing). What matters with any food, chew or dental product you give your dog is the quality. Where does it come from? What are the ingredients? Veracious chewers can unravel a rawhide bone and swallow large pieces that become lodged in their intestines. Dogs can break their teeth on hard material. Excitable dogs could choke to death.

I give the dogs marrow bones, preferably bison, because it is lower in fat. I boil them for several minutes. That is my choice! I separate them for the "chew festival" because it is high value and the dogs are ranging in age and personality. I want the shyer Greyhound to enjoy a good chew, without having to give it up to the other two dogs.

Treats, whether for training or sharing, should have the same healthy and whole ingredients as the food.

Grooming for Self-Esteem—Touch Me, I Smell Good!

Grooming is essential for Health and Self-Esteem. A well-groomed dog is healthier and aesthetically more pleasing to the eye, thus more touchable. People love to muzzle nuzzle and hug a dog who is well behaved and smells fresh and clean. They do not have to be doused in fragrances.

Dogs naturally get more attention, which increases opportunities for socialization. A well-groomed dog looks better, feels better and walks proud.

Your dog's coat is his crowning glory. Gleaming hair with a lively, resilient bounce sets off your dog's fine qualities. A healthy, shiny coat (coat applicable texture) is an indicator of good health and nutrition.

Coat and skin care start from the inside with a complete and balanced diet. In addition to quality food products, exercise and regular veterinary wellness care, grooming ensures a healthy dog.

Brushing and combing are essential to a healthy coat. It eliminates mats and tangles, removes dead hair, dirt and burrs. Brushing distributes the natural oils, producing a healthy skin tone. Grooming gives you the chance to train your dog to relax and enjoy it. While grooming you get to check for skin condition, warts, sores, fleas and ticks.

Establish a grooming routine as soon as your puppy or adult dog comes home. Remember to breathe, not struggle. Grooming your dog while stressed will scare puppies, and older dogs will avoid it.

Save your back by using a bench or table that does not wobble and is of adequate height and size. A rubber bath mat provides a non-slip surface for your dog. Plus, it resembles the conditions that your dog encounters with professional groomers and veterinarians. Secure your dog on the table and let him know that this is grooming time. Be firm, but pleasant. This "task" has been accomplished.

Never leave your dog unattended on the table. For larger breeds, a step-up stool will assist getting the dog on and off without injury. You want this to be a pleasant experience, so you will both enjoy doing it often.

Keep first grooming sessions short & sweet. Keep one hand on your dog for reassurance and to prevent scrambling for escape. Talk calmly; massage her ears and sides of the body, all the way down the legs to each toe. Brush a little, praise and do it again. Do this several times a week (daily if time permits). You will discover that most dogs love the sensation of being brushed if it is done gently, correctly and with appropriate tools (slicker and pin brush, comb, mat splitter).

Mouth / Ears / Nails: In addition to the above daily routine, gently touch (or massage) your dog's mouth, rub the ears and the paws. Get him accustomed to having his mouth opened for inspection. This will assist in making toenail clipping, although not always a favorite past-time for dogs, a more pleasant one.

Nails should be clipped on a regular basis. Few dogs get enough exercise on rough terrain to keep their nails naturally worn down. Overlong nails spread the paws which is painful and, in extreme cases, crippling. Neglected nails can snag fabrics, rugs, human skin, and cause injury by getting torn off. How often you trim depends on the dog's activity level and necessity.

Use commercial dog nail clippers/files. Trim the nails as often as needed (every two weeks at least) with a good *guillotine* or *plier style* clipper. The *plier style clipper,* with two cutting edges, works best on large and giant breed dogs. Grinders are terrific for smoothing nails but most dogs need to be desensitized to the noise first. I use a rechargeable grinder on my toenails. The dogs may not enjoy getting their toenails done, but will tolerate it, especially when they see me doing my own.

As the nail grows in length, so does the blood supply. A vein runs about three-fourths of the way through the nail. Be careful not to cut this vein called the *quick.* It is difficult to trim a long nail to its normal length without causing bleeding. Trim a safe amount and repeat trimming at 7 to 10 day intervals. The blood supply should recede. Gradually reduce the nails to their normal and safe length.

Can't stand doing this? Have your Vet Tech and/or Groomer help you. It may be less stressful for you both. A professional will simply and quickly get the job done as painlessly as possible. Dogs need to have a complete brush out at least weekly. Nails must be clipped regularly and at least once-a-month.

Keeping our dog's teeth clean and gums healthy can be a life saver. Kibble, biscuits, dental chews and "orals" that can be sprayed or rubbed onto the teeth helps remove excess plaque and tartar. Gently desensitizing a puppy by rubbing their gums and teeth creates an adult dog who will more likely allow it. Plus, it desensitizes hands around the mouth.

Clean your dog's teeth daily and at least weekly. Consider getting a tooth brush and dog toothpaste. There are mixed reviews on rinses that you can put into their water. Consult with your Veterinarian. At least once a year, at your dog's wellness check, the Vet will assess your dog's teeth and gums.

Breath of Awareness—Nose to Navel

Let's review breathing with awareness. Before you begin grooming, training or during any stressful situations, notice your and your dog's breathing patterns and energy levels. What is the energy like on a scale of 1 to 10? If you are at an 8, consider pausing to breathe. To be present and focused, the energy level needs to shift to at least a 5 or below before engaging in activity that requires attention to detail.

Listen to your dogs as they sleep and play. Observe how they relieve stress with big sighs.

Inhaling in, nose to navel, to the count of 1, 2, 3, 4,
holding for 6, 5, 4, 3, 2, 1,
and exhaling through your mouth for 8, 7, 6, 5, 4, 3, 2, 1 . . .
saying or imagining "so-calm."
Raising your shoulders slowly to your ears to the
count of 10, holding, and slowly lower them down.

Stretch your arms over your head (if you can).
If you can't reach over your head, how about to
the side, like an airplane? Do these several times
while breathing in and out. It relaxes your body
and desensitizes the dog to silly movement.

Clearing the Clutter—Calming the Chaos

What? Is this Feng Shui training? No, but clearing the clutter in our minds, house, life and with our dogs is freeing. Too much of anything can negatively influence or even completely block the flow of training.

The reason most people avoid clearing the clutter is not because it takes effort and can be time consuming. It is because clutter cleaning can be an emotional process that feels like therapy. It takes stamina to go through our "stuff" and let it go of the "excess baggage". I weep when I give an extra leash away because I just know I'll have a dog in the future that will want it?!

The good news is that once you clear most of your clutter and have a plan to avoid its accumulation in the future, you will start experiencing high energy levels, more clarity, and a heightened sense of well-being.

Equipment—Toys
Keep it Safe and Simple

Unless you are training in a fenced, safe area, you will need a comfortable collar and a six-foot leash and a few life rewards (healthy treats, toys and positive attitude). A positive, confident attitude and acting like you know what you are doing helps too.

I do not recommend flexi or other roll-out leads for training unless you are doing field work. Even then, watch your feet and hands. They can be dangerous. Read the safety labels. You have absolutely no control over a 120lb dog with a 16-foot roll up flexi cord. The flat strap, stronger models are okay for the beach, hiking or field work. Do not wear flip flops. *You may end up with half a foot.*

If you have a strong dog, I recommend any of the front mid-chest buckle harnesses. They are designed to guide the dog at the most powerful place, the chest and shoulders, without strangling or straining their throat and neck muscles.

Muzzle leaders are alternatives, but not my first choice. Any head controlling type of equipment should be gradually introduced. This is not something you throw on the dog as a last ditch effort. I have observed dogs that are fine with them. Others become anxious, spending more time trying to rub them off, then enjoying being with their owner. I tried it on my Newf and we were both embarrassed! She looked cock-eyed. That lasted 30 seconds.

Walking harnesses that clip on the back are best for small to medium sized dogs. I like a harness for my Border Terrier. It is easy on her neck and throat. Stronger, larger dogs will pull you with robust pleasure and strength. It is self-reinforcing. Drafting harnesses that clip on the sides of the dog are designed for powerful pulling. All require desensitization and used for appropriate activities.

Before we launch into Level 1, 2 and 3 training for you and your dog, please consider the following on "listening and observing" to help you on your journey living and learning with your dog.

Listening and Observing

Whether in class, at work, with friends or our dogs—observing and active listening skills are beneficial on so many levels. The foundation of communication with dogs is to simply listen and observe. You learned in "barkeology" that dogs bark for a number of reasons (excitement, boredom, communicating). Learning your dogs attention span, barking habits and what turns them with life rewards, gives you the vantage point of teaching them what to do, when and for how long.

Active or **Reflective Listening** is the single most useful and important listening skill. In active listening we are genuinely interested in understanding what the other person is thinking, feeling, wanting or what the message means. We actively check out our understanding before we respond with our own new message. We restate or paraphrase our understanding of their message and reflect it back to the sender for verification, rather than creating our own version of their story. This verification or feedback process is what distinguishes active listening, from pretend listening, making it more effective.

Here are a few tips on active listening skills that will help you with people you encounter with and without your dog.

1. State what you need directly and clearly.

2. Offer empathetic listening—what is the other being feeling and thinking? Are you listening to the words only or looking for the feelings or intentions beyond the words?

3. Don't interrupt, but do ask for time to speak w/o interruption. This can be with an employee, colleague, family or friend. If our dogs are barking and we are trying to talk, it's time for "quiet" and "go like down".

4. Clarifying (asking questions) can seed an idea, relieve misinterpretation, and save needless emotional energy. Offer suggestions in a non-threatening way. "How about I take my dog to play with that group of dogs. They seem to be larger and your dog is enjoying time with the smaller dogs."

5. Paraphrase the message in your own words or theirs to be sure you get it correctly.

6. Reflect: "I know you enjoy walking your dog with me, but it sounds like you are frustrated when my dog barks. Care to discuss it?"

7. Emotional Component: listening and looking for verbal and nonverbal cues—voice tone and volume, facial and bodily gestures, eye contact and physical distance—will facilitate more accurate reflection. Is the dog backing away? Is the person folding their arms scowling?

8. Summarize and Give Feedback—Too much information might overwhelm a receiver. Not enough could leave them confused. Feedback should be timely and non-judgmental, "Good Sit" or "that was a little slow, let's try again".

9. Mirroring—Direct conversation is not always possible unless the other party is willing to listen. Mirroring their behavior sometimes works. They cross their arms, you cross yours. Dogs mirror our behaviors often. If we are not getting the response we want, we need to tray a different teaching and communication path.

Spatial Bubble
Freeze / Don't Come Any Closer

Have you ever been engaged in a conversation with someone who gets so close that you can feel his or her breath? Intimidating isn't it? You step back a foot, they move in on you. You step to the left; they follow, almost swallowing you up.

One of my favorite *Everybody Loves Raymond* shows, Rob was talking so closely to Ray's face that Ray said, "don't do that again unless you're going to hang an air freshener from your nose".

Dogs have spatial bubbles just like people. Pictured is a young, enthusiastic miniature schnauzer (Mojo) with older adolescent Journey, the Newf. You can see by Journey's cocked head that Mojo gets the

message. Dogs let other dogs know that it is not
polite to step into their space without permission.

People and dogs have spatial boundaries. Intrinsically, dogs have extremely sensitive olfactory cells. Cultural diversification will lend itself to many different greeting rituals. The dog's greeting ritual is different than ours. It should be respected especially when you are interacting with others whether it is family, friends, strangers, veterinary staff, groomer, trainer, massage therapist or out on a walk.

The dog's spatial bubble is the area in which a dog will decide who and how close another dog (or human) may approach in a particular environment. An association in the past, when someone encroached upon their "spatial bubble", may have been positive or negative from the dog's perception.

We have shared how dogs meet / greet by circling and sniffing. They engage with each over the neck, pyramiding, splitting, yawning, rolling, mouthing, pumping, humping and other body bouncing behaviors. Some are fun, play enticing behaviors, while others are hierarchical communication signals saying, "stay away" or "knock this battery off of my shoulder".

A dog's place in a pack can be safe or tense, depending on how well they learn to use these communication skills. Dogs use these same communication skills with humans *only they can be misunderstood or neglected*.

Getting to know "your" dog's body language tendencies, especially with other dogs, is paramount if your intentions are to walk in high-traffic areas, parks and playgrounds. The following is not extensive, but enough to give you what you need to recognize what is usually "clusters of behaviors" that our dogs show us indicating what might happen next in interactions and responses to the unfamiliar situations. How we respond (or not) matters.

Body Language—Knowing yours and the Dogs

Often, we don't recognize signals that our dogs give us until it is too late. A dog's body language and senses are much keener than ours so it makes sense to be aware of them and use them wisely for communication. We expect them to learn human, so it is only fair for us to learn to talk dog.

It empowers training opportunities and prevents creating fearful dogs. It is sad to watch a dog cower or get decked because they didn't recognize that the dog's face they just dove into did not like it. Dogs and people prefer invitations. Dogs do too.

What amazes me even more, and I have heard this countless times from others, is when "walking a dog", someone let's their dog launch into the dog's space, at the end of a flexi-lead or off-leash. Worse is when the owner floats in with a dumb remark like, "my dog loves meeting dogs."

"Thank you for enlightening me but my dog is 120 lbs and yours is 10 lbs and hanging from my dog's chest fur. Could you please remove him? Here's my business card (dog training coach)."

Following are some signs of stress (body language cues) that all dog lovers need to be aware of. Respect for others, whatever species, prevents conflict, and most dogs (and people) do not intentionally want conflict. If they do, they need medication and therapy.

Most stress signals come in clusters. With awareness, unless a dog is unpredictable, you can recognize when a dog is scared, happy, sad or confused. It is essential to look at the WHOLE DOG and WHOLE PICTURE. What is going on in the environment?

If an incident happens, reflection will offer preventative wisdom. For more on body language and charts, visit my website www.dogtalk. com, The Learning Zone. Here are some of the more common signs. Be mindful that associations influence our dogs. Like us, there can be several meanings to body language and behavior depending on the familiarity and experience of the interpreter:

- Penis Crowning (can be arousal or can escalate to aggression)
- Lowered Head, Tucked Tail: Look at the rest of the body. This dog could be shy or fearful, or like our Greyhound, a tucked tail and lowered head may be a normal posture.
- Tail flagging high, ears or forehead perked up and teeth showing can be a direct message to "back off". Heed it!
- Teeth clattering and/or trembling (cold, stressed or connecting to an association / previous experience).
- Sweaty Paws (stress or sweating).
- Lip Licking (invasive). Maybe the dog is wiping something from their lips. What does the rest of the body look like? Think about your own body if you were scared or getting ready to defend yourself.
- Tongue Flicking—can be nervous, like us breathing heavy or blinking a lot.
- Dilated Pupils—Whale Eyes—Whites Exposed
- Tap-Out: The Phrase tap out" is a wrestling term and happens when an opponent taps the ground with an open hand requesting a release. In dog terms a tap out is a distance increasing signal. The dog will roll over almost vertebrae with

stiff or uncomfortable body language often accompanied by lip licking, puffing of the cheeks and kicking out of the legs. Ultimately the dog will end up on his back. Generally the dog's muscles are tight and the tail can be tucked into the belly or stiff.

- Roll-Over: In a happy flop, dogs roll for pleasure and in trusted company all the time. Rolling over for submission is usually accompanied with urination and about as low as a dog can submit.

- Freezing—Holding Breath: Be mindful of dogs that hold their breath and freeze. It has been misinterpreted. Some dogs hold their breath and freeze to listen. How long are they freezing? Try to change their mind with redirection to a place or activity that is more pleasant.

- Tucked Low Tail (some breeds unravel their tail when stressed—Akita, Basenji).

- Pacing, panting, excessive shedding (nervous, hot, and/or ill health).

- Stiff / alert posture versus, relaxed / grounded posture.

- Over Stretching (not the relaxing play bow).

- Urogenital Check-Outs—Assessing if equipment is still intact (body parts). This can be a form of displacement and detracting attention.

Stress Vocalizations

- Stress Panting—Dry/Shallow
- High Pitch Whining
- Dry Heavy Panting (wellness check—dehydration)

- Excessive Salivating—Panting—Whining (again—Clusters and can happen with Submissive Licking)
- Cheek Puffing (note—Newfies puff to keep water out of their mouths while swimming—this isn't stressful—it's breathing)
- Relentless and repetitive howling or barking (territorial, boredom, lack of management)

Calming Signals (Turid Rugaas)

Most trainers or behaviorists are familiar with Turid Rugaas. Turid is a friend of mine and many others. Based in Norway, Turid has travelled the world teaching us about body language and calming signals in dogs. It is used by organizations like Pet Partners for training pet assisted therapy dogs.

Not recognizing our dog's signals, and dogs not learning how to navigate their way with other dogs in interactions, can become a social deficit. Depending on the individual dog, it is important to look at the whole picture of the situation and the dog. Try not to make quick assumptions. As shared, just because a dog sniffs or rolls over, doesn't mean their displacing, submitting or avoiding you. Being mindful of loose interpretations from the so-called "experts" is relevant too. Don't take my word for it. Always ask yourself, is what happened with my dog true in the context of the environment?

Use the following illustrations as a guide to understanding a dog's signals. Use them yourself, like yawning, to calm your dog. Use your nose-to-navel breathing to calm yourself and your dog.

- 🐾 Yawning and Looking Away
- 🐾 Sniffing—(in 3D)—Keep in context with the situation and other behaviors. Sniffing does not always mean stress. Dogs enjoy it.
- 🐾 Sneezing and Snorting: This is usually not stress. Allergies can cause sneezing. The dog may be getter a bug out of its nostrils. Snorting is sometimes an indication of excitement.
- 🐾 Scratching / Excessive shedding is noticeable in clumps on the floor. Scratching happens in context with the surrounding criteria / environment / happenings. Scratching can mean dry skin.
- 🐾 Blinking or averting gaze (I am invisible or I have something in my eye)
- 🐾 Shaking Off—when not wet and frequently
- 🐾 Arcing . . . the dog chooses to arc away from a perceived threat or stressor. Arc along rather than pulling them into it.

*Notice behavior clusters like yawning / lip and
nose licking. Before becoming alarmed at your
dog's behaviors, consider how many times this
has happened (why, when, how, where).
Stress and displacement signals can happen in unfamiliar
environments. Eventually, dogs will become familiar
with the situations after repeated exposure and if
you remain calm. Guide them to safer distances.*

We can learn about our dog's behavior by observing their body language and signals that they use naturally. Watch dogs or wolves in packs interacting. It is the "best" learning experience from the experts (dog and wolf). Have fun and be safe. Enjoy the following illustrations and do not hesitate to visit Turid's website at www.canis.no/rugaas.

Sniffing is like us saying, "Hello, nice to meet you. What's your cell phone number?" Give dogs the opportunity to meet-greet in safe areas, where they are familiar with the environment, and you are calmly supervising.

Blinking, averting eyes, turning away is a dog trying to avoid perceived conflict. If you are angry and they turn away, the message is, "I get it and I am trying to avoid a conflict. You've made your point."

Lip Licking may indicate getting something off of the nose. Turning a head while lip licking and interacting with humans or the environment is a sign of stress or being unsure.

Yawning is used by dogs to calm themselves and others.
As illustrated, we can use yawning to calm our dogs
when walking in noisy areas. Be sure they are looking at
you. Be calm and breathe. If they get too stressed, them
create distance, redirecting to a safe, more quiet area.

Circling is how dogs meet and greet each other. When
it is safe, do not intervene. This gives dogs a chance to
get to know other dogs that they remember later on.

Yawning is used by wolves, dogs and can be by us to indicate many expressions. One is, "It is okay". The message is chill-out. Yawning can relieve stress in our jaws too, try it know. See!

In Yoga, it is called the Lion's Roar, where you stick out your tongue, tense up your face, hold and release, ahhh. Actively applying tension to any part of our body (close fist and hold) and releasing eases tense muscles and joints. Try tensing up your whole body now, hold, and release.

Yawning is being studied (Science Daily, April 2010) in many species (Wolves, Chimpanzees, Horses, etc.). Yawning is not only for stress release, boredom or calming. It is a social connection. Wolves have been photographed in tandem—yawning rituals. One puppy will see another yawn and join in. A human will yawn and others will join in too. Guess we really are from our relatives - the Chimpanzee.

Splitting, not shown in an illustration but I welcome you too www.dogtalk.com/dogtalkmedia to view dogs playing, with a specific Newfie splitting, even at 6-months old. I am sure you have seen it when dogs play together. It is remarkable. A dog will go between impending conflict and too much energy to break the cycle before it escalates. Again, most dogs do not want conflict.

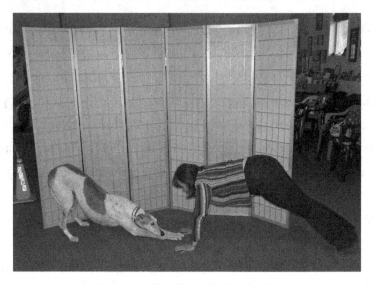

Play bow for dogs signifies, "let's play", not to be confused with stretching which is healthy. When you awake, take a deep breath and stretch. Pictured is Tia, the Greyhound and me. The dogs and I bow to each other. There are videos and images on line of wolves bowing and yawning in unison. It is contagious. Give this ultimate stretch-out a try.

Marking Signals

Have you ever been out for a walk with your dog, ready to rip your hair out, because they stop at every single tree, bush or pebble to pee? Both male and female dogs mark. You have to be observant to catch the females who lift their leg too. Females will urinate on each other's urine, like a female bonding experience.

Dogs leave urine in their bladder to continue marking as a throwback to ancient wolfdom. Together, they will urinate on each other, then on the urine, and then on the surrounding area just to be sure they haven't missed a spot. Here's why:

- ❧ Dogs (wolves) mark territories so they know their territories and warn others that this is their territory.
- ❧ Domestic family dogs mark for the same reasons. In a pack they mark on each other's urines repeatedly.
- ❧ Don't confuse this with the meet / greet ritual of sniffing and sometimes having a peeing and urinating party.
- ❧ Some dogs simply need house training and on walks be taught to urinate once or twice. Walk a bit more and reward with a, "go pee".

Hard Eyes (stay away)

You know hard eyes when you see them. The head is usually turned-away when human approaches and/or they stare straight at you, cold as ice. The eyes are whale-eyed (big) and the dog may freeze. A dog with hard eyes is warning you to back-off. It is a physiological response / signal saying, "get away from me" or "don't come any closer". It can be accompanied by a low-growl.

Soft Eyes (inviting)

A dog with soft eyes is usually friendly and may be a little apprehensive due to previous associations. It is distinguishable because the eye is open, soft looking, and you don't feel threatened.

Muzzle Punching

The first time I got muzzle punched was by a 60 lb American Bulldog who took me by surprise. I was going to counseling graduate school and showed up a pro-sem supervisory group meeting with a black eye and swollen cheek to talk about domestic abuse and violence. I had a hard time explaining that a dog, not a human, punched me out. If you have been muzzle punched you know it. Your jaw and nose hurt. The dog very quickly jumps to your face before you have a chance to turn around or redirect. You may be bent over greeting and they jump up and clock you. My advice, be prepared, and teach a "sit" in front of humans.

Resource Guarding

Dogs are by nature resource guarders (scavengers). RG drives (hard wired) are stronger in some dogs. Dogs can resource guard anything from a toy to the neighborhood. Refer to (Pawt 8) for ways to prevent, manage and rehabilitate resource guarders. Boundaries in the home and around children, food and toys are essential. Supervising children is crucial, as they will give the dog too much freedom. Supervision by adults is a must. Rehabilitating a serious (dino-dog) resource guarder requires professional help.

Alpha This, Alpha That, Forget About It!

Tap-Out is when the head goes down and the body flips, slowly into a roll. It can be accompanied with submissive licking. This dog is avoiding conflict, and if in a pack of wolves or dogs, is being submissive.

The roll-over or alpha roll, in slow-motion video of wolves or dogs, shows the more submissive dog "rolling" on their own. They are not being physically tossed into the position. There are quirks and imbalances in nature that can screw-up pack harmony. Chimpanzees stage wars against other chimpanzees, killing females, infants and elders. If I am not mistaken, I believe we humans do that a lot too. We have humans in prisons that have missing links and do unexpected behaviors.

A pure pack leader does not expend needless energy, nor do they want to harm their pack. Most dogs will avoid conflict, in favor of peace. Pack leaders are quietly stronger, faster and/or work as a team to hunt and survive. It would be nonsensical, from a survival perspective, to go around killing off pack members that pose no threat.

This debunks the myth that we need to be alpha and roll our dogs while staring them down with laser eyes. Our dogs know we are not wolves or dogs. If they wanted to kill us, they could, instantly, like in about 18 seconds!

More seriously, a child could get injured imitating a parent doing this. There are better ways.

Displacement Behaviors

Displacement Activity is performed to change the motivation in a given situation to escape conflict or threat. The individual tries to achieve a sense of security by performing an activity that feels safe and connects them to pleasure.

> DPB is something you do to look busy when
> you don't really know what you should be
> doing! If I don't see it . . . it's not there.
> If I look busy, they'll leave me alone.

Join me for a few minutes of nose-to-navel breathing. Get comfortable with your puppy or dog. Let activity around you float away. It doesn't matter. Only your dog does. Visualize what you want your dog to do today.

When you feel focused and centered, open your mind to new possibilities and begin the following joyful easy training with your dog.

Every day is a new beginning while living and learning with dogs. Enjoy the journey.

PAWT 5

Joyful Easy Training— Level 1—Beginning—Let's Go!

Be mindful that I will be adding visuals at www.youtube.com/dogtalkmedia

Whatever you do with your dog, it is okay to take three steps forward, two steps back; you are always one step ahead. Level 1 for puppies is easy. If you have an older or adopted dog, pretend they are beginning too.

In Level 1, words, cues or signals aren't as important as getting the behavior. You can add in the cues of stand / sit / down / stay / take-it—leave-it / wait / back-up / high-five and relax gradually as you teach the behavior. Simply get the behavior and praise it, without judgment, of yourself or the dog.

Set an intention. Being focused, even for a few seconds, increases learning. Intentionally faking it (pretending you know) is better than not being present. If you cheat (dog gets up and you say GOOD SIT), what's the point?

Shift positive intentional energy into the moment, being genuinely focused, one behavior at a time. That's all it takes. If you are teaching a sit and your dog happens to lie down, take advantage of it by saying, "good down". Later on, we'll get more specific, meaning when I say, "sit", I mean "sit".

Be mindful that while teaching novel (new) behaviors, we want to motivate the puppy / dog by lavishly treating and/or praising. Gradually, change delivery of the reward to equal the response of the behavior (good, better, outstanding). Some dogs will do puppy push-ups (stand-sit-down) for joy. Others need more encouragement. Some dogs get bored after 2 seconds, so you will have to use bigger motivators and shorter training opportunities. That's why taking advantage of training while living with dogs is so beneficial. We have to do regular routine activities for their health and wellness like walking, eating and playing to balance energy. Why not start from the get-go asking for age appropriate activity like "watch-me" and "sit".

All dogs should sit for dinner. They usually do anyway, while waiting for us to dish out their food. If you are doing this 2X a day, that is 14 training opportunities a week. When your dog knows what to do (learning plateaus are usually 45 days depending on the task)—begin rewarding only the best behaviors.

Building in anticipation is your vantage point and keeps learning fun. A dog that enjoys being with you, and voluntarily offers a behavior, is expending energy into acceptable outlets and learns quicker.

Is your dog ignoring you after months of training? Consider if you are a person to be ignored. I am sometimes too. How is their well-being? How is yours? Are they bored? Everything is good you say. Okay, then maybe this is adolescent stubbornness, manipulation or angst.

Reflect for a moment on the past few days. What's been going on—any transitions in your life? We all have our days. Relax; try again some other time. The dog will be fine.

About Physical Prompts: Physical prompts guide your dog into position, like the traditional butt tuck, sliding your hand down the dog's back and scooping in the back legs. If possible, evolve into hands-off. It is less distracting for the dogs. Touch is a reward, and if you are tense, and use your hand to butt-tuck your dog into a sit, they can feel the tension. It takes the joy out of learning for them. Plus, it is quicker and easier to reward them when they voluntarily offer you the behavior.

By the way, it is a huge myth that dogs need to learn how to sit, down or any other behavior from only one position, like on your left side (heeling). Dogs are very intelligent. Once you teach the concept of any behavior, expand the repertoire into various positions, places and activities. It keeps training exciting and challenging. There are very few limits to what you and your dog can learn with determination, focus and creativity.

The Voice

Listen to your voice. Tape recording is helpful. When you listen to different kinds of music, what happens? We dance in class to music like *Moves like Jagger (Maroon Five)* and meditate to *Listen to your Heart (Mike Rowland).* Music and noise affects the dog too in various ways.

Are you asking with a sing-song voice where the inflection sounds like a question? Are you asking with a low, monotone, linear (heart machine dead line comes to mind) tone?

Saying "sit-please" and "thank you" in a firm whisper or tone is polite. Asking a question is giving them a choice. *When requesting a behavior from our dogs, the voice tone should be pleasant, non-threatening, and meaningful. Sit—Please—Thank you.*

Practice Time—Enlighten Me!

In Focused Training (FT) and Relaxed Training (RT), practice creates success. However, there is a fine line between balancing effort and surrendering to the present moment. When you practice is as individual as your lifestyle, you and your dog. I suggest five to ten minutes of calm, focused training as often as possible and at least 3 times a week.

Relaxed training is integrated into daily living and learning with your dog, like Doggy Diner and Mine, Yours, Ours, or meditating/chilling out time with our dogs.

Our dogs stand, sit and lie down all the time. They come to us even when we don't call them. Capture those moments with praise and give the behavior a name—GOOD SIT, DOWN, COME, RELAX.

Greeting—The Social Sit

Take a walk around the block. Have two or three friends walk around the same block, (separately) in the opposite direction, so that you will meet one of them every couple of minutes. Each time you meet one, teach the puppy to sit, have your accomplice greet the puppy after she sits, and then carry on. Do several *social-sit-greetings* with each person. Practice this at the front door with friends, postman, or the UPS delivery person.

Walking Meditation

Walking is training with your dog. The environment is unpredictable. We can't control change. We can teach our dogs to be calm in chaos. Taking a walk, without expectations, to spend quality time, is renewing and relieves stress. To learn more about living and learning with dogs and meditations you can practice, visit www.dailydoga.com. We make better decisions and become better teachers when we are aware of our breathing.

Walking meditation is the same as meditating on your own. You are breathing deeply, observing your dog, but in a relaxed way and aware of what is going on around you without allowing it to control or distract you from having a lovely walk with your dog. Sure, there will be interruptions and unpleasant experiences, but you decide whether it will knock you off balance or not.

Watch-Me (attention please, and try to look me in the eye)

Getting your puppy / dog's interested is the first step to teaching any behavior. Using a charming voice or hand signal (hand to chest), call your dog and when they arrive, guide them into a "sit" and say, "watch-me". If you do not like this word, create your own.

Watch-Me Hand Signal: With arms outstretched (airplane), use your finger, point to your eye, and hold a treat in the other hand, while saying watch-me. The arms are kept still. When the dog looks at you say, "good" and hand them the treat. EYE CONTACT is not necessary for fearful dogs, and most puppies will look someone near your eye. That's fine. Trust takes time. You will know that magical moment because they will look at your eye knowing that only good things happen.

Eventually, begin swirling your arms in small circles one way, and then the next, getting some exercise and getting your pup use to spaghetti arms.

Integrative Training Alternative (ITA)

Whenever your dog looks at you, say GOOD WATCH ME.

Watch-Me and Stand

Stand is valuable for Wellness Checks and Grooming. To teach stand, sounds ridiculous, but have your dog sit. Using a toy, your finger or a treat (works faster), let them sniff it as you guide them forward into a stand while saying "STAND". Do this every day.

Hand Signal: I follow the contour of the dog's body. Using a treat, toy or finger (works best with treat), put it near the dog's nose for a sniff, and guide forward.

Integrative Training Alternative (ITA)

If your dog is standing there while you peel potatoes, looking up at you with adoring eyes, waiting for a hand-out or something to drop, say "GOOD STAND"! Whenever you catch your dog standing, say "GOOD STAND".

Bread basket works well. Take your leash while still on the dog, loop it around the mid section and hold the top gently to keep the dog standing. If you are flexible, and your dog is tall enough, get on your knees, put one knee under the dog's belly. Vets do this to keep the dog up and their back muscles calm.

Sit (a good manners posture)

How many things can your dog do (or not do) while sitting? Sitting and jumping are not compatible behaviors. Dogs should sit in front of humans before interacting.

a. Breathe | call your dog | if they don't come, use your voice, be more motivating.

b. Take the treat or life reward (toy)—let them sniff it | hold it in front of their nose.

c. Slowly bring it over their head. Even the most resistant dogs will automatically sit.

d. Click, Praise or Smile . . . give the treat / reward (whatever you are using).

Hand Signal: Palm up, raising it, indicating a sit. Some people prefer to point to the butt. Do what works for you.

Integrative Training Alternative (ITA)
Whenever your dog shows you a sit, praise with a
"YES, GOOD SIT".

Stand, Sit or Down-Stay are good manners behaviors that should be practiced in every room and outdoors. Begin training up close and personal, increasing distance and duration to the point of success! If you ask for a "Sit or Down-Stay", and your dog moves after 3-seconds, you know that you have to try again and closer. Practice in different postures, standing, sitting and lying down. Practice on one side and then the other. Simply try and learn.

Down

Down can be a relaxed or anxious position for a dog depending on where they are and who is around. Being supportive of your dog while guiding them into a down, especially if there are other dogs around, is essential.

a. Watch-me—focus—we know that our dog has to be paying attention to teach a behavior.
b. Using a treat, toy or hand signal, at the dog's muzzle (nose), guide them downward into a down while saying "down". The words in Level 1 aren't as important as getting the behavior and praising.

Hand Signal: Palm down towards the floor . . . holding the treat or toy. Be patience, don't give up. There is a tendency to smile, laugh and say, "he's not going to do it or she does it at home." Your dog can learn to "down" anywhere.

Integrative Training Alternative (ITA)

Our dogs lie down all the time. Next time your dog lies down say—**"YES, GOOD DOWN"**.

Stay (dancing with your dog could save their life)

If your dog ever escapes or is in a precarious situation (busy street) staying calm and saying —"stay"—could save their life. Incrementally teach a "STAY", dancing toe to toe, than side by side with your dog. If you rush stay, the dog will make a mistake, usually following you. The good news is if you ask for a stay, and they don't, then you know you have moved too far, too quickly. You are dancing with your partner. Teach the relevance of what, when, where and for how long.

a. Imagine dancing with the dogs . . . or square dancing . . . partners move in and out, quickly, while paying attention to their partner. They aren't sipping an iced coffee, talking on the cell phone or checking out the dog 10-feet away. FOCUS!

b. Watch-me | sit | stay | genuinely focus . . . don't scatter.

c. Step in front or out to the side and immediately step back. Do this multiple times before increasing the spatial distance to 2, 3, 4 or more steps.

d. When your dog remains in stay for 5-10 seconds, gleefully praise and reward.

e. Offer a challenge of up to 30 seconds, incrementally increasing time and distance.

f. Practice in different rooms and outside.

Hand Signal: Palm flat, facing and in front of the dog, but not close enough to poke their nose. You can choose your own comfortable signal too.

Integrative Training Alternative (ITA)

Wherever you are, practice, STAND, SIT, or DOWN STAY in each room, back yard and when the dog is sniffing. Call them and say "SIT-STAY". Pause and breathe. Like dancing, move in and out quickly, while reinforcing STAY. Reward them when they STAY with a piece of that turkey you are chopping up.

OOPS, not into human food treats? Okay, BE SURE you have the dog's treat in your pocket. If you walk off to get it, you are doing the Salsa with yourself. The dog does not have to dance with a non-attentive partner who steps on their toes or walks away.

Come (Be someone your dog wants to follow)

This behavior can save a dog's life. More importantly, I want my dogs to merrily come to me without fear. I want to be a pack leader they respect and enjoy being with.

a. In a safe area, puppies or dogs can be off leash. Call them. Praise when they come. Have them follow you.

b. Sit, always, in front of humans.

c. Unsafe areas—please use a leash. Call the pup. If they are pre-occupied or bored, make yourself more interesting using your tone of voice, clapping hands or back stepping in the other direction.

d. Still not coming—don't panic. Take a deep breath, walk slowly to them, and hold the collar (nicely), put on leash.

e. No need to reprimand, because you are teaching. Be more juicy next time, showing them a treat and then releasing them. They learn that coming to you quickly has perks.

f. Try again, even at home while in the bathroom. Call your puppy / dog. Enjoy it! Who else comes to you so joyfully?

Hand Signal and Body Posture: Enthusiastically, get them to come to you. A palm over the chest can be used or design your own unique signal. Squat, clap, jump up and down if you have too. It is good exercise. Coming to you must be a positive experience!

Integrative Training Alternative (ITA)

Go hide and call your pup / dog. Even though this is out of sight, they are in a safe place. Emergency Recalls are more intense, indoors, and eventually in other environments (parks, beach). When they arrive, praise lavishly GOOD COME. They deserve it. Whenever they come to you and sit (while you're cooking), say "good-sit".

Congratulations—Bravo—Woofee

If you have been integrating Level 1 awareness centered training into daily living with your dog for about six weeks, it is time to flow into Level 2.

To increase learning and self-esteem, for us and our dogs, we need to challenge ourselves. It keeps the dogs eager and out of trouble. Balanced exercise, healthy nutrition, humor, appreciation and feeling good will enhance well-being. Look at it as team work.

Continue on to Level 2 for a few new challenges. Notice that Levels are a matter of where you are with your dog, not a rule or timeline. You will know when to regress if your dog is not doing what you ask. **Make it meaningful, fun, relatable and enjoy the journey.**

Level 2—Moderate—A Smooth Energetic Flow
Calming Adolescent Energy
Adolescence is about 9-months to 3-years

Let's have a nose-to-navel breathe and connect with our dogs. Imagine "so-calm". Be present, centered and meaningful.

Level 1 segues into Level 2 without judgment. If you relax your connection / training with your dog it is okay. Life has other priorities. Do a check-in, reviewing behaviors like stand, sit, down and stay at the beginning level. How is it going?

You may be living with adolescent energy shifts. The attention span is longer than a puppy's but harder to capture and hold. *Doggy Diner* and *Mine, Yours, Ours* continues for a lifetime and will help you NOW.

Keep yourself and your dog engaged and focused practicing every day for short periods. Make sense? Let's review drives because teenage dogs thrive on drives:

Drives (that we share with our dogs)

Chase ✦ Prey ✦ Fight ✦ Flight ✦ Freeze ✦ Appease ✦ Faint

Orient ✦ Eye Stalk ✦ Chase ✦ Grab-Bite ✦ Head Shake ✦ Dissect ✦ Consume *(think wolf in the wild or Border Collie spotting the sheep)*

Be mindful of dogs, thresholds, toys and children . . .
Games require boundaries and rules to play fair and safe.

The Grid—Six D's
(Use gradually, safely and to the point of success)

Begin to add some Grid (and Grit): Gradually increase delivery, distance, distraction, duration, diversity and discrimination, but only to the place of success.

Delivery (rewards): Early on in the training game, begin to randomize the delivery of your reward (treat, toy). Reserve the best rewards for best behaviors that are offered quickly. Regularly, do a check-in. Where is your dog? Who are they paying attention too? It should be you and for longer than in Level 1.

Building in anticipation, and using a vantage point by rewarding the best behaviors, keeps your dog perky and interested. If you *treat (reward) mediocre responses*, than that's where the behavior will stay.

If you are teaching a new behavior, or it becomes blaze, jazz it up with treats and toys. Consider using props like *Dogs, Balls, and Balance* in Pawt 6. You will know when it is over stimulating because your dog will begin to do one of two things: tear your pants pocket off or act like the energizer bunny on crack. They stop connecting you and behavior to the treat, focusing on the treat alone. Be the motivator with or without the treat or reward.

Change where you put the treat or treat bag (back of pants, in a different pocket, on a table or no treat). When they calm down and get focused, try again.

Distance: Gradually increase the distance from your dog on sit, down, stay and come. At this level you might consider no more than 4-6 feet—on or off leash—so you can reposition, redirect and correct (gently). If they launch into space, remain calm, keep calling, walk slowly to them, take their collar (gently), hook up a leash and try again. *Alternative: walk away or end together time for a few minutes (time-out).*

Distraction: After only a couple of months of working with your dogs, distractions should be mild to moderate and only when you can supervise your dog. Distractions are sights, sounds and smells that are part of the real world. Observe the dog's body language. Is it perked up, frontal, and ready to launch into cyber-chase? Are they so distracted that they aren't paying attention? If you are concerned about walking by that house where the Labradoodle runs out to excitedly greets you, and the owner babbles, "oh she's okay, she likes to play,", either choose another walking route or plan a script to share with this dog person on your walk.

For example, "thank you for sharing, but honestly, my dog and I prefer to take calm walks. If you want your dog to greet mine, I'd prefer you ask and/or have your dog on a leash." Another that we find effective is, "I appreciate that your dog is happy-go-lucky, but mine isn't, so please restrain your dog. Thank you". If they do not pay attention, call the town dog officer.

The environment is a challenge for responsible dog lovers. Unfortunately, not all people have social skills or care. Role modeling may help, but sometimes we have to be more direct. An alternative is to redirect your dog, ask for a "sit-stay", then joyfully walk off in the other direction. When this happens to me, depending on the mood I am in, I ignore the blissfully ignorant. If their dogs are nasty and uncontrollable, they likely are too!

Duration: The dog is steady on her Stand-Stay, Sit-Stay or Down-Stay for 10 seconds or more. Try extending the exercise for 15, 20 or 30 seconds. Practice in each posture, in different rooms and environments. Set your dog (and yourself) up for success.

Diversity: The dog performs well in her usual, calm training environment (home, yard, and classroom). It's time to challenge matters by introducing to different people and places. Has your dog met someone of a different color or culture? Will she walk as nicely on a loose leash in the park as she does in the backyard? Will she "Sit and Stay" in your living room if you walk to the closet and put on your coat. Will she COME if called while the doorbell is ringing? Whether she did or didn't, you know where to begin.

Discrimination: In dog sports, dogs learn the difference between A-Frame or Dog Walk, Tunnel or Chute, little or big jump. Does your dog know a hand-signal, "sit", and a verbal one? I like to proof even young dogs with cross-training for positioning, with hand and/ or voice signals. It's fun, a challenge, it takes repetition and practice, and it's okay for the dog to make a mistake . . . let's explore.

It usually takes 100 to 1000 practice repetitions

to teach and/or change patterns,

habits and behaviors . . .

CROSS-TRAINING (CT—Hand versus Voice)

This is something you can try with generous and fair expectations on the dog's behalf. CT enables you to communicate with your dog, for a lifetime, with hand or voice signals. I had a deaf dog and have worked with blind dogs. This can be valuable as dog's age.

Integrate this while feeding and training. See what happens. Glue your arms to your side and ask for a "sit"? What happens? Your dog sat. Great, then you know that they get sit with voice signal.

Now try training in stillness (silence.) Use your hand-signal for sit only. Whisper the cue if you like, "sit". Dogs are experts at body language and watch our lips. What happens? If it is confusing for you or your dog, regress by adding the hand and voice signal together or use the treat. Keep practicing. Most dogs enjoy the "newness" and "quiet" of this interaction.

Dog's who have been lured into a sitting position by using a treat held at the muzzle, for a sniff and brought up over the head, automatically know sit from a hand-signal.

Practice this every day during Doggy Diner. Eventually, the goal of most dog parents is to have a relationship with their dogs based on mutual understanding. CT helps to create ways to communicate effectively up close and personal or from a distance, whether we can see or hear . . . how cool is that?

Watch-Me | Stand | Sit | Down | Warm-Up | Stay Skill Spotting—I see you

Getting your dog's attention is the first goal to teaching any behavior. Virtually, any realistic and relatable behaviors are possible to teach. Skill spotting is capturing behavior whenever and wherever you are *and quickly praising.* Similar to clicker training, where you click that sharp, come-to-me and sit front behavior, spotting the skills and praising it works as well. It works on family members and employees too. We all like recognition, dogs included.

Practice each posture, stand, sit, down, stay and come, increasing the amount of time to 10, 20 or 30 seconds. Play puppy push-up, having your dog stand, sit and down sequentially. If you have one of those spot-on dogs, challenge yourself to a minute of stay with each behavior while you stand and breathe.

Integrative Training Alternative (ITA)

Integrate this into daily living and learning with joyful easy training. Whenever your dog looks at you for a minute, like when waiting for food or play, then offers a down automatically, take a deep breath and praise with your style of, *"GOOD Sit or Down".*

Stay (Variations / Postures / Distance / Duration) – Stay Means Stay

A teenager (human or dog) needs a challenge and they will challenge you. When dogs reach adolescence, like human teenagers, they expect more freedom of expression. Along with that comes boundaries and continued respect. This stage of training requires vigilance. It is not the time to relax your boundaries with the dog by letting them get away with obnoxious behavior like staring at you when you say, "get off the sofa." It does not have to be mean, but needs to be clear, that "Lotus" can get on the sofa by invitation only. Again, this is individual choice, but be clear about your expectations.

How many things can your dog do (or not do) while performing a task or in a sit-stay?

Sitting is a good manners posture. Stay can save their life and keep them out of trouble. At the least, it can make living with dogs more pleasurable because they learn to stay on blankets, in a room while you are watching TV, meditating, eating or relaxing. At this level, it will need to be focused and reinforced for success.

a. Using hand or voice signal, ask for a "sit | stay".

b. Step to the side and back, or if you prefer, "stay"—and back-up several inches. What happened? Did they stay? Okay.

c. Let's try again with a challenge of stepping back a foot, maybe two . . . you get the picture.

d. Only go as far as your dog is successful. The only way to know this is to try.

e. If the dog moves out of the box—that's good! It gives you a chance to gently correct and re-position with a "sit—stay".

f. The Circle "Bone-us" Challenge: If your dog has his or "A" game going with a solid "sit-stay", try walking around your dog. If they get up, gently reposition—only go half way. The **CIRCLE** desensitizes dogs to people coming up behind them. It teaches them context. Stay means stay. Heads will roll and flex looking for where are you are going. That's fine. We use this reliably as part of the pet assisted therapy testing for registration. It makes sense because children and objects will move around dogs.

g. Are you having fun with this? If you can circle your dog, in a sit-stay, then try skipping while yawning, humming or singing. Do some jumping jacks or yoga warrior poses. The Goddess pose works well where you squat into chair position, with your arms turned up at the elbow, towards the sky. Dogs are so amused at us being silly that they sit-stay on purpose. It becomes self-reinforcing.

Practice Stand-Stay | Sit-Stay | Down-Stay several times a week. Integrate in creative, fun sequences

Integrative Training Alternative (ITA)

Whenever your dog shows you a satisfactory stand-stay, sit-stay or down-stay, praise. You can practice this anywhere in the house and especially at dinner time. Have your dog "sit-stay", pause for 10 seconds or more. If you have a genius, then place the dinner bowl with a "GOOD STAY".

Come
Be Someone Your Dog Wants To Come Too

To have a dog that gleefully comes to you is breathtakingly rewarding and joyful. With a Newf, it can be daunting to watch that big brown mammoth come towards me. She is amazingly graceful as she leaps into the air but not knocking me over. She knows that I am human and fragile. Early on, when she would dash to me, I would turn sideways and toss her toy as soon as she was within 3-feet. I have taught her, and you can too, that you can come to me without fear, and "be gentle", because you are a dog and I am human. Let's practice the three postures.

Stand | Sit | Down | Come—Remember to work incrementally and to the point of success. If you walk 10-feet away and your dog steps out of the stay box and wanders off, call again, keep calling until they come to you. There are THINGS and TRICKS you can use like walking to the door to leave.

Stand | Stay | Come
Breathe, Center, Focus

a. In a safe area, dog on or off leash, ask for a "Stand—Stay".

b. This is new so you can use a treat or a leash if your dog is wandering.

c. "STAY" and step back a few inches and right back in, reinforcing the stay. It is okay to say "GOOD", but be sure to follow-up with another "STAY". Otherwise you have released the sequence. Your dog is free to go. The goal is to have them "STAY".

d. Do this several times until you can accomplish a "Stand, Stay" for 10—20 seconds or more.

e. Do it again "Stay"—step back several inches and,

f. "Come" (you can use your hand to chest signal if you choose or just "Come" in firm, but non-threatening voice.

g. "PRAISE AND RELEASE, "Good Dog"!

h. Are you satisfied? Good, then don't do it again. Stop on a positive, successful note.

Sit | Stay | Come—*The Dance*

a. In a safe area, dog on or off leash, ask for a SIT | STAY.

b. Request a "Stay" and step back a few inches and right back in, reinforcing the stay. It is okay to say "good", but be sure to follow this with another "Stay". Otherwise you have released the sequence. Your dog is free to go.

c. Do this several times, adding in stepping to the left for 1-foot and to the right for 1-foot. When you accomplish a SIT | STAY for a 10—20 seconds or more . . . begin increasing the distance.

d. PRAISE and RELEASE, "GOOD DOG".

e. Are you satisfied? Good, then don't do it again. Stop on a positive, successful note.

Down | Stay | Come

a. In a safe area, dog on or off leash, ask for a DOWN | STAY.

b. "STAY" and step back a few feet and right back in, reinforcing the "Stay". It is okay to say "GOOD", but be sure to follow up with "STAY". Otherwise you have released the sequence.

c. Do this several times, adding in stepping to the left for 1-foot and to the right for 1-foot. Step back a foot and back in. When you accomplish a DOWN | STAY for a 10—20 seconds or more . . . PRAISE and RELEASE, "GOOD DOG".

d. Are you satisfied? Good, then don't do it again. Stop on a positive, successful note.

Reverse Circle Sit, Down or Stand /Stay. The dog's rear ends are facing each other while focusing on you. This is a trusting relationship position. Breathe and wait. If the dog gets up, calmly reposition. One at a time, call the dogs.

Family Circle Come to me Please

With family or friends, make a circle. One-at-a-time call the puppy / dog and ask for a "sit". If the pup jumps, nips or knocks someone over, please do not laugh. I know it is tricky with children and teenagers. We all laugh automatically at dog behavior that tickles us. Careful humor lightens even the tensest situations, but when it comes to teaching our dogs, laughing reinforces behavior (good or bad).

Take-It | Leave-It | Find-It (Ti, Li, Fi)!

Take-it, Leave-it and Find-It is practiced at different levels every day. Imagine all the things your dog cannot do if they listen to you when you say "LEAVE-IT". Dogs can learn to take the right toy or carry a bag, giving them a job to do. They can go FIND a stuffed toy before greeting (or mugging) you at the door when you get home.

a. Have a treat or toy in open palm, about 10-inches from your dog, say "Leave-It". If they try to take-it, close your hand. Very simple. Practice this about 10 times, 3 or 4 times a week.

b. If you dog patiently waits for about 10 seconds, and looks at you, say "Take-It". The goal is that *every time they look at you, good things happen.* You can add variations.

c. Put the treat or toy on the floor about 6 feet away. "Leave-it". Take a stroll around the leave-it-item. When they look up at you, "YES, let's go explore and then you decide if this is a safe Take-It".

d. Coffee table simulation: Using a chair, place a treat or toy on the end. Say "Leave-It". If they do, and look at you with adoration, DO **NOT** SAY TAKE-IT OFF THE TABLE OR CHAIR. Can you guess why? You will want to go and get it, explore it, and then decide if you want to give it to them or not. Otherwise, choose a treat or toy that you have in your pocket. Many people are teaching their dogs to "leave-it" from baby carriages, coffee tables and other "off-limit" places (poison mushrooms on the ground).

Grab Desensitization
Grab me, I love it, Really!

Eventually, someone will grab your dog. Gently and slowly touch your dog all over. Hold your pup's collar; give a treat, thus creating a positive association. You want your adult dog to be "unfazed" when someone takes his collar.

While smiling, make it slightly rougher without hurting. Offer a delicious, healthy treat. Add in a little more abruptness or quick motion, while making a funny face.

Walk around your pup. Gradually, work your puppy up to being very relaxed about grabs and bumps from all directions. This desensitizes them to children grabbing, veterinary wellness checks and grooming. Have fun!

Bravo! Keep practicing and when you are comfortable, take your dog for a stroll into Level 3 for some challenging behaviors and creative games!

Dogs naturally follow the flow of life with acceptance . . .

Level 3—Challenging Choices
Training with Clarity—Adding More Grid
Teaching with Compassion, Leadership, Acceptance, Integrity and Intention, Trust and Treats, YES more than NO

Sweet Spots—Capturing the Juiciest Behaviors

Challenging is letting go and moving forward as much as you and your dog want (a good metaphor for living). If you have been practicing regularly, this can be a smooth flow into adulthood for your dog, while still embracing the puppy or childlike quality in us and our dogs.

Whenever I visit the elderly for pet therapy, they reflect, wishing that, "they had challenged themselves more and worried about silly stuff less". That can be as varied as the individual, but the message carries powerful meaning, that you can interpret in your own unique way.

Not all children, teenagers, adults or dogs are the same. Some had better options early on in life. Some struggle with new challenges and change. Others wake up each day for the next adventure. Only you and your dog know the comfortable level.

If you have been practicing awareness centered training and would like to learn more challenging sequences, let's flow into Level 3 together. This is the time to get "focused" and "capture" the sweetest and juiciest behaviors, while teaching new ones.

Stand-Stay | Sit-Stay | Down-Stay
Delivery—Distance—Duration—Distractions—
Diversity—Discrimination—Breathe—Center—Focus

Let's review this dance with our dogs. You may notice that there is some cross-over and repetition. You are right. A behavior is only as strong as its weakest link. To continue bonding with the dogs and building a reliable training relationship, we need to continue the dance, creating a chain of reliable behaviors.

a. Practice each of the above as often as possible, indoors, outdoors, and add in a new place like the beach, park or parking lot. If you are in an unsafe environment, and not sure how your dog will respond, on leash please (safety first).

b. Discover opportune times, with less traffic and activity, and walk different routes, gradually increasing the activity level.

c. With the "Stay" position, pause and breath, and walk around your dog, one way, reinforce the stay, and walk the other way.

d. Add in silly faces and people behavior like laughing and giggling.

e. Wear hats, glasses, hop or skip.

f. Are you getting a solid sit | down | stand and stay? If so, next time when you circle, tap your dog on the rear end. What happened? Usually they are curious. Some dogs startle. Either way, smile or say, "oops, sorry" and give them a treat. Dogs will be bumped in real life.

g.   Using the same sequences, increase your distance and duration, as far as you want to challenge yourself and your dog. You will know if the gets it because either they will stay or not. If not, shorten the distance and duration, and do make it meaningful. Dogs when we don't care.

Journey, the Newf, practicing a sit-stay and watch-me.
At this level, she may wait longer before a reward.
I may ask for a down-stay or come and sit-front.

Cross-Training and Crossroads
Wait | Switch | Forward | Back-Up | Enough
Stop | Emergency Come | Gentle | Easy
With-Me—Where you Love to Be

We shared how important it is to honor various stages of our lives as well as our dogs. To review, cross-training is taking training with your dog to a higher level of communication. Dogs learn to discriminate between behaviors, like "wait" or "stay". With practice they learn the difference between items (ball, keys, gloves, blanket, sofa).

Proofing our dogs by using voice or hand signals for learned behaviors (sit, down, stand, stay, come) increases our ability to communicate more effectively. As the dogs ages, hearing or eyesight may diminish, so it behooves us to have an alternate way to communicate.

Life will present many crossroads to us, where we will have choose right, left, wait, move forward, back-up, or when it might be enough. We are happy where we are and can relax. If we let go of the struggle and breathe, it increases our awareness, enabling us to make better decisions at these crossroads, and in every area of our life.

I view the following behaviors as crossroad behaviors. Increasing our dog's repertoire of communication with us is the foundation for a long, happy and understanding relationship.

Wait—We do this Together
Stay—Means you Stay, and I'm Leaving!

Wait is valuable and not to be confused with Stay. Stay is when we want our dogs to stay in "place" until we ask them to move.

Wait is teaching your dog to pause at doors, before getting into or out of cars, and at stair landings when you are bringing in the groceries or laundry. Stay would work too but why not jazz it up with the "wait".

Next time you are heading out for a walk; ask for a "sit" and "wait". When the dog is calmer, then proceed. If you are practicing at the door with your dog, and you want the dog to stay inside while you leave, then you may want to revert to "stay".

Wait means you are going out together. Stay means you are going out and "Molly" is staying at home.

Switch

Switch is a useful exercise where you simply guide your dog behind you to the left or right, depending on what side you prefer dog to walk on, and switch back. You can do a dance with your dog that has the added benefit of creating a barrier (you) between stimuli in the environment that you may not want near your dog.

Go Forward (We can't fit through the door together)

Some trainers say our dogs should never walk in front of us. That's silly. I have more confidence in dogs than that. When carrying eight bags of groceries, I give my Newfie a **job to do; "carry and go forward"**. This is easy to teach because our dogs are usually dashing forward, especially if you have more than one. There is a natural competition.

A main complaint of owners is a lunging dog (pulling on leash). Solution: Teach the lunge. When your dog walks calmly, let them "go forward or pull". I am not suggesting allowing them to pull you onto your face, but enough for a reward. Think about dogs that compete in "draft trials" and/or pull carts for a living. Put it on cue with a "forward or pull", and then, "easy" and "stop".

Back-Up (valuable in tight squeezes)

Dogs back up all the time. Watch your dog next time they are between a sofa and coffee table. It is a tight squeeze. They back-up naturally and automatically. Back-up is valuable for pet assisted therapy dogs because the dog can be presented with situations where a wheelchair is coming out of an elevator. As the handler and advocate for safety, you can step in front of your dog or, if practiced, from the side, and ask for "back-up". It is very impressive!

229

How many other situations can you think of where your dog would benefit from backing up? If we are squashed between a rock and a hard place, and our dog is standing in front of us, "BACK-UP PLEASE".

a. Facing your dog, and depending on their size, start walking toward them without barreling them over. Be mindful of small dogs. Generally, they back up naturally so we don't step on them. Automatically, they begin backing up as we gently encroach on their space. Even dogs in a sit, will scoot back. This is hysterical. You can call it "scoot".

b. An alternative is to gentle guide your dog back by placing your hand on their chest (if your dog is tall enough).

Integrative Alternative: Wait till your dog backs up, capture and snapshot the behavior with "YES, GOOD BACK-UP".

Enough (Play Growls turn into Fights)

Parents know this one well. It works on dogs too. Enough means you are going overboard (calm down, play nicely, go lie down, time-out). The threshold of behavior is escalating to a point of no return where children, or dogs, switch from playing to arguing, growling, crying or whining.

For dogs, growling while playing is normal and healthy. If it escalates, and you recognize this by reviewing body language signals and thresholds, you can intervene, preventing a squabble or worse (something or somebody getting damaged or frightened).

Intervening between dogs is similar with children. The first goal is to calm down with "enough". Let's explore what this is all about. The next step is a choice. Neutrally direct the dog (or dogs) to their blanket or crate with a "toy" or simply to "settle down" for 10 or 15 minutes.

From this point, supervising play and intervening when the level of intensity is going to turn into atomic warfare is a good choice. Dogs (like children) can learn to play respectfully.

Be mindful of how you intervene with a dog when you want them to "give a high-valued item" up, (Pawt 8, Prevention, Management and Solutions). Dogs anticipate and associate from experiences. If a dog has learned to expect a "bad outcome" when people approach them around spaces or high-value items, they may act out of fear and growl.

Forcefully intervening, by physically taking away valued items, sets up the dog for future expectation. A child (or adult) who tries to take a toy from a dog who, in the past, has been physically "alpha'd" into giving up high-valued items could get hurt.

By far, the best way to teach a puppy or dog is with a trustworthy object exchange, then teaching drop it. We want our dogs to enjoy giving things up to us, not fear roughed up.

TIME-OUT is neutral. Neutral means the dog is escorted to a crate or confined area until they calm down.

Stop

Stop for me, and it can be different for you, means just that—STOP. This behavior is annoying, grating and I am on the edge. It's driving me crazy. Body language (hands on hips and a firm face) is oftentimes all I need.

STOP can be used for "fun" recalls. Place your dog in a "sit-down, or stand-stay". Step away to your level of comfort (success). Call your dog, and when they step about 3-feet, using your hand signal, say "STOP". You may have to walk forward a few times to teach the concept.

Some people prefer "WAIT". Again, the word is of less concern than the meaning to you and your dog.

"STOP" is teaching our dogs that enough is enough.

Come

Continue being someone your dog enjoys coming too by calling your dog to you in a variety of rooms and outside (safely). I realize this sound like a rerun but what often happens is we begin to relax our behaviors with our dog. When we do, our relationship suffers.

As with any good relationship, if it is not meaningful to us, and practiced, it will not be meaningful to the dog (or other person).

a. Continue working with your dog on various postures Stand, Sit, Down and Stay.

b. Walk away to about 10-feet, pause, be calm, and watch your body movements. Our dogs read our body language. Even a twitch of a little finger might cue them to come before called.

c. Call your dog. What happens? Are they spot-on—sitting in front of you? Great. Praise. If you are happy, "stop". If you ask for the same behavior too many times, they will get bored, and begin showing you some funky stuff, like walking off or lying down and falling asleep (you are boring ho-hum).

Integrative Variations: You can add in fun sequences to teach (and proof) your dog's response to come.

a. Choose a spot and have your dog "sit and stay". Leave your dog, but this time, do not face them.

b. Turn-around, pause. It is okay to sneak peeks over your shoulder to see your dog's expressions, just try to be subtle. What are they doing?

c. Call your dog. What happens? Often, they land in front of you, even though you are turned around. You can choose here to shape where you want them to be with gentle guidance either by your side or where they chose to land.

d. As always, gage your praise (reward) for the behavior (okay, outstanding). Only you can decide.

Emergency Recall—Trust Me

Emergency recalls can save your dog's life, but you don't want to frighten them. Use a friend or family member to help (teamwork). When your dog is roaming in the house, yard or park, or lying down, call them enthusiastically, like your life depends on it. Clap your hands, go in the opposite direction, but get them to come to you and PRAISE (always be kind to dogs who greet you nicely). "Sit-Front". Sitting dogs can't knock us over.

Find Me: Have someone hold your dog while you hide in another room or behind a tree (outside). CALL and praise when they find you. That's why we adore our dogs. They greet us every second like they just met us for the first time.

Depending on how this is progressing, you can have your dog find you in scarier places like a *room without lights*. This is easy in the house. I go to the bathroom at night, and if I don't trip over the dog first, I call them in.

Take-It | Leave-It | Drop-It (Ti-Li-Di—chant)

Continue practicing take-it, leave-it and drop-in a few times every week. Adding a "drop-it" is good to teach children. When a dog learns how to drop-it, hands are not near their mouth. Plus, it's fun. Let's review:

a. Just as with "object exchange", get two of your dog's high-value items (ball and treat or two toys). Offer one to your dog. Then offer the other while saying "drop-it". Most of the time, they drop-it because they want the other treat or toy.

b. How is it different from TI or LI? If they take something dangerous or that they should not have, you have the option of saying, "leave it" or "drop it". It is a handy request to add to your communication toolbox. With practice, you can phase out the extra high-value item, and simply say "drop-it".

Gentle, Easy and With-Me

"Gentle" is part of biting awareness. Dogs should take treats or toys gently from human hands. You can cue a dog to be gentle around fragile people, cats or other pets. Before they interact, cue "gently".

"Easy" is handy as a casual request to not pull, slow-down or come snuggle but—easy—please, so you don't leave paw tattoos on my legs.

"With-me" is used in agility and dogs sports but is useful anywhere. When dashing from one obstacle or contact object to another, handlers say "with-me" meaning by my side, then here, as they point to the jump. We can use it to mean "with me", "by my side", on or off leash. It can mean within proximity of a few feet or close by.

While walking our dogs in a safe place, smelling the flowers and sniffing the grass, "with me" may be in sight, within 10 or 20 feet. This is your choice. Some prefer **"STAY CLOSE"**.

Teaching our dogs to "quiet" and "be gentle" when taking treats or to stay by our aside, "with-me", creates a bond built on trust, compassion and kindness. These behaviors are taught and used with pet assisted therapy dogs.

Dogs that get moderate exercise every day are happier, healthier and stay out of trouble. Give them a job that is appropriate for them like find a healthy bone or toy that is buried in the sand.

PAWT 6

Have Fun, Get Fit, and Balance Energy

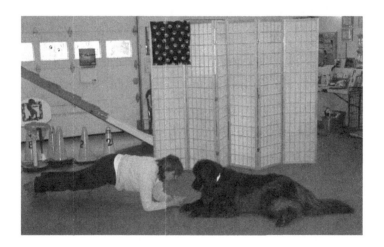

Teaching our dogs to be gentle and patient, no matter where we are or what we are doing, is essential for a respectful relationship. Pictured here, I am in plank position, activating a strong core and praying that Journey doesn't decide to jump over or go under me unless I ask her too.

Fitness, flexibility and balance are important for our well being. You can get fit while training with simple sequences using a chair, step or fitness ball. Have your dog "sit or down—stay". Before you leave, stand straight in Mountain Pose—a strong pose where you consciously, with awareness, plant your feet on the ground (floor). Stand as straight as you can, shoulders down and relaxed. Begin breathing in a full breath to your navel. Raise your arms over your head, into steeple position (index fingers pointing upward). Comfortably focusing on your breathing (inhaling and exhaling) is individual. It takes practice to increase inhalation and exhalation. However, try to make your exhale slower than your inhale, thus, the 4. 6. 8. Inhaling to the count of 4, holding for 6, and exhaling for about 8. It truly does calm the body and mind, giving it a chance to rejuvenate.

Mountain Pose is a good overall body stretch. While inhaling and exhaling, stretch to the left and to the right. If your dog moves, simply say, "stay". If this is new, have a leash on, and/or, step on the leash, so they don't wander too far. Most dogs are so curious at what we are doing, that they "stay" to watch. You are desensitizing them to movement too. All good!

Walk to a chair and do some airplane (arms up) squats (touching the chair with your bottom). Go back and praise. Next time, "sit-stay" and go to a chair and do a few lunges. You can sit on a chair while your dog watches in amusement. Stretch your arms to your side, and one leg at a time. It feels good (in yoga this would be a modified chair Warrior pose).

Return to your dog and praise at the level of success. Did they stay in the box? That's "GOOD". If they wandered off and you had to re-position them, that's a so-so, and "let's try again".

Let your dog join in on the fun while learning how to respond to you when in different postures. Reviewing generalization and context, it makes a difference to a dog where you are and in what place. Teaching our dogs to respond in a variety of rooms, while we do a variety of postures is beneficial for a flowing and trusting relationship.

Try this: Sit in a chair or lie on the floor. Tell your dog, "sit-stay or down-stay". What happens? They need to learn this in context, so you may have to do this several times. In the beginning, my dogs get up and try to rescue me, smothering me with sloppy kisses.

Sit in a chair, have your dog, "sit or down-stay". Pause and breathe. After 30 seconds, say, "STAY", and get up. What happens? You'll know where to go from here. Some dogs get up with you. Now you know! Try again, because the goal is for them to "STAY", while you get up and walk a few feet, then further, until you ask them to "COME". Enjoy and create your own sequences.

Creative Games
Cones, Chairs, Hoops, Blankets, and Paper Plates

Training your dog can change your life by opening our minds to possibilities, with our dogs, and in real life situations. Have you been at work or planned a day off and things did not go exactly as planned? Do we fall apart or look for alternatives? Alternatives give us an opportunity to make what seems like a disappointing or unachievable situation into a new learning experience.

Please enjoy the benefits of attending agility or other training classes with equipment. However, you can inexpensively create games to play with your dog, while getting some exercise, using cones, chairs, hoops and blankets. Create patterns and targets for your dog to stand, sit, down and stay. Some examples follow, but are not limited to these.

> Clients (dog and human) amaze me. I learn as much
> from them as they do from me. One special client, with
> challenges, came to dog sport class with her adopted
> dog. She taught her dog to climb the "A-Frame" (typical
> climb-up for agility competition) but instead of saying,
> "climb" or "A-Frame", she used the word "ramp". She
> knew she would eventually be in a wheelchair. How clever!

Arrange several hoops in various places. After a "stand-stay" in one hoop, call to the next hoop for a "sit-stay", then the next for a "down-stay", and then have them "stay". Walk away and ask for a "sit" and "down". What happens?

You may have to regress when asking for a new behavior, but this is what makes training fun. It isn't about perfection, but trying.

While placing your dog in a "down-stay" in a hoop, go sit in a chair. Call, and then walk around the chair in a circle and reverse the circle. "Good Dog".

You can create all sorts of fun sequences . . . have your dog "Sit-Stay" in a hoop while you place a stuffed toy or a food dish with something yummy about 6—10 feet away. Walk a few feet, but close enough to the dog, to prevent them dashing by for the food. The goal is to teach, "leave-it" and come directly to you! Extend the distance when you are more confident that your dog will come directly to you. Always make coming to you a better place to be than stealing food from an unknown dish.

Use **cones** in a line to zig-zag or weave. Create patterns like triangles, circles and squares. Cones are inexpensive. You can get soccer cones at children's stores or more hefty ones at Home Depot or Lowe's.

Have your dog "stand" at a cone, "sit" at the next, and then "down" at the third, and "stay". Walk away. Call your dog to a blanket, indicating which one. When they arrive, ask for "relax" (chill-out). You get the picture. Be creative.

Paper plates are useful for more than eating and chewing up! We have the dogs focus on paper plates teaching them to sit on them, not chew them. Some creative students have the dogs place each paw on a plate. Like with paper cups, you can place an "X" on one of them. Teach the dog to target that specific plate and find a treat underneath. The list goes on.

Laminated Signs: No, not blank, but with big bold letters typed on the signs like SIT, DOWN, STAY, COME, and one with the dog's name on it. Laminating these 8 ½ x 11 inch signs saves paper. You can teach your dog to read the signs by holding them up and asking for the behaviors. Eventually, the dogs become familiar with the sign and you fade out the request, just hold the sign. It is fund and impressive in front of company.

Dogs, Balls and Balance
My Favorite!

Does your dog have balls? As we age, the first thing to go is short term memory and balance. Other areas begin to jiggle, wiggle and droop. We can shape (spandex), laugh and use props and moderation for various stages of fitness.

Maureen and Journey hanging out while training.
I can no longer do a "wheel" position in Yoga, but
I can use props like this fitness ball. Be mindful
that these balls roll. The peanut style fitness balls
offer more stability for dogs and humans. I have
taught Journey to stand by my side so that I can
use her strong back to help me get upright!

Fitness balls, round and peanut, are used in yoga classes, gyms, physical therapy and children's play rooms. Like dogs, they come in all shapes, colors and sizes. Flat fitness disks are great for sitting on, forcing us to sit-straight. They can be used for balancing, crunches, pilate extensions or yoga boats (a posture where you sit on the disc (or floor) and, depending on your fitness level, make a V, legs and arms up, strengthening your core by holding in your abs, breathing and balancing.

We do not need to torture ourselves doing crunches or training our dogs. Integrating 10-20 minutes of quality exercise and/or dog training works effectively.

As we age (human and dog), the core (abdomen) becomes lazy. If we get too relaxed in this area, our intestines and other organs, lose support and bulge. Focusing awareness on our posture and core (sucking it in) will strengthen it. Planks, as shown with Journey the Newf, can be done on elbows or hands. It is important to maintain a straight back, relaxed knees, and strong core. Don't forget to breathe. Oxygen will help muscles become stronger and prevent us damaging tissues and joints.

Next time you are running up the stairs, pause, breathe, count five stairs up and give it up (5-10 or more push-ups). It only takes a few seconds. Park a little further away, walk five minutes more with your dog, eat a little less and healthier. A little more each day will increase well being, lower stress levels, improve attitude and quality of life.

Fitness balls are good to use sitting at computers or watching TV. They force us to sit straight and tall. Slouching causes you to roll off the ball and on to the dog!

Play training with dogs and balls serve a dual purpose. We get to stretch, balance and the dog gets to train in different positions and, eventually, at a distance.

Give it a try. The exercises are the same as in Level 1, 2 or 3. The difference is that you and/or your dog are using props (balls). The training sequences begin up close, slowly, and then extend the distance and duration.

Be creative by prompting them to put their front paws on the ball, targeting one or two paws at a time. Some dogs enjoy rolling the ball.

You have nothing to lose, but be careful. The dogs enjoy pushing the balls around. I find the peanut balls have more stability for me. If a dog hits the side of a round ball, while I'm doing a crunch, see ya! I'm on the floor.

Make sure they push their own ball, not yours. Be careful of balls at night. If the dog pushes the ball into the middle of the room or doorway, and you are a night-stroller, whoops-wee-plunk!

Dog Sports—Non-Competitive

I use to compete, so I am keenly aware of how challenging and stressful competition can be. The only competition the dogs and I do know is with us. Dog sports are as much fun and less stressful, as a non-competitive virtual playground for higher learning. It is contagious fun to share with the dogs without pressure.

DS is comprised of a maze of games using obstacles that dogs maneuver (with handler guidance). Feel free to use cones, balls, chairs and broom sticks (good for puppies or geriatric dogs to step over).

The dog learns to traverse a dog-walk, negotiate a see-saw, climb an A-frame, zigzag through weave poles, slinky through tunnels, soar over a variety of challenging hurdles, cones, chairs and challenging sequences.

Dog sports, along with your own creative games, are mentally and physically stimulating. It is a great way to balance excess energy and blow off steam in a constructive, controlled and pleasurable way.

Dog sports begins with an introduction to contact obstacles, teaching your dog to safely get use to cross-overs, dog walk, tire jump, climb the A-frame, weave poles, tunnels (chute and pipe) and tip the see-saw.

It is about team spirit. As with any training, DS is introduced slowly and positively. Become "aware" of what your puppy or dog excels at.

More challenging sports are comprised of target training, obstacle discrimination and simple sequence set-ups, like going over little jumps, than big jumps, and through a tunnel and chute.

We have discovered ways to use empty cider barrels that most farms who make cider will sell reasonably priced. You can cut them in half, making two smaller tunnels. We have them marked "geriatric and puppy tunnel".

> Age is not an issue with modifications. Anne's dog "Brandy", a 15 year old cattle dog, use to compete in agility and became a pet assisted therapy dog at 12. Brandy would air-jump beside the bigger jumps, over a broom stick. Her eyesight was failing, but it didn't seem to bother her that she could no longer traverse high jumps. What mattered was her time with Anne and being praised for doing activities that she enjoyed.

Let's Go To Bed—Really?

Many people ask me should my dog be allowed in bed. By the time they ask, it is because the dog has growled at someone, chewed pillows or messed the bed with dirty paws.

My dogs are allowed in bed with me (oh my). This is my choice and it is yours. Meditate on this before deciding. You teach a precedent when you allow your dogs to do anything, and especially join you on furniture, including your bed.

The bedroom is what it is for you, personally. Review the whole picture. Having a cute puppy cuddling in bed is one thing; Having an Irish Wolfound or Newfoundland another story. Having a wet dog on the bed can be a soggy, uncomfortable experience.

What is your lifestyle like? Are you someone who likes to change your comforter every season? Dogs cannot discern between white, peach or indigo blue. Do you want paw prints on the bed? Are you married, single or dating?

Looking at the whole picture for the dog's sake is important. If your dog is bonded so closely with you that no-one else can enter the "bed" territory, strongly consider having them sleep on their bed or crate.

Creating a relationship with a dog that is interdependent, not co-dependent is for their well-being. Interdependence creates a confident relationship, whether you are around or not. Co-dependence is stifling, where the dog can't function in unfamiliar situations.

Okay, you've decided that your bed is their bed. You like to snuggle, cuddle and do not mind getting kicked in the middle of the night by dreaming legs. Please teach the "UP" and "OFF" first. Do this multiple times.

The litmus test is when you ask your dog to "get off" what do they do? Dogs should have respect for you on or off "YOUR BED". When you say "off", it means off, and "Go to Your Bed".

Our dogs do get on the bed. The Newf stays for 3-seconds, says goodnight, and leaves. It's too hot. Here is the caveat. If you ask, or anyone close to you is on a bed and asks the dog to get off, and they do not, the privilege is over.

Teach them to go back to their bed, blanket or crate. And, you get on their bed too. The earlier you make sharing beds a positive experience, the better.

Does this mean your dog can't cuddle with you on the bed again or on a couch? I don't know, does it? This depends on the level of intensity. No "human" should be in fear of asking their dog to get off of furniture.

The solution is to teach them from the "get-go" "UP" and "OFF" many times. Dogs quickly learn how to respond, where to go, and when. They can discriminate between "this time and that time". Okay, tonight she says I can "stay on the bed", and maybe tomorrow night, "go to your own bed."

You may be giggling about this, but behaviorists, including myself, get called in often to resolve situations during divorce, death and transitions in family lifestyles. It affects the dogs too. Dogs that have been cuddled, and use to sharing a bed or sofa with someone, and are faced with change, need time to adjust. Some are more resilient than others. Dogs can learn how to be resilient and embrace change. Resilience can be learned by teaching them variations of different situations. Sometimes they can, and sometimes they can't. When in doubt, it is fine to have the dog sleep in their own space!

Dog Team Baseball

HOME HOOP

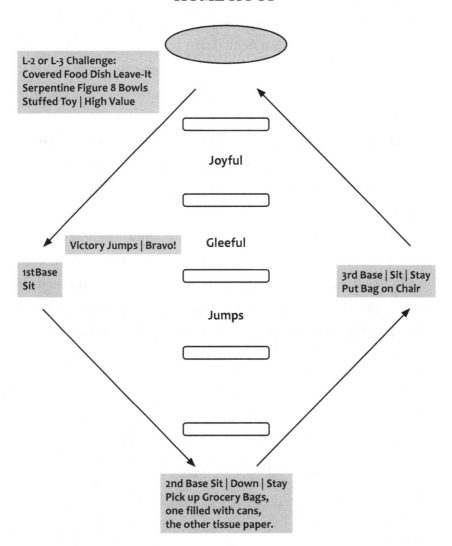

L-2 or L-3 Challenge:
Covered Food Dish Leave-It
Serpentine Figure 8 Bowls
Stuffed Toy | High Value

Joyful

Victory Jumps | Bravo!

Gleeful

1stBase
Sit

3rd Base | Sit | Stay
Put Bag on Chair

Jumps

2nd Base Sit | Down | Stay
Pick up Grocery Bags,
one filled with cans,
the other tissue paper.

Create challenging variations of Baseball by integrating
real life activity like having someone, at several feet
away, bounce a ball, skip, sing or do a few jumping jacks.
Add a bell at Home Hoop. We hang ours from
a child's basketball hoop. Teach the dog to
target the bell and ring. Create different levels
of fun and intensity with a variety of sights,
sounds and smells that dogs will encounter.

Hide and Seek (Who enjoys finding us as much as our dogs)

Search and find is a cool game you can play with your puppy. While they are resting or playing with a toy, hide in another room and then call. Some dogs like to look for toys or biscuits. Two people can take turns gently restraining the dog while the other one hides themselves or the toy. Encourage the dog to "go find" and help them the first few times.

Outside, in a safe fenced area, hiding behind trees and bushes is a hoot. Watch your dog's expressions. Appreciate the joy that is shown upon finding you, their favorite person!

PAWT 7

Stress and Survival Savvy

For You and Your Dog

Ready or not here it comes—adolescence—at around 6 to 18 months, and up to 3 or 4 years. The adorable and attentive pup who use to hang onto your every word, and follow you around, gives you a nose and tail up, and walks off. The scenario may go like this, "Excuse me, where the heck do you think you are going?" Pup, "What's it to you and any where I darn well please".

Being aware of this phase and breathing will help you survive it and beyond. What is important is to not give up. We tend to relax or behaviors after puppyhood, when this is the time to "ramp up" focused and awareness centered training.

Case in point: the largest number of dogs relinquished to shelters every year in the USA is usually 3 years old and under. That message flashes in neon. If you have a high-def dog, with lots of energy, now is the time to continue with education.

Instant Energy Assessment (IEA) I Yi Yi

You can do an instant energy assessment of your adolescent dog (or any dog) by observing your dog's "high def" energy times. What are they like when your first arrive home? Are you impaled onto a chair or denting the wall? What is it like when you begin a walk? Are you on the next block before you have closed the door?

Most dogs are more alert and active at dawn and dusk, and when left for long periods without adequate exercise. We change their circadian rhythms to match ours, leaving them with little alternative or ways to expend energy.

When is your dog most active, reactive or energetic? When are you? Only you can know for sure through observation and awareness of self and your dog. If you take a walk and your dog is focused on everything in the environment to the point where walking is a miserable experience rather than a pleasant adventure, there is your answer. Choose quieter places to walk until you can calm the energy.

You can deflect and redirect adolescent energy into positive outlets, while calming and preparing yourself for an activity. What I recommend to clients is to get the dog in condition before hard core running, exercising and avoid the "toss the ball a hundred times" activity without focus. By focus, I mean with boundaries and rules like in any game. Have the dogs "get-it", "bring-it" and "sit".

Let's explore ways to tame energy with benefits.

Taming High Def Energy with Benefits

The Teenage Stage: Puppy hormones awaken and distractions begin to compete for attention to "you". Response to requests like "come" become optional. The pup begins to exert influence in familiar surroundings. Mildly annoying behaviors such as jumping on visitors and lunging on leash become pronounced because the pup is now a dog, and getting bigger and stronger.

Around 9—18 months, your dog's need for leadership and boundaries is vital. Pushy, and often more vocal in this stage, your active youngster will find impulse control challenging. Many dogs look like adults at this stage, but still lack confidence and polish.

Like with human teenagers, things may become heightened and dramatic. With dogs, it appears as funky behavior like fear of familiar items. They have passed the garbage can a hundred times before, but now it is a big spooky monster. Armed with a baseball bat you may find yourself going to the basement to face a burglar that your dog is barking at to find your dog standing there, eyeballs huge, frozen in fear staring at their dog food bag. Flip the switch, lights on, and "oh, that's my food bag, duh, I'm embarrassed". Relax and say, "That's a silly bag, it scares me sometimes too, let's go find your stuffy".

Continue with joyful, easy training. Here are some paws of wisdom to survive the teenage phase:

1. Breathing—always helps reduce stress and increase focus. Your calm energy will relax your dog's "high-def" energy.

2. Continue practicing confidence building skills using what comes naturally like eating, playing and loving. Channel energy with controlled games and exercise (Baseball).

3. Continue using the mantra, you do something for me, and I will do something for you. Those few moments a day of asking your dog to "wait, sit, down, stay, come" helps keep them focused. Focusing is a form of expending energy.

4. Balance Energy with Adequate, Healthy and Safe Exercise—most people will stop exercising their dog at this stage because the dog is getting stronger and harder to control. Every day, they need two or three exercise sessions. That's how they continue learning boundaries, becoming familiar to the environment, and paying attention to you.

5. Become a motivator with life rewards. Make it more enticing. Simply having them "sit" and "wait" for diner is expending energy.

6. Where is your dog? Where are the children? Children and adolescent dogs should be supervised. Bigger dogs are powerful and can knock children over.

7. ACT with prevention. Begin to give your adolescent a little more freedom, in successful increments, but still with boundaries and supervision. Clients say that they have left their dog for 2-hours—to come home to a house torn to shreds.

8. Whoops! Too long, too soon. It is a heck of a lot of fun for a bored dog to chew a sofa. Be mindful that after the fact is too late to correct. If you do, you create a downward relationship spiral. Instead . . .

9. Continue using confinement, while giving the dog more freedom of expression, for shorter periods, and only when you can supervise and teach.

10. There is a tendency with adolescent dogs to start walking and hiking off leash. I strongly recommend you consider where and when you do this. Most parks and recreational trails have rules. Is it on or off leash?

   a. When confronted by unusual situations (a hiker with a backpack) the dog may become intimidated, learn to alarm bark, or worse, lunge at the strangers or any fast movement (squirrels).

   b. Dogs should be on leash, and practicing distance control, until adulthood and/or in a safe, fenced area. When you have practiced and are sure of emergency re-calls (dog comes to you no matter what), give it a try.

   c. If you accomplish this, please patent this approach. You may become very wealthy. In the big picture, we have to be extremely exciting for an adolescent dog to come to us, especially if they have been inside all day!

11. Look around before unhooking the leash anywhere. Is your dog paying attention to you or the kid on the skateboard?

It is possible to shift energy levels, in any direction, for us and our dog with practice. If your top half is going right, and your bottom half is going left, you are going to hurt yourself. Getting calmer first helps.

"You can say any fool thing to a dog, and the dog will
give you this look that says, "My God, you're RIGHT!
I NEVER would've thought of that!"—Dave Barry

Whoa, Time-Out for a Brain Break

This is not guess work anymore. Powerful and empowering research is being done all over the world on the mind, body connection. The East has met the West. Breathing techniques, Reiki, massage, acupuncture, acupressure and aromatherapy, healthy nutrition and lifestyle changes, and pet assisted therapy accompany recovery plans in hospitals to enhance recovery and well being. Unfortunately, some do not get the benefits of this until after they have become ill.

We can prevent illness particularly from stress with awareness and integrating small, but significant changes into every living.

Calm in Chaos—You can Find it and
Stop you Head from Twitching!

We have all been to that edge where if one more thing happens, over. Our dogs experience this too, and especially adolescent and misunderstood dogs. Oftentimes, the very thing that is driving us crazy, like our dogs bouncing all over the place, is exactly the kind of dog we were attracted to (the puppy who dove into our lap).

Traditionally, people think that they need to exercise long and hard, and meditate for hours, to calm the chaos in the mind. I hope you are discovering that even in today's multi-tasking, fast paced society that we can and should take several ten minute brain breaks through the day. It benefits us and our dogs. If we are not calm, they cannot be. And, they usually reflect our behaviors, like living in a house of mirrors.

When I am at the edge, and one more thing happens, I become scary not only to the dogs but me. How do we prevent this? Good question. Awareness is the beginning. It is not easy to change, but as we have shared throughout ACT, we can integrate little changes, like nose-to-navel breathing, several times every day, anywhere and anyhow.

No-one will know that while you are taking your dog for walk that you are secretly breathing in one and exhaling two, while doing Kegal exercises (internal pelvic lifts to strength Kegal Muscles— helping to prevent urinary incontinence in men and women). Focusing on strengthening our core (ab muscles) while walking our dogs, helps us hold on to them. It is a matter of perception. Instead of looking at it as a walk from hell, consider it exercise, while training the dog to "calm down" and "walk calmly".

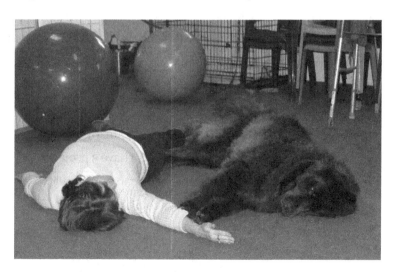

As illustrated with Journey (Newf), we can teach
with kindness, showing them they are safe, not

threatened. Teaching a dog to lie on their side or roll over is beneficial for vet exams, grooming and to lie down quietly when we have visitors.

Relax, Rejuvenate and Reconnect
Calm the Chaos

We all have days when our stress levels are worse than others. The days when we are being tugged in multiple directions like Gumby. Some stress is healthy, and jars us into motion, urging us to prioritize, plan and get moving. Too much stress causes blips in our radar and ill health.

Learning to relax and breathe, even for a few minutes, several times a day, will help rejuvenate our brain cells, and ultimately help us reconnect with ourselves, our dogs and others more consciously and coherently. I say coherently because oftentimes when we are stressed out, we ruminate (babble) and replay negative tapes in our minds that make no sense in the present moment. Letting it happen, learning and letting it go (Liha-L-Ligo) is like having an Hawaiian cocktail. It relaxes us, knowing that what is past is past. Now is the time to focus on changing ourselves or our dog's behavior.

Here is a typical day described to me by many multi-tasking clients: 3-phones are ringing, I have 3 project deadlines, I work from home—so I can be around when the kids get home. I have to pick up the dog at the vets and stop at the grocery store—making it quick because I want to get the dog home to rest, and get supper going—my husband has hockey tonight. Oh yeah—the laundry is still in the dryer,

and I left the click-to-pay online—I just know my
information is now in some foreign country. I need
help, but everyone else is busy too. AHHHHH—My
hair is falling out and I need some rest—NOW!

Sound familiar? Sure it does, because we all have similar days, perhaps with different stories or dilemmas. Take solace that you are not alone. There is a reprieve, but it has to come from the source, and that source is you. Give yourself permission to take back control of your breath, your dog and your life.

We all experience chaos. So do our dogs. How we deal with chaos matters. Some end up on medication or self-medicate because life is controlling them. Whatever this means for you, and whatever help you need, it is okay, as long as you are aware that you need it.

In the moment of chaos, and this takes practice, it is possible to experience calm by simply saying, "stop" and "breathing". This does not mean that life will be strawberries dipped in dark chocolate and whipped cream. Projects and chores won't poof into completion. You WILL be better able to navigate the day knowing that "you" are in control of how chaos affects you. You are not alone.

Honor yourself and your way of engaging in life. I enjoy multitasking, but if it starts affecting me or my dog's well being (I'm screaming at them), then I know it is time to breathe calm into chaos. The stuff still needs to get done—but I have choices. I can take a moment like my Greyhound who rolls in the grass, or the Newfie who nose-dives through the snow, and the Border Terrier who stands in silence for 10-minutes at the hopeful chipmunk path.

I can take a walk, choosing to set aside fifteen minutes. What absolutely needs to be accomplished right now? Can it wait? It does not have to be "perfecto".

However, letting things pile up isn't the answer either. Organized chaos and clutter is fine in small dosages. Procrastination creates more chaos, and usually has deeper-seated issues like—what are you avoiding? Is being caught up scary? How come? There will always be more chaos. Clear the clutter and breathe easy. Don't worry; you can collect more later on.

How we deal with daily chaos is a matter of breath. Taking a few breathing brain breaks at least a few times a day cleanses your brain with oxygen and your body of toxins and toxic thinking.

> Stop: Take a deep belly breath now—slowly breathing in to your abdomen to the count of 4 counts—not speed dial 1, 2, 3, 4. Holding for about 6 seconds, and exhaling for about 8 counts. This is 24 seconds of your time to pick your twitching head up off the floor. Read on —

Chaos swirls around us, like being in the eye of a storm. We can be safe in chaos, by becoming observers. Let things float by without getting sucked in by saying, "STOP". Taking a deep breath changes every cell in your being and your body's response to bedlam. It calms the endorphins and cortisol (which causes belly fat) and regulates serotonin and dopamine (fight / flight response). It does for dogs too!

Shut off the music, turn off the news and walk away from the computer. I'm going to do that right now. Ahh—better.

Have you ever noticed how you get injured more often when you are doing things too much or too quickly? I've cut myself more times (while pretending to be a master chef) when I'm rushing to cook. I become an automatron, not paying attention to the task. When I'm playing Rachel Ray, I have to have several band aids available. It is way too dangerous, and blood doesn't add great taste to the meal, maybe a little coloring.

When things seem at their worse, looking at others put it into perspective. Our chaos is usually much smaller than living in a shanty tent while excrement, from the tent next door, is rolling into ours. Wondering where our next meal is coming from is a scary thought but happens to millions. Have you ever considered what life would be like if tomorrow you didn't have arms or legs? Most of the time, we are better off than we think or feel.

Schedule a pity-party to sit with the stress, sadness and anger for awhile. Explore the places that scare you, and then, let them go and move on.

There are ways we can organize our lives, delegate and do it a little less than perfect. Ask for help—it only hurts for a minute. Outsource (hire or ask someone to temporarily help). It won't get done the exact same way, but occasionally it is okay to delegate walking the dogs to someone you trust.

> *OPIUM helps*—organizing, planning, implementing (action), understanding flexibility, and making changes if necessary. Life is not fair, it is challenging, change will happen. *Tony Robbins* has a saying: "life jars us into motion." We become use to a comfort zone. That's fine, if we are content, but do not become complacent. If we are frequently complaining and tired, it might be because we need a change, even a small, planned one. Big changes will shock us into movement, whether we like it or not. We can find new beginnings in small changes every day.

Remember I shared that some thrive on chaos, thinking that without it life is meaningless. That *puddle of nothingness* you feel when you sit still and breathe is exactly what you need. It is called peace, even for a few moments. This peace gives you a chance to truly listen to your body, thoughts, needs and concerns. It clarifies the message your dog is trying to tell you with their behavior (good or bad). It gives you a moment to put life into perspective—chaos into calm—well being into you and your dog's life.

Manage your chaos, like your well-being depends on it, because they are interconnected. Sit with your dog and breathe for a few seconds. You may discover an abundance of energy from this little siesta that teaches STOP to what you don't want your dogs to do, and STOP for what you need, a deep breath and a smile. Eventually, you will be unfazed by chaos by using what you can control—*your breath.*

> Have you ever watched how many things a dog can do in a few minutes? They can eat, go out—pee, poop, play, sniff with delight, roll in pleasure, de-stuff a toy, empty the trash cans, wag their tail, run in circles, trip us, then lie down, yawn, fart and go to sleep. We can accomplish a lot in a short period too, as long as we take short, frequent calming breaks.

Private v Play Groups v Walking—The Difference

Group classes in a motivating environment, using positive, and awareness centered techniques can be advantageous for dogs and people. You get to network and connect with guidance from a skilled and dedicated trainer.

Group classes, with the exception of open enrollment in upper levels, where people and dogs are more experienced, should be kept small, no more than 8 or 10. Otherwise, it is nearly impossible, especially for a novice trainer, to effectively and safely manage the chaos.

Group classes must be family oriented which means that one puppy could be accompanied by several humans.

With this in mind, there are questions to ask when searching for a good training group. If they have a website, and you are computer savvy, use it first. Calling a trainer or behaviorist to roll-out-a-scroll of issues will waste your energy and theirs. Aside from the obvious like location, price and experience of the trainer, consider first:

1. What are your goals?
2. What approach does the trainer use? Does their experience match your goal or are they simply cheaper?
3. Do you have specific goals like pet assisted therapy or competition? Are they familiar with this?
4. How many people and dogs are generally in the group?
5. Will there be supervised puppy socialization before or during class?
6. Do they insist on clicker training or do you have a choice?
7. Will there be hand-outs or homework?
8. Do they listen with respect? Do they genuinely enjoy teaching?
9. Lastly, if you bounce into voicemail, don't be disappointed. It is today's world. Many trainers / behaviorists work in private practice or have only a few employees or volunteers.

A professional will call you back as soon as possible. If they do not, then you have your answer.

Group classes should be well-rounded and include at least some guidance on nutrition and well-being, the whole dog, not just training. Beyond that is anyone's guess until you arrive. Practice 10/5. Be aware of what is going on around you within 10-feet, and ask before treading into someone else's spatial bubble within 5-feet (dog or human).

Private classes are rising in popularity for obvious reasons. People are busy. Social media and DVD's offer many options for self-training. Nothing beats hands-on experience and connection. Experienced puppy people can successfully train on their own, as long as they offer continual socialization and manners training (SAM).

Private Coaching can be more expensive, but more comprehensive. Coaching in private sessions gives you confidential, one-on-one support. If you have specific training goals, like becoming a pet therapy team, it can be advantageous and cost effective.

The same questions apply as with group classes with the addition of gathering information about specific behavioral modification and treatment planning approaches *(Pawt 8, Basic Behavior Problems and Treatment Collaboration)*.

Dog Parks v Play Groups v Walking—The Difference

Trending is that some people are swapping traditional training classes and walking time with their dogs for dog parks and play groups. Yikes!

A **dog park** is a facility set aside for dogs to exercise and play off-leash in a controlled environment under the *supervision of their owners*. Parks vary in accessories, although a typical dog park offers a 4' to 6' high fence; separate, double-gated entry and exit points; adequate drainage; benches for humans; shade for hot days; parking close to the site; water; tools to pick up and dispose of animal waste in covered trash cans; and regular maintenance and cleaning of the grounds. Better parks with sufficient space, will offer separate areas for puppies under 6-months, adolescents and older dogs. Dog parks may feature wheel-chair access and a pond for swimming, and a separate enclosure for small dogs (under 20 lbs).

All dog parks must have guidelines for dog and people etiquette. Towns and cities require health certificates and some charge a nominal fee. These ensure that dogs are healthy, licensed, and have their required vaccinations. All dog parks must have maintenance (clean-up) on a regular basis to prevent spreading of infectious diseases.

In the United States, the first official dog park opened in 1979 in Berkeley, California's, Ohlone Park. Today, more than 600 city or county sanctioned off-leash areas in the U.S. exist, and more than 1,100 exist in the United States and Canada combined (Dogpark. com, 2002).

> *Dogs can release energy and learn to navigate their*
> *way with other dogs in a supervised environment.*
> *Other dogs should know how to play safely, enjoy*
> *interacting, and with biting awareness (no bloodshed).*

In Australia, dog parks feature water taps rather than hydrants, garden benches, and mature trees for shade. Some (e.g. Pymble, New South Wales) have solar lampposts for after dark use.

In Toronto, Canada where some of my relatives live, it was a breath of fresh air to discover on and off-leash beach areas for dogs and owners. We loved it because it was managed well.

There is no doubt that most, not all, dogs enjoy running free. When all is well, and the dogs are healthy and get along, dog parks are pleasing. Please do not confuse free-running-exercise for training. Unless you are a focused owner, who is paying close attention to your dog, and other dogs that join the group, dog parks could be dangerous.

Dogs, dog parks, training, socialization and owner perception have different meanings. Incidents bring people, and dogs that have been decked, to private coaching for rehabilitation. Before releasing a dog in a park, prepare the dog. Look around and observe your dog's behavior. Is it safe? Are they feeling safe?

Ask yourself, does my dog want or need to run with other dogs in a dog park? You can tell by observing your dog's interactions and body language. If after several attempts, your dog is sitting under a bench, by your side, or off in a corner, screams "not ready".

Begin desensitizing them from a distance first, like across the street, or 20 feet away.

To keep your dog happy, healthy and out of trouble, you'll need to find ways to exercise her brain and body. If she enjoys the company of her own kind, visits to your local dog park can greatly enrich her life. Benefits of going to the dog park include:

Dog Park Upsides

Physical and mental exercise for dogs: Your dog can zoom around off-leash to his heart's content, investigate new smells, wrestle with his dog buddies and fetch toys until he happily collapses. Many dogs are so mentally and physically exhausted by a trip to the dog park that they snooze for hours afterwards.

Opportunities to maintain social skills: Most dogs are highly social animals. Many enjoy spending time with their own species. At the dog park, your dog gets to practice navigating their way with other dogs, if the other dogs are safe. They learn about body language and communication skills. They frequently get to meet unfamiliar dogs (and people). These valuable experiences can help guard against the development of fear and aggression problems around other dogs. Conversely, it can also create them.

Fun for pet parents: Dogs aren't the only ones who enjoy dog parks—people do, too. They can exercise their dogs without much effort, socialize with other dog lovers, bond and play with their dogs, practice their off-leash training skills, and enjoy the entertaining antics of frolicking dogs.

Dog Park Downsides

Despite the many benefits dog parks provide, it's important to be aware of the risks before you decide to become a dog-park junkie:

Health risks: Healthy, vaccinated dogs are at low risk of becoming ill because of visiting the dog park. There are health risks any time your dog interacts with other dogs, just as there are for us when we interact with other people. Talk to your veterinarian about the risks and whether s/he recommends vaccinating for Bordatella ("kennel cough") if you become a regular park user.

Fleas are everywhere-including on squirrels, rabbits and raccoons. The solution to flea control is providing adequate protection, of your choice, on your pet (topical, spray, internal).

Dog Fights: Your dog could get injured in a fight or during overly rambunctious play. It's highly unlikely, but small dogs could even be killed at a dog park because larger dogs sometimes perceive smaller dogs as prey or they can step on them.

PTSD (Post Traumatic Stress Syndrome): Dogs and humans can suffer from PTSD after an incident at the dog park. I have counseled several. When a dog is injured at a dog park, emotions, grief and guilt abound for the dog parent. No-one wants their dog or a person to be injured. If you are not paying attention, sucking on an iced coffee, or not sure of the dog (especially new or adopted dogs) then proceed with caution.

I do NOT advise taking a young puppy, or newly adopted dog, immediately to a dog park, and unhooking the leash. This must be a gradual introduction. The dog park must be managed well. You, as the dog's advocate, need to realize that a dog park may or may not be the best thing for your dog. Observe your dog. If they are shivering, afraid and do not attempt to interact, honor this request. Walk around the periphery and/or find a less stressful way to exercise your dog.

Dog problems: For shy, fearful or easily overwhelmed dogs, a visit to the dog park can be more stressful than exciting. If your dog has unpleasant experiences with other dogs—if they bully or fight with him, intimidate her or just play roughly-s/he might decide she doesn't like them at all. Dogs who prefer gradual introductions to unfamiliar dogs could begin growling, barking, snarling, snapping, lunging and even biting to drive other dogs away.

Aristotle Airedale bullied our deaf bulldog, Casidy, once! We had to remove her in fear of her learning behaviors that she would bring home to the other dogs. Interestingly, this dog's owner was a bully too.

People problems: Everyone has a different story. Dog people are passionate people. They have strong opinions about dog behavior. Pet parents or behaviorists don't always agree about what's normal dog behavior, what's acceptable during play, what kind of behavior is truly aggressive, which dog behaviors are obnoxious, whether or not one dog is bullying another, or who's responsible for the altercation. People might argue about how to respond when problems between dogs arise. Since there's rarely an authority figure to appeal to at a dog park, disagreements can get heated and result in human behavior problems.

Play Groups or Fitness Groups are springing up everywhere, including Veterinary Clinics. The same advantages and disadvantages apply with the exception of you are closer to a Veterinarian and Vet Techs who may have more experience about matching dogs with dogs. If a dog gets sick or hurt, at least they are at a hospital.

Be sure your dog is healthy and enjoys play groups. Like human hospitals, if their well-being is compromised, playing in an environment where sickness, bacteria, urine, feces and disease are bountiful is not the best place to leave your dog to play. Interview the supervisor. Who will be managing the dogs? How long will they be allowed to play and with who?

Being promised a look-and-see video? Great! Just be mindful that the video must be longer than a few minutes. Videos can be edited and/or taken at certain times. The best eye view is your own, in person, to see how your dog interacts with other dogs, before leaving them for hours or a whole day.

Walking—Common Sense Prevails

Walking (exercise), at any level, is healthy for dogs and humans. You do not have to run a marathon, but if you and your dog are conditioned, go for it. Walking puppies is a joyful activity of exploration. They paw along, sniffing, wagging their tail, discovering all sorts of new things. They teach us how to stop and enjoy what matters. Like infants, they are learning every second. Make the seconds count by capturing and praising good behavior like looking at, or for you, sitting, waiting, and walking calming on leash.

Choose your pleasures, poisons and walking routes. You can SAM your dog on walks by choosing calmer routes first, then incrementally increasing onto paths with higher levels of activity. Walk by the dog park and check it out from a distance. Sit on the bench. If someone nonchalantly approaches, let them know you are, or are NOT, socializing today.

Walking is good for our health and our dog's. One of the primary complaints I hear from owners is lunging. Walking gives an opportunity to redirect them, traverse steps, circle trees and bushes, and practice watch-me, sit, down and come to me, while expending energy and calories. Dogs cannot lunge if sitting or turning in multiple directions. Use "switch" (Level 3) where you direct your dog behind you to the other side, creating a barrier between your dog and other, more unfamiliar people or activities.

But I want my dog to run free! Okay, you can do that too in a safe place. Ask your dog first. A 4 lb Miki may not want to run free in a park with a 180 Great Dane. This is like a fly looking up at the bottom of our shoe! This is not to say that a Chihuahua can't rule over a St. Bernard. They might, but can get killed if stepped on by one. Common sense prevails.

Breathe and relax—the good news is that you and your dog have choices to enjoy healthy and safe exercise to increase overall well-being.

Prevention, Management, Solutions (PMS)

The following are joyful, easy and preventive solutions for shaping and re-shaping most commonly complained about behaviors. You have heard me parrot that every owner and dog is an individual. Whether you have a new puppy or adopted older dog, there are actions you can take to re-shape behaviors that may have unintentionally escalated out of control.

Remember PMS: Prevention of behaviors you do not like is the solution to almost all behavior issues. In the real world, things happen spontaneously and unintentionally. We can't be in five places at once or in control of everyone our dog meets. The environment is unpredictable and a powerful behavior shaper.

Management in the home and outside is 50% of the solution, especially if we don't have time to be hyper-vigilant, 24/7. Some behaviorists would say that we manage behaviors 80% of the time. I think we can get to 50%, or less, with awareness centered training. It depends on time and commitment. Otherwise, yup, we are managing more than teaching.

Solutions are win-win, meaning respectful, fair and relatable. Sound good so far? If we are aware of what we want to change, and make a commitment to change it in a way that the dog (or anyone) can relate to, then we are on the right path. Let's explore some of the most annoying, and over diagnosed behaviors, that are preventable and/or manageable in peaceful way.

Behavior Adjustment Plan (BAP)
Lifestyle Adjustment Plan (LAP)

I am going to brag a little. Being a counselor, I have developed a lifestyle assessment tool that probably causes me to lose money. I have clients answer several questions, then email it back before coming in for their first coaching session. It sparks the thinking process.

Once potential clients calm down, and a day goes by, then they read a few questions and honestly answer them, they realize that the puppy knocking over their toddler, then chewing the toddler's stuffed doll, followed by throwing it up on the new carpet could have been prevented. Other issues, after breathing and calming down, may not seem as bad as when it happened either.

Visiting a dog behavioral counselor is like going to any professional for help whether it is a veterinarian, doctor, therapist, plumber or personal organizer. Forms need to be filled out and information gathered. The obvious is name, address, phone, dog's name, breed or breed X, when they acquired their puppy or adopted dog, from where, how long ago and is the dog a male or female, neutered or spayed.

Beyond that I like owners to share what is going on in their life that might affect the dog, but not have to face me personally, yet. I find that people more easily write what's happening on paper first. It gives them an opportunity to consider how they may have contributed, or not, and without judgment. Most haven't thought about it yet while embroiled in the heat of emotions, depending on the situation. Obviously a dog bite that required multiple stitches takes on a whole new meaning and crisis compared to a dog that was left alone or attended, and pooped on a bed.

Clients and this happens to me too, are focused on what I call "rolling the scroll" of the damage, cost and unemotional ungluing. Focus tends to be on the negatives of what the "dog" did "wrong", rather than teaching them what to do. More often than not, the puppy or dog hasn't done anything wrong, simply doesn't know what to do, or was left in a position to do what they use too (adopted), and way too soon.

An intake (lifestyle questionnaire) is non-threatening. If one loves their dog and is committed to creating change, then they need to be honest with themselves about what "really" happened. That isn't always easy. People can't change their dog's behavior until they explore the causes and commit to changing their own behavior.

I am happy to share this with you, but encourage you to seek help, if needed, in resolving any issues you and your dog may be struggling with. Here are the basic questions to ask yourself, breathe, and then consider seeking help with someone you trust and feel comfortable with.

Brief Lifestyle Intake

Who does the dog interact / live with? Children, Other Pets, Family Members, Other

1. Describe Presenting Problem Behavior(s) / Other Concerns
2. Describe Your Dog(s) Lifestyle & Well-Being (we'll explore this more in session)
3. Date of Last Wellness / Health Check
4. Veterinarian(s): Name(s):
5. Is your dog in good health? ⑨ Yes ⑨ No
6. If not, please describe and bring your Veterinarian's Treatment Plan including medication . . . (I happily collaborate with Veterinarians who respect me)
7. Nutrition / Food / Treats / Supplements
8. Feeding Schedule (who, what, when where)
9. Exercise—who, what, when, where and for how long?
10. Grooming—who, when, how?
11. Any Major Lifestyle Changes or Stressful Transitions Recently (briefly describe and we'll explore in session)
12. Goals—Describe which behavior is the one you want to change the most.

Whenever something goes awry in my own pack, I go through these same questions, once I get past denial, anger or any other emotion that is clouding my thinking about a situation with the dogs.

The full intake is longer and includes a sheet of behaviors that we review and check-off in the first session. With more experienced people, I will offer the behavior check-off sheet in advance, because it saves them, and me, time, money and energy. This list gives indications of clusters of behaviors and is educational even for first time puppy parents. The only glitch is that if you are a first time puppy parent, behaviors can seem amplified, when they are pretty much normal, like jumping, pawing, whining, growling, chewing and knocking things over.

As in group class, when an individual or family arrives with their dog for a private coaching session, we sit, calm down and breathe. If it is safe and the dog is fairly housetrained, I let them explore the area off leash.

Then, we begin exploring what the clients have already begun with the intake. It is empowering us to feel aware and part of the learning process. Much of the session is observation of the dog and interaction with the human. Training and homework are part of every coaching session.

Treatment Planning and Collaboration

Treatment planning and behavior modification, for humans or dogs, is a collaborative effort (teamwork) that is in the best interest of the individual, family and dog. This is the most effective approach, especially for serious intervention and behavioral change.

Sessions with people and their dogs require a Lifestyle Adjustment Plan (LAP) for them, and a Behavior Adjustment Plan for the dog (BAP). The plan is flexible and revisited every 1—2 weeks. Results are equal to the effort and commitment given to the recommended changes and honesty.

Clarity and Sanity

It may take 2 sessions or 1-year, depending on the severity and number of behaviors that an individual or family feel they have with a dog or multiple dogs. Most are pleased to discover that with some clarity comes sanity. Many of the issues are simply natural behaviors. With awareness, guidance, compassion and education, they learn how to resolve "dog conflict" and "human conflict", creating a more manageable and peaceful lifestyle.

Together we learn how to create positive, achievable and realistic changes to living with dogs. Training your dog can change your life because when you love your dog, and want to continue sharing a life with them, you have no place else to go but to open your mind and heart to new possibilities. The skills learned while training a different species, with empathy and compassion, are transferrable to other areas of living (work, career, friends and family).

Let's explore a little about how our dog's tick internally and how it projects externally. Some of the topics may or may not appeal to first time puppy parents, and you can skip around. I am adding it into ACT because, as a behaviorist, I see this happen on a daily basis. With the exception of those delightful situations when new puppy families have done their homework, and come to training classes to learn, the majority of trainers / behaviorists and veterinarians get called when things have gone too far or someone (dog or human) has been hurt. The following is for enlightenment before it happens (prevention).

Dog Fight Prevention and Intervention
Let's be Sensible, Sensitive and Safe

As shared, a puppy will growl and bite. It's natural for them with other puppies, but can hurt us if they bite too hard. The goal is to teach the dog what to bite how hard or soft, for how long, and know when to "leave-it", "drop-it" or "easy—gently".

If you have multiple dogs (pets) or have adopted, err on the side of caution for many months, until you know how the dogs will interact with one another, around children, and in a variety of environmental situations.

I am going to be realistically blunt to save you future heartache. Most dogs do not want conflict and what we do, as humans, matters. I have lived with multiple dogs and counseled hundreds of families, individuals and dogs. In many cases, situations could have been avoided with some common sense, sensitivity and safety measures. Along with that comes putting the ego aside and realistically assessing each situation. Knowing our dog's body language and thresholds (trigger points), through observation and body language, is relevant information that increases our awareness. It helps us, and the dogs, prevent or avoid future conflict.

For example, when you see a dog lie down, either with a human or around boisterous dogs, they are sending a message, "let's calm down, I don't want any trouble". Now, I don't mean a Border Collie lying down, eyes oriented, ready to herd sheep. You will know the difference by observing dogs in play. A dog that is not sure, especially when a bully arrives, will lie down in wait. Some uneducated people will say, "you dog is a woos". This dog is "smart". They are doing exactly what needs to be done to diffuse a confusing and fearful situation.

As shared, some dogs *will never* cohabitate comfortably without vigilant supervision. Not everyone is the "dog whisperer" or "dog guru" or has a staff; camera crew and money to rehabilitate and/or manage and care for multiple dogs. I learn from and enjoy watching the dog "celebrities" too, but realistically.

It is magical thinking that we can add two or three dogs to a pack and have instant peace. It requires focused training, oftentimes several months to a year of rehabilitation, and integration into a new pack (human and pets).

Non-celebrity trainers and behaviorists are WSYWYG (what you see is what you get). We don't have the privilege of a back up crew or opportunity to edit for the sake of ratings. What I agree with is that more often than not we are training people and rehabilitating dogs. Humans get mixed up when they start treating dogs as humans. Dogs get sucked into the family dynamics including emotions, alliances and coalitions.

I think it is courageous of the people who expose themselves on national TV with their personal issues that reflect their dog's obnoxious and sad behaviors. I agree with the "dog guru", behaviorists and trainers are therapists too. There are truly very few "dog only" related behavior issues.

What concerns me when I coach people and dogs is safety and commitment. For example, intervening in a dog fight is scary and the solutions come in a variety of old, interesting and new. First, prevention is always preferable and safer. Second, be sensitive to the people around you, including children, older adults and other pets.

If you must intervene in a dog-fight, team work is safer. Picking up the rear legs and turning the legs sideways (not breaking them), can throw the dogs off-balance long enough to separate them. For safety, you need two people to hold both dogs. Otherwise, the dogs will go right back at each other and someone will get hurt

Some behaviorists say, "squirt them." Squirting is relative, especially at dog parks. What are you going to do throw an iced coffee at them? It might work. I have seen very few dogs get squirted with water and have it matter, especially a Newfie or Labrador Retriever—who laugh out loud.

Air horns (Correctors) or making a loud noise (banging) can HALT the behavior, it won't teach the appropriate behavior. It simply gives you time to intervene and get the situation under control.

The following is going to be "boring" to some, "interesting" to others and hopefully "educational awareness" to all. Dogs that are fearful of humans (physically or emotionally) react with coping mechanisms for survival. Like us, they have a fight or flight instinctual response. Like us, it kicks in due to experience and associations. The body reacts to defend itself.

What is Fear?

Fear is a chain reaction in the brain that starts with a stressful stimulus and ends with the release of chemicals that cause a racing heart, fast breathing and energized muscles, among other things—also known as the fight-or-flight response. The stimulus could be a spider, a knife at your throat, an auditorium full of people waiting for you to speak or the sudden thud at the door.

For dogs, it could be fear of new situations, people or simply having a bad day. Dogs may be conditioned to fear from living in the streets or in homes with lack of gentle and relatable training. Dogs that have been trained with aversive and fearful techniques are more likely to become aggressive and bit when pushed to the edge. Some will become unpredictable snappers / biters, but this is rarer than you might think. With information gathering / history, it usually can be traced to not only genetics, but the puppy or dog's environment and training techniques.

The limbic system is made up of the amygdala (where aggression and fear are generated), the hypothalamus (the control center for stimulating secretion of hormones throughout the body), the hippocampus (is important for memory), and parts of the cerebral cortex (where behavior is organized and contributes to pleasure), and other structures.

The endocrine system and the limbic system are intrinsically linked; this is where hormones are produced and released. The limbic system is linked to the autonomic nervous system that is responsible for the fight-or-flight response. This is why physical responses are caused by emotions. Our emotions affect the dog too.

Dogs react to stimuli in various ways. Some bolt, while others freeze. Many dogs drink excessively when their owners come home after having been away a long time. The secretion of hormones causes the dog to feel hungry and thirsty when the limbic system induces the positive emotions of happiness and excitement. Sadness and confusion suppresses hunger and thirst in dogs, resulting in some dogs refusing to eat, drink or respond.

I have seen dogs that begin to itch and pant while the owner is sharing concerns in a coaching session. I watch the dog's response to inflection (rise and fall) of the owner's voice and emotions. The family dynamics plays out in front of me, as I observe the dog winding up or down, to the tune of the child's activity level. You can observe and learn these signs too, knowing when to intervene and redirect to quieter behavior.

What is PTSD?

Posttraumatic stress disorder (PTSD) is an anxiety disorder that can occur after you have been through a traumatic event. A traumatic event is something horrible and scary that you see or that happens to you. During this type of event, you think that your life is in danger. You may feel afraid or feel that you have no control over what is happening. Anyone who has gone through a life-threatening event can develop PTSD, including dogs.

Change disrupts and confuses a state of normalcy. The natural reaction to interference of homeostasis is for the limbic system (command central—brain) to engage, creating the proverbial fight or flight response.

With dogs, it may engage a "reactive" versus "curious" response—to a situation—depending on experiences, associations and what they perceive as a threat or not. We have all encountered those "what was that" moments where are dog is fine in most situations then notices someone or something and goes nuts (barking and/or lunging). Become a CSI detective asking, "is this an isolated event or has it happened before?" Start taking mental notes when you are walking, in the yard, or when visitors come. The more information you gather about your dog, the better the opportunity to help them overcome fear of certain people, events or unfamiliar situations.

Breathing and bringing yourself and the dog back to a state of calm is helpful. Adopted and/or a dog whose routine has changed due to lifestyle transitions comes to mind. Change can cause the body to react as if it is threatened. We know that everything will be okay, and that it is temporary, but the dog may be confused.

Ironically, the body grieves familiarity and reacts to emotional pain the same as if it were physical pain. Change, whether from trauma or transition, can become emotional pain. A dog cannot express it to us by writing letters or talking to a therapist. Instead, they act it out using familiar coping mechanisms that helped in the past. This can be barking, lunging or hiding.

It is interesting because when a human has a traumatic event and needs time to heal, we tend to offer compassion, "take the time you need to heal yourself". With dogs, there is a tendency to want them to bounce right into "I'm okay, You're Okay". Each dog and person has a different level of resiliency and bounce back. Some need more, or less, empathy, time, patience, guidance and compassion.

The Nervous System
Sensory Overload and Balance

We all know what stress feels like, tight shoulders, headache, shortness of breath, panic breathing (shallow), insomnia, upset stomach, nausea depression. We know what can trigger it, deadlines, rush hour traffic, insensitive people, and unexpected changes in our lives.

We also know that too much stress can make us ill. Ulcers and high blood pressure are prime examples. A recent study noted that

19 percent of employees who call in sick on any particular day do so because they simply felt they needed a day off.

Compared to our stress-filled lives, many people think that our dogs have it easy. Well, sometimes. The fact is, our dogs can be and often are stressed by many factors too. The stressors may seem insignificant to us, as we grapple with the multi-tasking processes of making money, paying the bills, and handling the relationships in our lives. But, from the dog's perspective, their life can be very difficult too. Once you are familiar with the body-language indicators of stress, you can easily observe that many dogs are tense much of the time. And, some dogs, like us, are more sensitive than others.

We explored body language; now let's look at some of the indicators of excessive or unhealthy stress, and how it happens physiologically:

- Diarrhea
- Vomiting
- Excessive scratching / skin conditions / flaking / shedding
- Panting
- Excessive barking, whining
- Chewing
- Biting the leash
- Sweaty paws
- Foam drool
- Red eyes
- Tense muscles
- Dilated pupils / freezing / whale (whites of eye)
- Excessive tail wagging
- Shivering (when it's not cold)

Stressful situations can contribute to a number of health problems in dogs and people. The more we understand the external contributing factors that lead to stress, and the better comprehension we have of the physiology of stress, the better equipped we will be to help our dogs (and us) relax into a long, healthy life.

It doesn't take an expert to determine the more obvious canine stressors. This can be gleaned from our own observations, and I hope that ACT is helping you with this. Many dogs dread going to the veterinarian's office and some on walks. Panting, sweaty paws, and diarrhea may accompany these necessary visits, and the vet's examining table will be covered in shed hairs.

Riding in the car, while a delight for some dogs, is a form of torture for others. Tense muscles, vomiting, foam drool or excessive barking may accompany automobile trips. Being left home alone is highly stressful for some canines, who are highly social pack animals by nature. These individuals may develop bloat, dig, pace, chew, or bark excessively.

Dogs who attend training classes should have an enjoyable time meeting other dogs and learning. Some are so stressed by the time they get to class that they lie down and zone out, or chew their leash to pacify themselves. Fearful dogs, when feeling pushed into a corner, may act out with unwanted aggression.

Many clients have genuinely expressed that they actively play with their dog for 30-minutes at a time, every day, and sometimes twice a day. Some say they come home from work and start throwing the ball or Frisbee for 10 or 15 minutes. This intense play after being in a crate or confined area may not be healthy physically or mentally for the dog. We need to warm up before exercise, and oftentimes, this revs up an already high-wired dog. What I suggest is that you give the dog a chance to decompress, so you can too. Let them out if they need to eliminate, but wait a few minutes before taking a walk or playing an energizing game of fetch.

Too much of anything can cause undue stress. I use to compete with our Newfies. Three days of conformation, followed by draft or water work was fun, but our adrenaline was in overdrive. It was like getting home from an exciting trip to a spectacular place, being exhausted, but can't sleep.

Dogs experience this too. While intense activity, over a long period, may not seem like a problem, combine that with a host of other identified stressors that their keen senses take in at magnifying rates, boredom, excessive noise or other life transitions in the family, and you have a recipe for trouble. There is a solution, but first let's explore what happens to our dogs and us internally when we are barraged with external stressors.

The Physiology of Stress

Medical encyclopedias define stress as any emotional, physical, social, or any other factor that elicits any response in a subject. The stresses we are concerned with, however, are factors that trigger the release of what is commonly called the "fight or flight" chemical: adrenaline.

In simple terms, the brain "tells" the rest of the body what to do, by sending messages through the nerves that branch from the brain down the spine and out to the periphery of the body. Half of this communication system is comprised of the voluntary nervous system—the part of the system under our conscious control. We decide to move a muscle and the body responds. Thus we can choose to brush our hair, pet our dogs, or take a walk on the beach. And our dogs may give us a paw, heel at our side or scratch behind an ear.

The other half of the nervous system, called the involuntary or autonomic nervous system, projects to organs besides skeletal muscle and controls the less conscious bodily functions such as blushing, sweating and getting goose bumps. For dogs, it can be raising hackles (pilo erection) and shedding.

Action / Reaction

The *involuntary or autonomic nervous system* is further divided into two halves: the *sympathetic and the parasympathetic nervous systems*. The sympathetic nervous system is activated by our response to stress, kicking into action when our action is called for.

Whenever life gets exciting or alarming, the sympathetic nervous system releases adrenaline into the bloodstream. Excitement can happen visiting the dog park, playing ball or a game of tug-of-war, or at the approach of a stranger.

The 4 F's of instinctive behavior—flight, fight, faint and fooling around (pretending I am invisible)—are all accompanied by production of adrenaline. Constant activation of this stress–response can deplete the body, create fatigue and eventually lead to muscle atrophy. Note that past experiences for us and our dogs makes a difference: if we have experienced a traumatic event, our system has kicked into overdrive, and it has left a lasting impression (association). The body and mind need time to recover depending on the severity. If an event happens soon after that traumatic one, and even remotely resembles what happened before, it can trigger a fight or flight response. It can be an insidious cycler if we are not given the change to recover, renew and gradually introduce ourselves (or our dogs) to situations that may trigger this response.

Adrenaline is secreted by the sympathetic nerve endings in the adrenal glands. Noradrenaline, a related substance, is secreted by all of the other sympathetic nerve endings throughout the body. These are the chemical messengers that kick various organs into gear, within a fraction of a second, causing the heart rate, blood pressure, and breathing rate to increase in order to transport nutrients and oxygen at greater rates of speed. Digestion is inhibited, as is growth, in order to conserve energy. This is why a continually stressed puppy (or child) may not reach its full growth potential. In the frequent presence of adrenaline, the immune system is also inhibited, which can make an animal more susceptible to disease.

Over long periods, the presence of high amounts of adrenaline can cause serious damage to the body. When the dog's blood pressure is continually high, damage begins to occur at branch points in arteries throughout the body, and fatty deposits begin to form a thickening of the blood vessel linings. It may take time for the negative results of chronic stress to become apparent, but because they are invisible doesn't mean they don't exist.

The second half of the involuntary or autonomic nervous system, the *parasympathetic nervous system,* complements the sympathetic nervous system. Whereas the sympathetic nervous system is activated by stress, the parasympathetic nervous system is suppressed by stress.

The parasympathetic nervous system helps the subject engage in vegetative, relaxing activities. Digestion and rest are mediated by this part of our nervous system. The parasympathetic nervous system secretes chemical substances that encourage the opposite functions as the sympathetic nervous system. Where the sympathetic system elevates the heart beat, the parasympathetic slows it down after the crisis has passed.

Stress Reduction

Some situations—like shipping a dog on an airplane across the country, networking dogs to stay in an animal shelter—are well-known stressors that can alter a dog's physiology for days or even weeks. Dogs should be given at least a week to adapt to the stressful environment before making decisions to euthanize based on behavior.

Providing a den to hide out in will help new arrivals cope. When adopting a dog, be flexible and forgiving for the first couple of weeks. Let your new family member take it easy and have time to adjust. Some apparent problems may vanish as stress hormone levels decrease.

Balance

The key to a happy, healthy life and dog is balance and moderation. Too much or too little exercise or socialization can be harmful. Major life changes—new pets in the family, a divorce, a move to a new home—are usually stressful.

Inconsistency can stress your dog, be it an irregular feeding program or lack of follow-through in training. Boredom may be your dog's bug-a-boo, or it may be harsh training methods. Please be sure that your dog has regular veterinary wellness exams. Pain and injury can be the core of unwanted aggressive behavior.

Besides acting out as a way of protecting herself, your dog may be experiencing chronic stress from unrecognized pain. Older dogs may have arthritis and many dogs have had past injuries—whacked tails, a bad fall, or an old bite—that, even when healed, still cause them to exhibit a protective attitude. Be careful about pushing any dog into situations where she may be uncomfortable

Relaxation

Is there anything we can do besides being mindful about keeping stressors to a minimum in our dogs' lives? As a canine massage and acupressure practitioner, I can vouch for the effectiveness of body work and how it affects the nervous system. Gradually introducing exercise, like dogs, balls, and balance, or dog sport can help strengthen the immune response. Be sure to begin slowly and condition yourself and your dog.

Any gently touching, gradually introduced like www.TTouch. com can change the hormonal balance in the body. Ear slides can help relax dogs, improving their response to loud noises, car travel, nausea, shock, trauma and indigestion. This, in turn, can help strengthen the immune response. The easy-to-learn circular touches and gentle lifts may actually help to change the hormonal balance in the body. These TTouches can also help a dog gain awareness of his own bodily tension—a stress response—and help with its release.

Pictured is a 5 year old Leonberger, Eli, receiving
TTouch ear-slides to help calm stress. Eli and the TTouch
Practitioner, Cindy Fischer, were both battling cancer.
It was endearing to watch them help calm each other.
Unfortunately, both lost their struggle and are at peace.
Massage and simple techniques like ear-slides can
help calm your dog before, during and after stressful
events or treatments. Consult with your specialist to
ensure what you are doing is not contra-indicated.

Being aware of our rhythmic breathing, taking deep nose-to-navel breaths, will help our dog remain calm, focused and relaxed.

Isn't this exciting to learn that we share many things with our dogs including stress and how to balance it together? Knowing this will help when we are faced with what I call "discovery shockers".

A firecracker goes off and the dog dives for cover under the sofa while taking down the coffee table, snacks and red wine (yuck). Or, a dog is adopted and the new owners are informed that the dog is housetrained, loves other dogs, children and is cat tolerant. She loves to exercise. The owners discover that a 60lb American Bulldog can pull up to 2000 lbs. She doesn't love to walk; she loves to pull them right into a gravel pit. I am sure you can name several incidents where you stood in utter amazement saying, "what the heck was that?"

Consider all that you are reading about the dog's brain, fight or flight response, the nervous system, and how it relates to reactions to experiences, and it all seems to make more sense. Dogs are reacting, very much like we do, to a variety of situations. Therefore, they can learn, like we do, to relax too. With this awareness, we can recognize when things are getting out of hand, and why, like barking and regularly noted behaviors like resource guarding and separation anxiety.

Barking (Communication)
Barking Festival

The only way to change or manage a behavior is to have the behavior. Sounds redundant I know, but consider this: if your dog never barks (maybe yodels like a Basenji) then you have nothing to worry about. If your dog is barking, and you want to manage it, this is good news for you, but maybe not your ears! Whether city or country living, dogs bark more at things they are unfamiliar with. The win-win solution to barking is to seek the root cause (boredom, too much activity, paying more attention to barking than quiet).

Putting a behavior on cue reduces the cause of many noise inducing headaches. For example, teach "whisper" or "speak". Put barking on reward, letting them bark 3 times as loud as they can (barking festival). Bark with then if you like and then request "quiet".

Be aware of the busiest, noisiest peak times of day. Choose walking routes where you can manage the barking more effectively. Does the school bus arrive at 2:30 every day? Do your dogs stand in the window barking? You have a choice. Move the sofa, close the shades or relocate the dogs to a more productive activity—elsewhere, that is, unless you have the tenacity and time to stand there at least 100 times teaching "quiet" at the window. Doors are different matter altogether. We want to teach our dogs to "alert" bark, for a few barks, then "thank you, quiet".

Barking tends to bother people at certain times like when they put their dogs in a crate or confinement area, the door bell rings, or tied outside. Tying dogs to lines is dangerous. Leaving dogs for long periods unattended in kennels is careless. Dogs that run back and forth on cable runs can learn to lunge and chase children or other pets. Not a good idea.

If you can't be home for 8-hours, then have someone come in to ensure they have shade and water if outdoors or can be let out for some exercise. Enjoy these helpful solutions:

1) Prevent the barking with barriers and/or choose less active times of day to walk.

2) Redirect the barking if you catch it in time to a more positive and incompatible behavior like "sit" or "get your ball". Change their minds with something constructive and quieter.

3) Do not reinforce the barking by paying more attention to it. If you YELL, "QUIET"—5X, and your dog is still barking, what have you accomplished?

4) Teach the dog when to bark, for how long, and then "quiet".

5) Socialize more often to familiarize the dog to a variety of sights, sounds, smells and activities.

6) When the doorbell rings, let them be part of the process by barking a few times, then teach them, "thank you, and quiet now".

Dog Interrupted
Transforming Dino Dog into Respecto Dog

Does your dog growl at you or anyone (children) near a food bowl or toys? Do they get so excited that it is nearly impossible to get the bowl down before it is empty? I have a 120lb Newfie who will dance across the entire kitchen floor to her "diner" backwards on her haunches. She knows exactly where her diner is, but does not want to take her eye off of the bowl. She manages to dance "backwards" around the kitchen island, then the table, and left to the diner. Very adorable, and I believe she can do this blind-folded.

Resource guarding is the new contemporary word for anything that a dog does these days that involves growling or showing teeth near anything they covet like food and toys. What I have discovered is that this is being used as a catch-all "buzz word" for many behaviors that can be prevented and/or are brought on by other reasons, like lack of awareness centered training, and/or being roughed up around their toys and food.

If you have a puppy, begin early with *Doggy Diner Training.* You can reverse turn and re-read it many times. I still do and I wrote it. Add on *Mine, Yours, Ours and Object Exchange,* and I can guarantee you 98% that you will have a dog who is gentle and/or tolerable around food and who knows that to eat and play with their toys; they need to trust and respect the food and toy story owner.

Serious resource guarders, if truly diagnosed, can be difficult to rehabilitate. On top of this, they are sorely misunderstood. Today, we know that it is questionable whether a dog is territorial, resource guarding or fearful, due to previous incidents where they were physically forced to give up food, items or toys. Adopted dogs who have lived on the streets may have struggled to maintain their survival by learning to hoard and protect what they have found. Each dog, and owner, requires careful assessment.

Does this mean that the dog should be allowed to growl or bite at the food bowl or with objects? This is a resounding "no". But, the way to rehabilitate is not by adding more stress or manhandling the dog into giving things up. That only frightens them more, and the dog will NEVER be trusted around children or other pets. Instead, whenever possible, rehabilitation involves a plan that needs to be adhered to, with love, commitment and perseverance.

Dogs that are use to a particular lifestyle, and have it disrupted through transition (new baby, death, and move to a new location) can become possessive of their space, food and toys. Maintaining composure and keeping their lifestyle, feeding times and schedule as similar as possible helps. How do I know? It's simple. Was your dog like this before? Keep a journal, making a note of what the dog was like before the transition and after.

If at any point you are fearful or feel inadequate, call a qualified behaviorist. Only adults should implement a program for Food Bowl Aggression (FBA) or Resource Guarding (RG). It should be positively reward based and with awareness centered training.

Seldom are puppies serious resource guarders, but left to much liberty, in the pursuit of adolescent, puppies can turn into resource guarders. Some street dogs that had to vigilantly guard their meager supplies may not have social manners, and need to be taught. This can take time, commitment and patience.

For prevention of RG, remember that you if you feed your dog 2X a day, that is 14X training opportunities a week to hand-feed, while requesting a "say please" behavior like "SIT". The dog should be "watching" you, not looking around every corner to see what or who is coming near. And, others should not be allowed to intervene or interfere with the process of rehabilitating either such as a toddler or other pets running free, in and out, of this dog's spatial bubble.

Be mindful of other dogs, cats and small children.
This is focused training that requires
commitment and a steady heart.

The following is necessary if you have a dog that you feel uncomfortable with around food, toys or other items. Pick up all toys and put them away. The only time you play is when you can safely take toys from the dog. I am not kidding. This requires some tough love that in the long term will reap positive results.

If you have multiple dogs, and you fear for their safety, you must feed the dogs separately in the beginning. There is "no guarantee" of safe and positive interaction when you introduce an unfamiliar dog to your family life. You must get to know the dog first, and even then, management may be the safest approach, especially at high activity times like playing and feeding.

Stage 1: Taming Dino Dog may take Several Weeks

First, breathe and focus. It is important if you have multiple pets to work with "dino dog" separately before feeding around other pets.

Place the dog's daily meal in a bowl on a counter in his (or her) designated feeding (safe) room. Include some high-value treats (turkey, cheese) as part of the meal. Schedule several feeding sessions throughout the day. The goal is to have the dog rely, trust and enjoy taking food from you.

Be mindful of caloric intake. Feed only ¼ of the day's ration at each session, a piece at a time, by hand. Preferably, you have taught the dog to sit first and/or at least be calm for a moment. Be patient, wait, breathe and the moment you sense curiosity and even a little calmness, hand feed, "good".

Is the dog climbing the walls? Consider tethering to a door knob or hook in the wall. This is temporary until the dog learns self-control. You can try tossing one piece of kibble at a time creating a positive association. Ask for a "sit". Stay at a safe distance if you aren't sure of the dog's behavior.

Stage 2: Empty bowl, single pieces
(about two weeks, can be more)

Schedule at least two feeding sessions throughout the day. Place the dog's daily meal in a bowl on a counter in his feeding room. Place his empty bowl on the ground at your feet.

Alternate between feeding several pieces from your hand, one piece at a time, and drop several pieces into the bowl, one piece at a time. Wait until he has finished each piece before dropping the next.

A dog that hasn't been use to eating with manners (kennel, street) is learning some and what a bowl is for. It is kind of like us eating our meal with a knife and fork instead of diving in with our fingers or shoving our face in the plate.

Stage 3: Empty bowl, multiple
pieces (two to three weeks)

During feeding sessions, place the dog's daily meal in a bowl on a counter in his feeding room. Place his empty bowl on the ground at your feet. Drop *several* pieces of food into his food bowl and wait until he has finished them. Then feed him several pieces one at a time, from your hand. Now drop several more pieces into his bowl. While he is eating those drop more "treats", one-at-a-time, into his bowl from waist height. The goal is to introduce a positive association from you to the bowl, as long as he is respecting you.

Stage 4, ACT-2: Two partial bowls (two weeks)

While he is eating from the first bowl, place the second bowl on the floor a safe distance away. "Safe" will depend on your dog and could be as much as 10 to 15 feet. Err on the side of caution. Return to the first bowl and drop treats (or kibble) into it as he continues to eat.

When he has finished the first bowl, very gradually—a few inches at a time—place the bowls closer and closer together. Watch for signs of tension or aggression. If you see any, you have closed the distance too quickly; go back to the distance between bowls where he was relaxed and work at that distance for several days before moving the bowls closer together again.

Stage 5: Several partial bowls (two weeks)

Repeat the previous stage, using several bowls (up to six). You can prepare all of the bowls at the same time and set them on the counter. PLACE THEM ON THE FLOOR ONE AT A TIME, while he is eating from the first bowl. Continue to drop treats into the bowl he is eating from, and occasionally pick up an empty one that is a safe distance from the dog. Look for opportunities outside of feeding time to drop treats near the dog when he is in possession of other reasonably valuable items like toys.

Stage 6: Calling the dog (two weeks)

Repeat Stage 5, except try to call the dog to you from a distance of 6—8 feet just as he finishes the food in the bowl. Have the other bowls set out so he must pass you to go to another bowl. Be sure to give him a very high value treat when he comes to you, but request a "sit".

Gradually start asking him to come *to you before* he finishes the food in the bowl—first when he is almost done, then when there is increasingly more left. As long as he stays relaxed, gradually move closer to the bowl he is eating from before you call him.

Practice this stage for at least one full week. Look for opportunities outside of feeding time to call him to you to feed him high value treats when he is in possession of other reasonably valuable items.

I'm guessing you are getting this by now. It sounds tedious, but if you have a dog (perhaps adopted) who is scaring you or other pets in the house around food or other items, this desensitization process works well. You are gradually teaching a dog to eat out of a bowl, and trust the person who provides the food, which h/she needs to live.

Stage 7: Adding two people (two weeks)

Have a second person, who is close or familiar with the dog, and not fearful. This should not be a child or stranger. Have the person move through the stages, spending up to a week at each phase or longer if necessary. If the dog is doing well with a second person, add a third, then a fourth. Be sure to use people who are well educated as to their responsibility—no heroes—no rushing—no interruptions.

Stage 8: Coming out of the closet

Starting back at Stage 1, move the food bowl exercises out of the dog's feeding (safe) room into other areas of the house or where you intend for the dog to eat their meal (kitchen, dining room, family room). Assuming the training has been progressing well, you should be able to move through the stages relatively quickly.

Continue to look for other real-life resource-relevant opportunities to reinforce the message that *human presence means more good stuff.* Embrace the mantra, "you do something for me, and I will do something for you".

Gradually introduce this, as mentioned, to other areas too like toys, children's toys and outdoors. Yes, outdoors! Some dogs feel as if they have to take on a "King Kong" personality in their backyards, protecting who knows what from the entire neighborhood. The only resolution is to teach them that you are grateful for their "alert" but are in charge of the situation, as their respectful pack leader and friend.

Separation Anxiety (SA)

Separation Anxiety (SA) is suffered by dogs and humans. We experience it in the form of panic attacks and stress. The best approach is to prevent anxiety from the get-go with early desensitization and counter-conditioning. Highly recommended are the Canine Noise Phobia Series of CD's that desensitizes dogs to city sounds, thunderstorms and firecrackers. It cleverly helps prevent anxiety in dogs with mild to moderate sounds while playing calming music, a winning combination.

How we respond / react when our dogs are anxious matters. Please do not cajole or get overly emotional if your dog gets stressed. Touching our dogs when they are stressed can add fuel to the firestorm.

Using massage, energy balancing, TTouch or acupressure can help. To learn more visit www.dailydoga.com.

Be aware and proactive (ahead of time) of your dog's stressors and allow them a safe place to be quiet. If you have a serious separation anxiety (SA) problem, seek the help of a qualified behaviorist. This does not have to be a Veterinary Behaviorist. Many excellent behaviorists / trainers focus on behavior only. Working in collaboration, if a dog needs medication, is preferable.

Many anxiety issues are conditioned and avoidable. Genetic predispositions for anxiety are as rare as they are for aggression. Playing soft music and having a stuffed toy or familiar scented piece of clothing may ease stress and pass time. Usually dogs will fall asleep. In the wild, they are *crepuscular*, meaning most active at dawn and dusk. We humans condition them to be awake when we are.

Using a safety cue like soft music helps during desensitization sessions where you are preparing your dog for time alone. The music becomes a signal to the dog that only short, non-anxiety-producing absences are in store. Music, reliably paired with tolerable levels of aloneness, creates a relaxing environment. Where you leave them (confined area or crate) prevents them from being destructive.

Gradually increase time-away, but for no more than two hours at a time. Be sure the dog is in their confined area with safe toys and water to keep them amused and comfortable.

Homecomings should be pleasant and non-anxiety producing (leash the emotion). Teach your dogs to get a toy and bring it to you. This can begin with minutes and increased to several hours. Quicker or more is not always better—and breathe—nose-to-navel. If you must be away for 8 hours a day, be sure to have someone come in to check on your dog's well being and take them out to relieve themselves. It is impossible for a puppy to hold their bladder for more than 30 minutes to an hour. To simulate this, try drinking a liter of water and holding the urge to pee for about 8-hours.

Is it Play Growling or Fighting—Do We Talk Loud or Chant

It depends. People can go crackers over puppies play growling. Adolescents wrestling are perfectly normal and healthy, but it can appear and sound like atomic warfare (visit www.youtube.com/ dogtalkmedia—puppy social). Owners fly in like Mighty Mouse or

Mother Theresa to save their dog from learning how to navigate with other like-matched puppies. Like-matched are the operative words. If you aren't sure, then be an advocate and calmly go and get your dog. In most interactions, there is no blood. If whisked away while sobbing, the pup has learned that playing with other dogs is sad, bad and their owners go bonkers.

Can it get dangerous between dogs? Absolutely and people can get severely hurt if they intervene. If you sense this, listen to your intuition, be wise and safe. Expediently contact a behaviorist who specializes in dog-to-dog or dog-to-human aggression. For a quick assessment guide I defer to the following—*Dr. Ian Dunbar's Bite Scale Assessment that should be in every veterinarian, vet tech, trainer and behaviorist's toolbox.*

Biting Awareness

Severity of biting problems must be based on an objective evaluation of wound pathology. Fortunately for us, Dr. Ian Dunbar has clarified the severity levels of bites, so that we can better assess and provide effective prevention, management and rehabilitation for dogs who bite.

As a behavioral coach, I am grateful, and wish more "professionals" would laminate, post and READ the following. It is distressing for owners to be told that their 4-month old puppy is "aggressive" because s/he nips a child. The behaviorist / trainer get the royal job of de-stressing the owner when it is discovered that this is a normal, happy puppy doing natural behaviors.

95% of the time it is not aggression between dog-dog or dog-human. It is **lack of** awareness, socialization and manners (SAM) and prevention, management and sense (PMS).

Dr. Ian Dunbar's Bite Scale Assessment

Level 1—Obnoxious or aggressive behavior but no skin-contact by teeth.

Level 2—Skin-contact by teeth but no skin-puncture. However, there may be skin nicks (less than one tenth of an inch deep), and slight bleeding caused by forward or lateral movement of teeth against skin, but no vertical punctures.

Level 3—One to four punctures from a single bite with no puncture deeper than half the length of the dog's canine teeth. May be lacerations in a single direction, caused by victim pulling hand away, owner pulling dog away, or gravity (little dog jumps, bites and drops to floor).

Level 4—One to four punctures from a single bite with at least one puncture deeper than half the length of the dog's canine teeth. There may also be deep bruising around the wound (dog held on for seconds and bore down) or lacerations in both directions (dog held on and shook its head from side to side).

Level 5—Multiple-bite incident with at least two Level 4 bites or multiple-attack incident with at least one Level 4 bite in each.

Level 6—The victim is dead. Not good.

The previous list concerns unpleasant behavior, BUT let's adds some perspective:

Levels 1 and **2** comprise well over 99% of dog incidents. The dog is not dangerous and more likely to be fearful, rambunctious or out of control. This is a wonderful prognosis. Quickly resolve the problem with basic training (control)—especially oodles of Classical Conditioning and repetitive positive reward based training with come / sit / food treats taken gently and/or retreat and treat sequences.

Reward and Back-up/Approach/Food Reward sequences are progressive desensitization handling exercises, plus numerous bite awareness exercises and games. Hand feed only until resolved, as described in "Dino-Dog—Resourced Guarding Help".

Level 3—Prognosis is fair to good, if you are committed to change. However, treatment is both time-consuming and not without danger. Rigorous bite inhibition exercises are essential. Please contact a professional behavioral coach for guidance.

Levels 4—The dog has insufficient bite inhibition and is very dangerous. Prognosis is poor because of the difficulty and danger of trying to teach bite inhibition to an adult hard-biting dog. Absolute owner-compliance is rare, but necessary to save this dog. These dogs require a collaborative effort, working with an experienced behaviorist. Owners must sign a form in triplicate stating that they understand and take full responsibility that:

1. The dog is a Level 4 biter and is likely to cause an equivalent amount of damage WHEN it bites again (which it probably will). The dog should be confined to the home at all times and only allowed contact with adult owners while vigilantly managed.

2. Whenever children or guests visit the house, the dog should be confined to a single locked-room or a roofed, chain-link

run with the keys kept on a chain around the neck of each adult owner (to prevent children or guests entering the dog's confinement area).

3. The dog is muzzled before leaving the house and only leaves the house for visits to a veterinary clinic or to the behavioral coach.

4. The incidents must be reported to the relevant authorities— animal control or police. Copies of the report should be given to the owners, veterinarian and behavioral coach.

Level 5 and 6—The dog is extremely dangerous and mutilates. The dog is not safe around people. I (Dr. Dunbar) recommend euthanasia because the quality of life is poor for dogs that have to live out their lives in solitary confinement.

PAWT 9

Pathways of Grief—Celebrating Life

There is one sure thing in life—we will experience happiness, sadness, anger, joy, change, illness, aging and death. When a dog dies, we grieve hard and strong. Many grieve more for dogs (other pets) than humans, for good reason. They go on adventures with us through life's peaks and valleys. We share things with our dogs that we never would with anyone else, even our therapists, partners or close friends. When we take our stress out on them, they instantly forgive us.

Dogs make us laugh and most of us aspire to be the person that our dog thinks we are—special, beautiful, loving and the center of their universe. They don't care what we look like or how smart we are. They accept us.

When you lose a dear friend, grieving is individual and all yours. No-one can tell you how to grieve, for how long, when or where. If you feel like carrying around your dog's ashes for 6-months—go ahead. We have multiple cans of ashes in our closets with stipulations in our will that when we die, we will all be scattered together. If anyone thinks we are odd, tough s—!

Coping Skills
A Journey of Transition: Loss of a Pet through Death or Divorce

As an author, counselor, dog training coach and yoga therapist, I am grateful to have opportunities to breathe, share, learn and grieve with families and their dogs.

Heart-centered stories are shared that are joyful and sad about family pets, domestic abuse and violence. Families have enlightened me to the emotional and oftentimes intense physical pain that accompanies the loss of a loved one through death and divorce.

The following is a connection that we share. Enjoy the journey knowing that your pet forgives and thanks you.

Understanding the Loss of a Pet

A loved one can be any being that shares your life and heart. That love knows no species boundaries. The same range and intensity of emotions are experienced. As Moira Anderson, M.Ed. states, "Grief is like a swamp without a map. It is easy to lose any sense of where we are going or where we have been. In time, as we progress through the grief-swamp to the solid ground of a normal emotional state again, that hole will change from a bitter gap to a well of pleasant memories."

It is like trying to get through each day as if wading knee deep in mud. Every step is torture, physically and emotionally. You wake up fine, then a song plays, or you glance over and see a collar, or smell a pillow where your dog use to lay their head, and a bucket of tears flow.

The Value of a Pet (Perception)

No matter what anyone says, thinks or interprets, we *have every right to grieve the loss of a pet.* The relationship is every bit as precious and meaningful as one we may have had with a human being or cherished memorabilia lost to disaster. People share that losing their dog was worse than a parent, husband or friend.

Like any relationship, love is an investment of emotions, with an unlimited potential for returns. A good relationship with a pet has been shown to relieve stress, lower blood pressure, and give people a new purpose. They allow us to nurture, be needed and reward us with unconditional positive regard and companionship—even during the worse situations or events in our lives. Pets are used widely in therapeutic situations to meet treatment goals.

Emotional Reactions, not Etched in Stone

Dr. Elizabeth Kubler-Ross lists the stages of grief in her book *On Death and Dying* as follows:

First Stage:	Denial & Isolation
Second Stage:	Anger
Third Stage:	Bargaining
Fourth Stage:	Depression
Fifth stage:	Acceptance

Be mindful that there is no absolute pattern for grief. These patterns are experienced differently at various stages of life, from childhood through older adult, whether grieving or not. One may be depressed before denying that one's pet is ill, dying or passed on. Each experiences these stages in different combinations and intensities.

Our personality, the type of relationship one has with a pet, a personal situation at the time of death of a pet, and cultural and religious beliefs all play a part in how each of us individually cope with pending loss and change.

We need to give ourselves permission to grieve in our own way, time and place. When denied an outlet, whether at home or at work, emotions do not go way . . . they simply manifest inside of you, twirling around, looking for a channel to release the pain.

Emotions will find that opportunity eventually and unexpectedly. Unresolved or repressed emotions can keep one embittered and hurting for years. Acknowledging these emotions is a good way to begin. Writing your emotions can be cathartic. Metaphorically releasing them like helium filled balloons to the sky is another way. Sharing with supportive friends & family, who genuinely listen, helps. Seeking professional help is an alternative.

Say thank you to well meaning people who may go "over-board", then walk-away, shut off the cell phone and be still, if that is what helps. For others, being around activity is beneficial.

Denial may be one of the first defense mechanisms to help us on a temporary basis to avoid mental anguish. It enables our mind and body to shift our attention, for the time being, away from emotions too painful to bear. It temporarily says, "ignore reality", because impending death is often too painful to accept on a conscious level right away.

If we are the caretakers, we cannot take time immediately to take care of ourselves even though we may be falling apart inside. We may need to keep ourselves together for a variety of reasons (work, sole financial provider, parenting, drive home safely, get food, taking care of the pets, taking on sudden additional responsibilities due to lifestyle changes). Eventually, we need to take time for our well being or suffer the consequences (mental and physical exhaustion and illness).

It is a natural response to be *angry* when we have lost a loved one (pet or human). We may look for someone or something to *blame*. If all of our energy is focused on anger, we will have little time to *feel the pain*. Striking back can be gratifying, particularly if someone or a situation is to blame for our loss. Acknowledging our pain (anger) is an essential part of the grieving process so we get let go.

It is natural to ask, "Why did this happen to me, my child or my pet?" Why did s/he have to die (or endure a trauma)? Rationalizing that it wouldn't have happened "if only I'd done this or they'd done that" may enter our thoughts. This is normal. Breathe and be with the thoughts. It is natural to want to seek retribution if the death of a pet is malicious. It is helpful to pause and take-a-deep-breath, then consider the circumstances / outcome of how we choose to respond. Whatever our particular situation is, eventually we need to come to terms with acceptance of emotions and loss.

Forgiveness is a choice,
but acceptance will help us move on.

Depression can result from physical and emotional exhaustion. It can range from "feeling low . . . in a funk" to "emotional paralysis" (can't get out of bed or function). Those in helping professions and volunteers know the wrath of empathy and/or compassion fatigue. It can last a few days or drag on for weeks or months.

The loss of a pet is traumatic, painful and stressful. It plunges a person into a whirlpool of emotions and one may want to withdraw from the rest of the world. It is true that no-one can possibly understand how we feel, but they can empathize.

Depression can feel like struggling in quicksand. You can feel as though you are slowly sinking. Seeking out help with supportive friends, family members or a professional who specializes in depression, pet loss and grieving can help.

Will I ever get past this?

Yes, in time and in your own way. Letting go and moving on belongs to you. The light starts to flicker at the end of the tunnel.

We begin to embrace and celebrate positive memories. We feel joy in simply breathing and doing simple things. We look at their picture and smile instead of cry.

Volunteering with others helps as long as we (and they) honor our grieving process. The connection with others and knowing that we can make a difference by helping them ultimately helps us.

Choosing to focus on well-being, breathing, learning something new, meditating; anything that helps us feel grounded and centered, sane and alive will rejuvenate us.

Some of the steps to help you acknowledge your feelings about grief are:

- If you know a pet's death is imminent, prepare yourself, children, family and friends by sharing feelings in your way. Writing notes—emails or verbally expressing to "others" helps.
- Embrace grieving, allowing it to flow.
- Create a journal and photo album to celebrate the pet's life.
- Rearrange your surroundings—to help with immediate reminders like removing the food dish that sits beside the dinner table.
- Change your schedule (filling in empty spaces that use to be a walk with your dog).
- Focus on surviving pets, children, family and friends . . .
- Get another pet when you are ready, not as a replacement, but as an individual, living and unique being.
- Listening and sharing with others who have experienced a loss.
- Seek outside help if necessary.

What to tell the Children

When a child loses a pet either through death or divorce, parents (all adults) must be extra-sensitive. I focus on divorce because I was a child with pets who suffered through the confusion and fear of not knowing what was going to happen to me or my pets. As a mediator, I sat with people who used pets as pawns during divorce, paying no attention to the needs of a child whose pet was her only comfort.

Divorce is a death of a relationship. Families (and especially children) grieve the loss of a lifestyle that was, while wondering what will be. It can be a scary and confusing time wracked with emotions, especially fear of the unknown.

How death is explained to children and how adult's role model their own grief will leave a lasting impression on a child. Age makes a difference:

- Children less than 5 years old usually don't understand death and its permanency. It's important to be concrete, but gentle when explaining that "Buddy" isn't coming back.
- Children between 5 and 10 usually want the gory details and often ask many questions out of curiosity. I suggest answering them honestly and gently with as much information as they can handle. Journaling, photo albums and scrapbooks will help ease the pain and celebrate the pet's memories.
- Children from 10 through the teenage years are generally capable of understanding the meaning of death and experience all of the emotions.

- ❧ Teenagers may shuffle feelings off, but they are suffering in their own private way. Patience and understanding is a virtue. Give them some space. Encourage them by sharing your feelings.

- ❧ Honor cultural diversity (socioeconomic backgrounds and personal values). In some cultures, life on earth is a journey to a higher-place, therefore an honor to die. Many do not grieve they celebrate.

- ❧ Some find solace in writing. Others believe that their pets will be waiting for them at *"Rainbow Bridge"* to guide them on their life's journey.

Children, Pets and Divorce

Grieving is an inevitable part of living, as is death, trauma and life change. Grieving can be a learning experience at any age and in many ways, depending on the situation.

There are transitions that can be difficult like when teenagers leave their pets behind for college. Fortunately, in these situations, the pets are usually loved and well taken care of.

One of the most poignant (and painful) experiences is when there are children and pets involved during divorce. Having been a child of divorce, I am keenly aware of what my dog and other pets meant to me. THEY ACCOMPANIED ME TO MY SAFE PLACE. Some of the scariest moments of my life were "not knowing" whether my pets would be taken away from me. I packed my little suitcase several times, not really knowing where I would go. I was always sure of one thing: *my pets were going with me.*

The trauma and grief that accompanies divorce affects the pets as well as the children. When possible, the best situation is to keep the pets in one household, at least for a transition time or place them where they will be safe and can be visited by the children. Otherwise, parents are not only dealing with emotional issues that go along with divorce, but the children's grief and behavioral issues of a dog (or multiple pets) who simply can't process emotions in a human way.

During divorce, parents are flooded with questions and decisions to be made for the future. In some states, families are mandated to attend mediation and for a good reason. They need a place to sort this out with facilitated guidance.

In the Child's Mind

In a child's mind, the conflicts that arise from divorce are amplified like *BIG FURRY MONSTERS WITH FANGS*. The emotions are too complicated for any child to sift through on their own. Inadvertently, most of the energy (and emotions) seems to go into the parent's decisions on liabilities and assets. Decisions around the parental and physical custody of the children are key elements of the proceedings. Oftentimes, the child's fears of being abandoned by one or both parents, and of losing their beloved pet, are ignored. Often, depending on their age, the children aren't asked or involved in the proceedings. Many times, they are used are "tools or weapons", in an alliance, triangle and/or coalition between emotionally distraught and arguing parents.

A Safe Haven with my Pet

This is a "must" consideration for all adults involved with children, divorce and pets. The same emotions of hurt, anger, fear, abandonment and the strong feeling of loss need to be gently addressed in a way that a child understands. Children need a safe haven to express their feelings, away from the distraught parents. In that safe haven, the children need their pets for support and safety. The child relies heavily on the support of their pet that sits and listens for hours. The child trusts the pet and may temporarily not be able to rely on support from emotionally distraught adults.

Mediators, Parents, and Attorneys

Another consideration at the time of divorce is **role modeling and responsibility** of parents, mediators, counselors and/or attorneys involved in the proceedings/transitions where children are present. Depending on the age, it can be threatening, misunderstood or **copied later on in life.** They are observing their parents and other people with decision-making power. You want the child to feel empowered and loved. They need to know that their feelings, and the care of their pets, are being given a "priority" and "careful consideration".

Pets with a capital "P" should be an integral part of the divorce proceedings, with the parents first, then the children—appropriately and safely included into sessions (counseling, mediation, and caucus):

- 🐾 Who will have physical care of the pets?
- 🐾 Who will cover expenses for their care?
- 🐾 What is the best alternative to the negotiated agreement (BATNA) and the gentlest transition for the Children and Pets?

Children need extra assurance that everything possible is being done so their pets will remain with them. If this isn't possible, then they need to know that their pets will be taken care of. This needs to be expressed in an age appropriate way from the parents, guardians and counselors.

<blockquote>
Oftentimes, parents may not know how to express this to the children, so offering facilitative guidance is helpful and valuable.
</blockquote>

What to Tell the Children

The impending loss of a relationship with a pet, or having the pets suddenly "disappear" out of the home, is experienced the same way as losing a pet by accident or natural causes. It is compounded by the emotional trauma of losing one or both parents. Life as the children knew it, whether healthy or unhealthy, has abruptly changed, and now their pet is gone.

Many of the same tools like drawing, writing, memory books and other creative ways to express feelings, while holding onto whatever is positive, will be helpful.

- ❧ **Best scenario:** slow transition of pets out of the home, preferably where the children can visit them and "see" that the pets are okay. Perhaps an arrangement with a family, friend or relative, with the understanding that the pets will be reunited with the children later (or in a new location).

- ❧ **Children and Pets will be separated:** Children and pets that have been together for even a small amount of time have bonded. If is determined that they cannot keep the pets, they need to know how come and what will happen. They need to be reassured that their pets will be safe and loved EVEN IF THEY CAN'T SEE THEM AGAIN.

- ❧ **Call a No-Kill Humane Society and/or Rescue Organization** (for specific breeds): Most rescue organizations will consider taking dogs that they know can be re-homed. Maybe relatives or friends in pet-friendly homes will help.

- ❧ **Worse Scenario—Domestic Abuse and Violence:** In situations where children have been removed from parental care and placed in alternative / foster homes because of domestic violence, then the pets should be removed as well and put in a safe place. It is a well-known fact that when a parent or child is being abused, chances are so are the pets. Being an advocate for pets teaches children to respect all living beings as adults. (www.latham.org)

❧ Trauma and grief that accompanies divorce affects the pets too. When possible, the best situation is to keep the pets in one household, at least for a transition time, or place them in experienced care where they will be safe. Otherwise, parents are not only dealing with keeping themselves and their children safe, but the behavioral issues of a dog (or other fill-in / impulsive pet buys) who simply can't process the human emotion / trauma.

Oftentimes, adults emotionally latch on to the pet during times of separation and divorce. The pet is a soft place to fall. Children can act out their anger and frustration toward the pet.

I have worked in situations where the dog is being chosen to fill the void as partner, playmate, child-sitter and much worse (the target of residual abuse). The dogs (and other pets in different ways) adapt to changes extremely well, but not without a price.

Many dogs become confused and overprotective. A sweet mellow canine companion is suddenly called upon to take on the responsibility of therapist, protector, mediator and resource guarder. It is best to try and keep the pet and child's life as normal as possible. When in doubt, seek professional help.

Do we ever really put Closure on Grieving?

I don't know. I think about all of my pets from the time I was a child. Each holds a special place in my heart. It depends on the individual. I believe it helps to process grief appropriately, but that it is DIFFERENT for everyone. We place it in a soft place in our hearts for safekeeping.

One may process and move on quickly, another may process for a lifetime, and some become delusional, thinking that if pay enough money to someone, they can see or speak to their deceased ones again as before. Maybe they can, who knows.

Tips for Helping

1. Be present and supportive without being pushy.
2. Genuinely Listen: "I can only imagine what you are going through; it is different and personal for all of us; I've lost a pet too" is helpful.
3. Encourage a friend (or child) to express grief by writing or drawing.
4. Assure that it is safe and confidential; allowing an opportunity to express emotions.
5. Books or visuals (age appropriate) as a gift can be helpful.
6. Acting as a buffer—offer to accompany a friend to the Vet, suggesting a memorial service, errands or help cook dinner.
7. If pets are involved in a divorce proceeding, offer to care for the pets.
8. Going to a movie, yoga class or having a cup of coffee/tea as a gentle distraction.
9. Sharing insights that you have gained on coping with grief.
10. Sending a condolence card.
11. Making a donation in the pet's name to an appropriate charity.

12. Sharing your pet, if your friend seeks the company.

13. If you think it will be well received, using a special talent of your own to make a memorial for the friend (frame a favorite picture, calligraphy, a poem, needle point).

14. Employers and employees: Be understanding and considerate. Offer time off.

Pitfalls / Blunders to Avoid

1. Take a deep breath and consider "what or how would I like someone to say and do to me at a critical and emotional time like this?"

2. The selection of a new companion is a personal one.

3. Saying "good-bye" happens in different ways for different people. Avoid statements like, "you should have been there".

4. Offer support without forcing them into action.

5. Don't take it personally if your friend doesn't want to come anywhere near your happy, bouncy, living pet.

6. Don't dismiss your friend's (or anyone's) pain with glib statements like "time heals all wounds" or "you'll get over it".

7. Don't regale anyone with horror stories of a "friend's pet who is dying of cancer" to fill up space.

8. Don't let yourself be sucked into family arguments. If you sense that the loss of a pet is creating stress on family relationships, step back and lend your support from a distance.

9. Don't measure everyone's experience by your own yardstick. If a friend seems to be reacting differently or their grief is

lasting longer, honor it. There are gentle ways to draw them out. You might share, "how you cried for three days when your dog died".

10. Professional counselors, mediators and health care professionals can help. Contact your family practitioner for referrals and/ or support groups when you need assistance.

Resilience and Letting Go

Resilience is bounce back in its simplest form. Studies have been done on siblings and identical twins separated at birth. One may turn out strong and successful, the other a drug addict. Puppies from the same litter may go to similar homes and turn out differently.

Resilience and flexibility go together to form a strong bond that gives us the ability to go with the flow of life as it changes, and it will. If there is a room without a door, look for a window. If you can't find a window, create one. A curve in the road is not the end of the road, only a new path. Life deals us many opportunities to grow.

Known now as Counselor Cali-Rose (Greyhound),
Cali was adopted from Second Chance Greyhounds.
Since, she is blending in well with our pack and
BTW (by the way), "I only wear Poochi". Cali is
the spokes-dog for Daily Doga Inspirations.

Celebrating Life—Let the things in your life wake you up.

I think I'll Stay
by Counselor Cali-Rose
They tell me about a greyhound,
That they miss.
They say I'm unique,
And give me a kiss.
I pull away,
They say it's okay.
I like it here, they need me,
I think I'll stay.

Centered and Safe

Energy is all around us. There is negative and positive ions (water) and energy. Keeping energy balanced is a challenge but worth the focused effort. People who love pets are oftentimes more sensitive. We know that dogs are because of their keen senses. Our sensitivity can overflow to our dogs.

We are receptive to the energy of the people and the environment around us. When something happens around us, our body and mind react or responds. We want to be part of situations that involve people and pets, especially today when socialization often means living in isolation for long periods. We do more with technology than people and pets at times. We can enjoy media and let our dogs reconnect to what matters—living beings.

With a few simple strategies, many that we reviewed in awareness centered training, we can entertain, socialize, work and support friends and family, without losing ourselves in someone else's energy. Our dogs can learn self-control too.

With a little practice and breathing, stress and overload take on a new perspective. We are in control, rather than being controlled.

Get lost with your dog (or alone) for a few minutes, several times a day to calm the chaos. Go to bed at night grateful and wake happy to be alive. Do you have a difficult time falling asleep? Try breathing in to the count of (1) and exhaling while imagining or saying, (2). When you intentionally focus on this, your mind has no choice but to quiet down. Chatter may happen, but go back to breathing in (1), and breathing out (2).

Take several brain breaks throughout the day for a few minutes, breathing. Lose yourself in that inner sanctuary that no-one owns or can penetrate unless you let them.

Forget rules about meditation. Say "stop" and "flow" with 4.6.8 breathing. Be still with your dog for a moment. Breathing in through your nose for 4 counts, holding for 6, and exhaling through your mouth, slowly for about 8 counts, while imagining, "so calm."

Teaching our dogs to "relax" may be one of the best behaviors you ever teach. Create a mantra while sitting with your dog, calmly, such as "We are calm, centered and safe" or "I can flip the switch and deal with this (issues) later." Imagine your dog peaceful, relaxed with no one to protect, no child to play with, no ball to chase, no one to visit; simply enjoying a few peaceful moments with you, centered and safe.

Choose to turn the energy volume (around you or in your mind) higher or lower with a metaphor like "safe shield". If it becomes too intense, switch to "safe shield", as if a bubble is protecting you and your dog. You are inside, observing, witnessing, but no-one can enter the bubble, until you say, "you may come in".

This may give you the time and space you need to check in with yourself, being aware of energetic imbalances.

Patience and breathing is a way to de-escalate aggression and its accompanying pain. When we feel aggressive—there's a seductive pull to want resolution. We feel wiggly and agitated. It hurts to feel aggressive or angry. At this moment, we can change the way we look at discomfort, breathe and practice patience. Will it matter ten minutes or a week from now?

PAWT 10

Bone Journals—Dog Reflections

Channeling Betty White

I love dogs and I know you do too. Dogs can change our attitude with their jovial sense of humor. A dog's approach to life is simple and that is exactly what we need today. They ground us in reality and love us no matter what.

As Betty White shares, "I have more in common with animal people. I find myself disappointed with those who are not interested in animals; they lack a certain warmth and tend to be a little self-centered. Animal people have empathy. Research has shown this to be true."

I agree with Betty who credits her positive attitude, through some tough times, to her pets.

> "Watch your thoughts, for they become your words;
> Watch your words, for they become your actions;
> Watch your actions, for they become your habits;
> Watch your habits, for they become your character;
> Watch your character, for it becomes
> your destiny." ~Unknown

Personal Renewal

Creating a personal renewal program for yourself will benefit your dogs too! One strategy for protecting yourself from the ill effects of a toxic environment or stressful lifestyle is to take frequent brain and breathing breaks throughout the day.

Balancing exercise, healthy nutrition, spending time with friends (including our dogs), meditating or quiet time and enjoying hobbies are what everybody needs—including our dogs. For people who face psychologically draining situations, on a daily basis, it's even more critical.

Our dogs learn how to get their needs met by communicating vocally or behaviorally (destruction or depression). We can tell if stress or life is pitching too many curveballs too. Our well-being slowly begins to unravel and fall apart. Learning to recognize these signals, rather than allowing them to control us, or our dogs, will help.

Honor differences in ourselves and others, and letting go of controlling and struggling with what we cannot change relieves stress. The only way to create change is through change and change begins with self, unless life does it for us. Ask any victim of a disaster what was the most important thing they lost and it will not be their car, house or stuff. There is regret, pain and sadness for the loss, but it is the memories and grateful feeling of being alive that prevails. For some, it is a new beginning.

With awareness, clarity and breathing, you will find sanity and peace even in chaos.

Awareness Centered Meditation (ACM)
Unconditional Openness

Simple serenity and peaceful moments is not a dream. The peace that we are looking for does not crumble as soon as there is chaos if we know how to be centered and safe. Whatever happens around us does not have to enter our heart-space. Whether we're seeking inner peace, global peace or a tranquil relationship with our dog (anyone), the way to experience it is to build on the foundation of awareness and openness to all that arises. Life is not an experience free of challenges, rough or smooth. Whatever unveils, we can handle it without feeling threatened or unwoven.

Listen to your dog's breathing. Listen to yours. Observe them dreaming, playing and exploring. Dogs can enlighten us with simply being. Let's practice awareness centered meditation. This can be for one minute or twenty minutes, you decide.

Assume a comfortable and natural position with your dog. You can sit cross-legged, lie down or sit on a fitness ball. Maintaining an upright, balanced posture will ensure that you are physically centered and prevent fatigue. Getting our dogs calm with a little walk will make this easier for them to focus, especially if this is novel.

Close your eyes and lay your hand on your dog. If this is too stimulating for them or you then just sit or lie down. See what happens. You have been practicing ACT training, so even adolescent dogs should be use to controlling their energy for a few moments when you ask them to "relax".

Notice any physical sensations. What are you feeling? It is common to feel like you have to get up and finish task number ten on the list of twenty-two. Try not to. It will still be on the list in ten minutes. When you are relaxed, breathe through the nose at your natural pace. With each inhalation, draw air deep into your abdomen. Allow the area surrounding your navel to rise and fall. Gradually focus your attention on the sensations caused by the inhaling and exhaling. Feel the air flow (wolf spelled backwards) in and out of your nostrils. Allow your tongue to float freely in your mouth, relax the tension in your jaw and body. Wiggle your jaw back and forth if it helps. Slowly lift and lower your shoulders. Feel the expansion and contraction of your abdomen. Feel your dog relaxing. If your dog decides they want to wander off, let them. If they come back, delightful. Keep breathing; stay focused—at least for a few minutes.

You may notice that your mind continues to stray. It's okay. Don't attach any significance to this. If you get frustrated or bored, honor it. Simply bring your attention back to your breath. You body and mind will thank you.

Eventually, the surge of mental noise flooding your mind will slow to a trickle. You will learn to control the current of thoughts, noticing them, but not be at the mercy of your reactions. Your dog will be learning to respond to and be grateful for your peaceful nature. Ahhh . . .

You can use this any time of day, anywhere, anyhow. Your breath belongs to you.

Relationship Performance Evaluation—Evolving

I worked in corporate for 25 years and dreaded performance evaluations. Afterward, I felt better because I knew areas I was doing really well at and strengths I needed to develop. I was lucky. I had managers / mentors, one a psychologist who was working as a corporate head, who knew that positive reinforcement would get employees to accomplish more. I still dreaded PE's but it gave me an opportunity to clarify my manager's, and my, expectations.

As a self-employed business manager, co-founder of a non-profit organization, and a dog training behaviorist and author, I have changed my approaches to living many times over the last 20 years, thanks to the dogs. They have changed my life. I have had the opportunity to explore how it feels, internally and externally, what it is like to teach another species, give myself performance evaluations and get them from another species, sometimes in odd ways. I gather constructive feedback from humans, and regard how the dogs treat me, as a reflection, of how I am communicating what I expect.

Our relationships, whether with partners, friends, families or our dogs can be easier and healthier with regular check-ins and relationship performance evaluations similar to those we get at corporate jobs. It gives us an opportunity to know where we are, what needs improvement or whether to stand pat (all is well). It gives others the same opportunity to express themselves whether child, adult or dog.

The following approach has successfully been used in businesses and works equally well in relationships too:

1. Know your Top Ranking VIPs (Very Important Principles):

   a. Make a list of the top five things you need from your partner / spouse / employees / volunteers / dogs! Write or type them down and have them write or type theirs down too. The dog will know what theirs are and so will you because you are using "life rewards" (eating, playing, toys, love, touch). A dog will show you how they are feeling by how they act with you and others.

   b. At any job / project, even if you manage your own business and work out of the home define what is important and expected of the relationship and the goals.

   c. We all have our stories, but do not know another's. The lists should be respected and honored—age, species and skill appropriate.

   d. Here is an example | create your own:

The Human:

   i.   Remember to call when late
   ii. Be engaged in the conversation and genuinely listen
   iii. Work as a team to finish a project by a certain date
   iv. Have my back like you would your team at work
   v.   Create laugh, play, humor, no expectation time —
   vi. Treat me with respect
   vii. Do something nice even when not expected

The Dog:

    i.   Dog: Remember to bark when you need to pee

    ii. Be engaged in the training or walk instead of lunging

    iii. Have my back by sitting and waiting before jumping

    iv. Make me laugh

    v. Come to me when I call or just because . . .

2. Think Three to One (3:1): How is it that five positive things can happen and we highlight the one negative? The magic formula is 3:1. Offer three positive messages (rewards) to one negative. Clarify expectations about the negative.

3. Bad/Good Dinner Table Game: Let's share today's bad things that happened and then end dinner by sharing the good things. "My dog dug a hole in my garden today and I was really upset. The good news is, I learned that if I put up a little garden fence and buried a bone for her to discover, she digs in her garden instead of mine".

4. Most of us have knee-jerk reactions, at different levels on the hurt-o-meter, depending on what kind of day we are having. Decompress and allow others to decompress first before launching into the day's tribunals. With dogs, it is best to let them eliminate and sniff around a bit before attempting a calm walk. Whatever bothers us will re-surface. If it does too many times, then you know it is time to address the issue or continue suffering the consequences.

5. Don't send your dog to horse school. Employees, family members or dogs deserve to be given jobs that have clear

descriptions and suit their current abilities and capabilities of learning something new.

6. Clarify the tasks, split the tasks, and share your feelings. Putting yourself in the other person's moccasins (or dog's paws) is one of the oldest, universal metaphors. Do not assume they know what you do not share. Be sure by having them repeat it back to you and vice versa (paraphrasing).

7. Perform a 360 degree review of your relationship: Be open to receive and give constructive feedback in a relatable way. The *review* helps clarify and balance how much, when, where, and for how long. In busy relationships, it helps to establish a set of guidelines (organizational plan) around the pets and children too. On a scale of balances, are you feeling overwhelmed? Are they tipping in someone else's favor? If it needs tweaking, let's clarify and make some changes.

Walking away from our dogs when they are acting out (jumping) usually works! Waiting for the calm behavior we want, and then praising shapes the inspired behavior.

8. Win-Win the Client: In mediation there is something called BATNA (best alternative to a negotiated agreement). In business or dog training, win-win is a favorite of mine because I know how I like to be treated. I get excited when I can get another species to voluntarily and joyfully do something to create positive change, even it means negotiating, and letting go of my own convictions. Both parties are satisfied.

9. Leadership can be win-win too. Sometimes, being more directive and assertive works best. Present assertively, with clarity and ask the recipient to repeat it back so we know if

it is understood. With dogs, it is easy. If they aren't doing something we want, then we know we aren't communicating clearly.

In long-term relationships, we do it more often because we get into a comfort zone. We do with our dogs too by getting lazy with our training. Then, "BAM", something happens to wake us up.

Energy levels vary. Take time to decompress together and apart from partners and dogs before dealing with questions, answers and decision-making. Everyone deserves a time-off from decision-making, so take turns and stick to the agenda such as, "we are taking turns—remember? Isn't it your turn to cook or clean the litter box? I thought you were deciding which Vet to choose this time"?

Delegating and directions make life easier, especially for women. I know because I am one. Letting go of perfection and thinking that we need to pole-dance while whistling "Moves like Jagger", while juggling a platter on our nose, wears us down. I like to dance, so someone has to carry the platter. This is a true story. I have been there, done that. Spaghetti and meatballs on the floor are a messy clean-up. We had a good laugh though.

Checking in with our dogs to see if we are being good dog parents improves living with dogs dramatically. Trainers will share, at least those who are honest, that after working with dogs and human clients all day, oftentimes into the evening, having a few dogs greet you wanting attention when you walk through the door is enough to send even the strongest minded person over the edge.

We want to collapse but see those big eyes pleading with us longingly to play a few rounds of catch. And, by the way, when's dinner? We all need a break, support and relief from day-to-day jobs, and, I love my job. The only one that can create the change to balance our lives is—you guessed it—us!

> *"In my late fifties, I began to embrace myself in a way that I hadn't been able to before. I find that I'm not as worried about what other people think. That's a comfortable place to be. And I'm starting to let go of the feeling that I need to push myself to do things I don't want to do."—Sally Field*

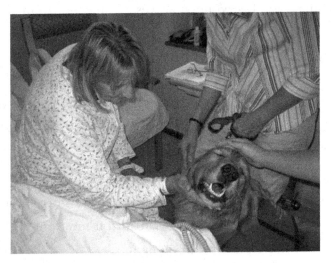

Team Jake, Registered Therapy Dog with his partner, Kathy DeLong, RN, visiting patients at Saints Medical Center.

Pet Assisted Therapy Resources—*Healing Dogs*

Making a difference, in our distinctive way, is a natural extension of being human and kind. What we give—we reap in bucketfuls.

Anything we do, on a small level, will automatically ripple into positive waves throughout planet Earth. It bodes us well to respect her resources.

Sharing our pets is one way to joyfully make a feel-good difference. Pet assisted therapy enables us to become qualified to visit health care facilities, schools and libraries. Sharing our well behaved and healthy pets with those in the community who enjoy pets brings a bright spot to what otherwise might be a boring, lonely and long day.

Registered (or Certified) teams are specially trained to visit with their pets (dogs, cats, horses, other) professionally and with integrity. The benefits of well-being are mutual (to follow).

I began working part time in a nursing facility called "The Old Lady's Home" when I was fourteen. I worked my way through high school. The seed was planted then and continues today. As a student counselor, I interned with horses in therapeutic riding and with dogs in hospitals and senior care centers.

My passion segued into co-founding New England Pet Partners, Inc., a non-profit dedicated to enhancing well being and education with pet assisted therapy and canine assisted learning. We use the Pet Partner's Program for training and registration. It is important to be registered or certified if your intention is to visit a facility on a regular basis, as a team. Team is the operative word. It is not just about the dog (or other pet) but about the collaborative team work between handler and dog, who set out on a mission to make someone smile, and end up doing so much more.

Social skills and being an advocate for your dog in what can be very stressful situations is a mandatory requirement. Understanding infectious disease, and how to interact with a variety of cultures, staff, populations and challenges are must have skills. Tops on the list are what you have been reading in ACT; that is recognizing and reducing stress in clients and the visiting dogs (or other pets).

As a licensed evaluator and instructor and an active volunteer, I am amazed at the way a dog can shift the energy of the room for a patient or group, within about 3-seconds.

Emotions can be raw for some people. Imagine never being able to touch or see your pet again due to financial or medical reasons. There can be tender situations where you have to sense when to regress or move forward.

Silence, not always easy, can be a gift, one that the dog offers naturally, but humans tend to feel they need to fill this space. Oftentimes, it is a knowing, where no word has to be spoken, just being there is enough.

The benefits of pet assisted therapy are many:

1. Psycho-social (acceptance by pet)
2. Fine and Gross Motor Skills (reaching, touching, grooming)
3. Balance (energy, bending, sitting up, standing)
4. Endurance (throwing a safe toy, walking with the team)
5. Memory / cognitive (remembering names, stories, reflecting and reminiscing)
6. Problem Solving (choosing games, naming dogs)
7. Range of Motion (tossing a toy, stretching, grooming)
8. Sensory Stimulation (feel the fur, body warmth, attention)
9. Speech (offering requests like sit, speak, high-five, engaging in conversation).

The strongest benefit is the attention that a dog (or other species) gives to the person they visit. They offer non-judgmental company and socialization. On occasion, not a word has to be spoken. The dog can translate.

The following is example of a story that was printed and published in many venues including The Latham Foundation, a good resource for materials on teaching empathy, compassion and breaking the cycles of violence.

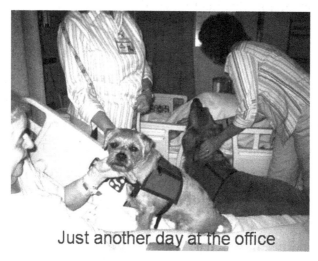

Just another day at the office

Team Tate visiting patients.

Dog as Translator

By Maureen Ross and Detective Tate McSniff
A short story about a Spanish speaking cancer patient, an English speaking woman and a dog, who helps to break the communication barrier creating a meaningful connection

Precious moments leave us feeling grateful to have the opportunity to share our pets. Tate (Border Terrier) and I are a registered pet assisted therapy team. We have worked together for several years and visited many people.

All visits are meaningful, but some are unforgettable. We visit the cancer unit at Saints Medical Center. One snowy day, at first glance out the window, I thought about rescheduling, which would have been fine with the Volunteer Director. I wondered how many people would show up for treatment today, or did they have a choice. Every infusion chair was occupied.

We ended up parking on the 6th floor of the circular garage, around and around. Deciding to take the stairs to release some energy and a little stress, Tate and I made our way to the main lobby for check-in. Visiting begins meeting and greeting dozen of people, including staff, who have gotten use to the little powerhouse Tate. The smell of Dunkin Donuts (located in the lobby) is an aphrodisiac. A dog is a double-aphrodisiac, ah, coffee, donut and Tate!

After meeting up with our volunteer guide, we headed to the cancer building. It was busy because people wanted to get their treatments before the holiday. We made our way down the aisle to anyone interested in seeing or touching Tate. Upon reaching the last curtained cubicle, we met Anna (name changed). Anna was busy playing with a camera. She was looking at pictures of dogs—perfect timing. When Anna spotted Tate, little needed to be said. The smile expressed more than enough to welcome us. Carefully placing Tate on Anna's lap I pointed to the camera.

Anna spoke a lot of Spanish. I speak a lot of English and some dog. Tate was our translator. Gleefully, we learned some new Spanish words like "Hola—hello" and "me ilamo—my name is Moe and this is Tate". Anna asked us in "pseudo-sign-language" to take pictures of Tate and her, not me, but that's okay. I'm use to being addressed as Tate's chauffeur, secretary, groomer, massage therapist and owner.

When it was time to say "adios" to our new "amigo", we hope we see Anna again. We never know.

This is one of many opportunities that dogs help us to break barriers of communication, put a smile on someone's face, share some joy, and makes a connection to be stored in a lifetime of memories. Language doesn't matter. Dogs know people who need and enjoy them.

As we left that day, we decided to climb back up to the 6-flights of stairs to the top, and outside floor, of the parking garage, much to Tate's chagrin. She would prefer to be carried or take the elevator. We both need to lose a few pounds for our well-being.

It was snowing. Tate and I pleasantly collapsed in the car and sat, watching the snow, grateful to be living in the present moment, and hoping that we made a difference.

"Becoming a bag lady. Getting Alzheimer's. Ending up alone or broke. All of these concerns speak to a fear not of aging but of living. It is being preeminently afraid of dying. It is not doing what you came here to do, out of timidity and spinelessness. The antidote is to take full responsibility for yourself—for the time you take up and the space you occupy. If you don't know what you're here to do, then just do some good." —Maya Angelou

Note: New England Pet Partners, Inc. was one of four non-profits chosen by Oprah Magazine in February, 2010, for "Giving Back Beautiful."

Daily Doga Inspirations—An Invitation Mindfully Living and Learning with Dogs

Practicing yoga and meditating has saved my life many times. I may have survived, but not without self medication (and I did some of that too, but not as much as I would have). I had to learn how to give myself permission to get in touch with my mind, body and soul. I had to connect my heart string to my brain stem. Yoga seemed like a good start because I liked the animal names of the postures. Exercise, in moderation, is a life saver. My current favorite is cross-training because it keeps me from getting bored. I may do yoga one day, weights the next, and elliptical three times a week, then back to yoga. I do what floats my boat, not someone else's.

I would like to say I have epiphanies, but Oprah will be disappointed. For me it is more like repetitive whispers that get louder over time. If I hear it often enough I know that I am either hallucinating or need to pay attention to the message. It's meaningful.

I do not have gurus, but possess an insatiable curiosity and flexibility that lends itself to exploration (body and mind). Life is like a giant quiz with multi-choice possibilities that all end with this equation: me plus you = let's talk about dogs.

I am not enlightened but I am inspired. Highlighted moments, good or bad, sparkle of dogs and their people—so I give up and let it flow. The more I share, the more people share—endless stories about how dogs have changed their lives. I know they have changed mine.

Daily Doga is a purely evolving well-spring of inspirations. I am inspired by people like Louise Hay, Madsyn Taylor and Cheryl

Richardson, all, by the way, connected to Hay House. I just know when something feels right, and for me, publishing with Hay House feels exceptionally right. That doesn't mean if somebody wants to offer me a lucrative contract that I will say "no", but for "ACT", Hay House was the chosen path.

Doga is not about doing postures with our dogs, but naturally we do if we pay attention. The dogs greet me with a downward facing dog (play bow) and seem to enjoy the newness of doing poses, or as previously described, training with dogs, balls and balance. It breaks up the monotony of regimented training (sit, down, come, sit, down, come).

Rolling in the grass (or the deep—thank you Adele) with the dogs is silly and feels good. We know we are different species, but if they have to yield to my quirks and desires, I should be able to cede to theirs. I do and enjoy every freedom of expression. I am not sure what the neighbors think, but no-one has called the police or come to take me away.

Daily Doga Inspirations are bi-weekly sharing's about making relationships better with ourselves first, our dogs, and others.

Intuitively (I) and instinctively (dog) invite you to www. dailydoga.com. Enjoy the gallery and mini-meditations (medis). You can practice yourself or with your dogs. Join the Doga Community sharing your life-changing stories with dogs in mind. I look forward to sharing stories with you.

AFTERWARD

Beyond the Positive— Enjoy the Journey

Journeys of lifelong evolution often begin simply. Mine has been with dogs and their people, who have graciously allowed me the privilege of their company. What is yours?

No matter how complex the goals or desires we are harvesting, the first steps are usually basic and uncomplicated, especially with puppies and dogs. We can offer them very little and they give us lot back. We can be good enough and they will be great dogs.

One of the easiest ways to create a freer and less stressful life is to expand our awareness. Knowledge empowers us to do almost anything we set our minds too. Dogs help us break down barriers of ignorance and open new communication paths. We can use our passion for dogs, with their simplicity and curiosity, as bridges of mindfulness.

Dogs help us look at ourselves through a different being's eyes. We can expand our horizons, one breath and dog at a time.

Training our dogs can change our lives. I cannot change the whole world for dogs, but we can positively make the world a better place for them through awareness, education, relationship and well-being. If we ACT a little every day, we can make a difference together.

WINDING DOWN

Expanding Awareness

Thank you for sharing this journey with me. Sit with your dog(s) for moment, and share a nose to navel, deep belly breath. Listen to your dogs breathing. Exhaling, imagine "so-calm—so loved—so what—so woof."

Enjoy the journey with love, compassion, empathy and awareness.

APPENDIX A

Big Confusing Word Behavior Guide

Clarifying big confusing terms and some small ones too!
Breathe in . . . Exhale . . . Use as a Reference

Awareness Centered Training (ACT): The cornerstone of this book and Maureen Ross's beyond positive dog training approach. ACT is teaching with kindness and understanding, while honoring differences and respecting relationships with our dogs.

Alpha: Equals breeding and eating rights. This is generally not an issue for dogs living with humans. We give them food, shelter, care and direct their breeding rights.

Antecedent: An antecedent is a preceding circumstance, event, object, phenomenon or precursor. It is the history, events and conditions of a dogs or humans earlier life. There can be association to a word, phrase, sound or happening leading to a behavior.

Association: Dogs live in the present moment but associate through sight, sound and smell, and in a variety of environmental situations. What is happening in the moment matters.

Balance: A sustained sense of well being for dog or human. Life is not perfect. There will be stress. What we can do is be aware of and balance stress for ourselves and our dogs.

Barking: Canine vocalizations / communication that is like us talking, crying or screaming. Harmonic barking is humans joining in chorus while yelling at dogs to be "quiet". Dogs cannot stop barking anymore than we can stop talking, laughing or singing.

Behavior: Observable activity in a human or animal. This activity can be good or bad.

Behavior Modification: A plan, over a period, to change a behavior by shaping a new and achievable one.

Behavior Shaping: Every creature has a repertoire of behaviors that they have performed at least once. If any behaviors are reinforced, chances are they will increase in probability and with greater frequency.

Brain Break: A five-minute focused breathing rest to rejuvenate the brain's hypothalamus (wishbone).

Bridging Stimulus: Auditory marker that the behavior we just did will get us something good. The something good will be as good as our behavior / response.

Classical Conditioning (CC—Ivan Pavlov's Salivating Dogs): CC involves placing a neutral signal before a naturally occurring reflex. Pavlov's dogs would begin salivating (visual and olfactory) the moment they saw the "food" person coming. The reflexes are involuntary.

Clear the Clutter: What we do with our closets, minds and life when we have too much stuff.

Clicker Training (CT): A marker for an acceptable, desired behavior. Think of whistle blowing for dolphins. CT is crisp and clear. It can shape or reshape positive behaviors. The handler needs to be capable of clicking on time.

Conditioned Reinforcer: A cue or signal that will tell the dog that positive reinforcement has been won (whistle for a dolphin, clicker, smile or praise for a dog—enthusiastic YES).

Conflict: Conflict is a disagreement where parties involved perceive a threat to their needs and interests. Dogs usually do not want conflict. In the wild it would threaten the survival of the pack. In human families or dog-to-dog, conflict may arise from lack of training, boundaries, management and leadership.

Consequence: The effect, result, or outcome of something that occurs earlier and because of the behavior. It is associated with safe or dangerous, pleasurable or painful, this or that.

Counter-Conditioning: CC is the extinction of an undesirable response to a stimulus through the introduction of a more desirable, often incompatible, response. A dog who sits calmly and watches you cannot chase a cat up a tree. A dog who listens to calm music gradually becomes more relaxed around loud noises. Desensitization and counter conditioning are more effective used together, depending on how strongly rooted a behavior is.

Delivery: In training a behavior, randomize the delivery of rewards to only the jackpot (best) behaviors. If you change, modify or add a novel—new behavior, simply begin again using more life rewards.

Differential Schedule: As soon as a behavior is put on schedule, select the best example for shaping—reinforcement. Choose the one you like the most.

Distance: Once a behavior is learned like sit / stay, incrementally extend the challenge (a foot, two feet), to the point of success. If the dog makes a mistake, regress, a few inches or feet (successive approximation).

Diversity: A behavior is performed well in one spot / place. Extend this to every room in the home and a variety of environments.

Diner Training: If you feed your dog twice a day, you have 14X training opportunities a week to kindly integrate training with life rewards (sit, watch-me, down—thank you).

Distraction: Behaviors will remain as is unless you incrementally add in distractions from the environment like noise and activity. While doing this, praise for calmness with a life reward.

Duration: Your dog is constant on her sit/stay for 10 seconds, so extend it to 15, 1-minute and to the point of challenge that is successful.

Effective Praise: Different for each dog and giver. If it produces an expected desired result on a regular basis than it is effective.

Energy: The strength and vitality required for sustained physical or mental activity. Energy can be good, bad or out of control.

Fair: Free from bias, dishonesty or injustice. Train with reasonable expectations and always look at the other's point-of-view.

Flexible: Capable of being bent without breaking; susceptible to modification or adaptation, tractable. Flexibility enables you to be resilient and see the dog's point-of-view.

Focusing: To enter into a special kind of awareness, different from every day. It is open and centered on the present and on your body's inner sensation. You genuinely ask, "How am I doing and how is my dog doing now?"

Forgiving: To learn and let go of resentment against your dog for a perceived offense especially after 3-seconds.

Fun: Training should be fun, in appropriate dosages, providing pleasure, energy balancing and learning with boundaries.

Grateful: Appreciation of gifts received from the Universe, our dogs, work, friends and family and self.

Grieving: What we do when we experience a loss. That loss can be big or small. How we grieve is our right as individuals. No two people grieve the same way.

Habituation: A decrease in response to a stimulus after repeated presentations (diminished response). Do you jump EVERY time the phone rings? Anything that occurs repeatedly may lead to habituation.

High Value Motivators (HVM): If you know them (toys, treats, touch, play) training is easy.

Housetraining: Teaching a puppy or dog how to live in a human house, where to pee and when to sit (see Housetraining at a Glance).

Jackpot: The BIG BAM prize for the best behavior.

Joyful Easy Training (JET): Lazy easy training, focusing on the behavior you want, when you get it, and praising the heck out of it, on a regular basis, to shape it.

Learned Irrelevance: A dog (or human) will tune out irrelevance, that without connection or meaningful consequence.

Life Rewards: Anything we need and will work for (food, attention, play, love).

Listen: Listening is an active sport and art. Listening comes before understanding. Understanding comes before wisdom. It is something you do, not have done to you. It takes practice.

Mantra: For dogs this may be howling, barking or whining in unison. For humans, it is a relaxing affirmation like inhaling in to "SO" and exhaling to "CALM".

Marguerites and Meditations: Whatever it takes to relax *(personal renewal)*.

Negative Punishment (NP): A behavior makes something good go away. If you want your dog to repeat a behavior less frequently, remove any reward or perceived award for the behavior. Example: your dog jumps, you leave, your dog sits, you stay.

Negative Reinforcement (NR): A behavior makes something bad go away—removal of a bad consequence. Dog is stepping onto the sofa, you scowl, they stop, and you smile.

Olfactory: The dog's extreme sense of smell. It is much stronger (about 75X) than humans. They sniff in high def, so consider using this as a reward.

Operant Conditioning (OPC—BF Skinner's ABCS of request, response, reward): This is the A.B.C.'s of behavior. A. Something happens B. behavior happens and C. a consequence happens. These can be good or bad.

Opium: Organize, Plan, Implement your Plan, Understand that even the best laid plans are subject to change and make the change.

Orienting Response: If someone walks into the room, you would look. Dogs will do this every time a new dog enters a training, park, house or pack. If it occurs repeatedly, the dog will begin to ignore it. Your emotional response / reaction can help to redirect the dog to a more calm response (i.e. barking, redirect, turn-around, relax or sit).

Personal Renewal: See Daily Doga Inspirations www.dailydoga. com. Quiet your mind, breathe and be still. Take time for physical, spiritual, mental, social and emotional renewal. You don't need to sit like a pretzel or meditate like a Buddhist Monk. A few minutes (breathing at a red stoplight) will help to quiet the mind for clarity and sanity.

Positive Punishment: Presenting something bad and behavior is less likely. You request a sit and dog walks in the other direction. You yank the leash hard or throw something at the dog. Not kind or instructive . . .

Positive Reinforcement: Positive Reinforcement is anything that, occurring in conjunction with an act, may increase the probability of that act occurring again. If you want your dog to repeat a behavior more frequently, reward that behavior more frequently. Present something good, in a timely way, and behavior will improve.

Premack Principle: This is a principle of operant conditioning originally identified by David Premack in 1965. The principle suggests that behavior that happens reliably (or without interference by a researcher) can be used as a reinforcer for a behavior that occurs less reliably. If a being wants something, they will likely perform an activity they do not like. The reward of getting what we want is contingent on if we do what we don't want. For dogs, this can mean sit for a treat. Children will wash dishes if they get to watch TV.

Primary Reinforcer: In operant conditioning there are Primary Reinforcers and Conditioned Reinforcers. Primary reinforcers are naturally reinforcing (there is no learning necessary.) For example, we will feed our dog no matter what. The conditioned reinforcer is learned like a cue or signal before feeding.

Reactive: Behavior that is not internally motivated but manifests in response to a situation or the actions of others or the environment.

Relax: What every dog should learn early on, on a designated spot (blanket) or haven.

Request: Ask for a behavior (Example: sit, stay, stand, down, come, take-it, leave-it, relax, wait).

Response: Any behavior from a living organism that results from an external or internal stimulus (dog sits or doesn't sit). Dogs bites or doesn't bite.

Reward: Something given in return for services rendered or achieved. Big kiss.

Reward Marker: Yes, Click, Cluck, Smile! This is signal indicating the behavior is good!

Responsive: Being responsive is acting appropriately to the issue at hand, rather than being driven by habitual knee-jerk reactions. It is the ability to think voluntarily, from experiences, and maintain self-control and perspective. Well socialized dogs who have been trained make better choices even under stressful conditions.

Socialization and Manners (SAM): Socialization and manners creates a dog who enjoys or at least tolerates people, other dogs and the environment without collapsing into a puddle or feeling threatened. They are welcome in the community.

Stimulus Control: Anything that causes some kind of behavioral response. Some stimuli can cause response without learning or training: we blink at bright lights and jump at loud noises. Other stimuli are learned through associations. Traffic lights make us stop and go. Dogs learn to fear people who hit.

Systematic Desensitization: A technique developed by Joseph Wolpe in which the patient imagines a hierarchy of anxiety-producing situations under conditions of physical relaxation with the goal of weakening the anxiety responses. Slowly build toleration as opposed to *FLOODING*, (leaving a dog alone for long periods).

Timing: The cornerstone of training, timing a behavior or correction as quickly as possible shapes or changes that behavior more quickly.

Unconditional Reinforcer: Something a dog is going to like and get regardless (food, love).

Variable Reinforcement Schedule: Once a behavior is learned (supposedly), reinforce it occasionally rather than constantly to maintain it at the present level.

APPENDIX B

An Enlightening (fun) Quiz about Interpretations

Please make a wish before you start this little quiz. Be honest, don't analyze, just have fun and answer these questions.

Number 1: Arrange the following 5 animals according to your preference (1,2,3):

Cow
Tiger
Sheep
Horse
Monkey

Number 2: Write one word to describe each of the following:

Dog
Cat
Rat
Coffee
Ocean

Number 3: Think of somebody (who also knows you) that you can relate to a color. Don't repeat your answer. Name only one person for each color:

Yellow
Orange
Red
White
Green

Number 4: Finally, indicate your favorite number and favorite day of the week. Are you done? Make sure your answers are what you truly feel. Last chance! Don't peek!

Interpretations

Number 1: This will define your priorities in life.

- ♥ Cow means Career
- ♥ Tiger means Pride
- ♥ Sheep means Love
- ♥ Horse means Family
- ♥ Monkey means Money

Number 2:

- ♥ Your description of Dog implies your own personality.
- ♥ Your description of Cat implies your partner's personality.
- ♥ Your description of Rat implies your enemy's personality.
- ♥ Your description of Coffee is how you interpret sex.
- ♥ Your description of Ocean implies your own life.

Number 3:

- ♥ Yellow = somebody who will never forget you.
- ♥ Orange = someone whom you can consider as your real friend.
- ♥ Red = someone you really love
- ♥ White = your soul mate.
- ♥ Green = a person whom you will always remember for the rest your life.

RECOMMENDED

There are many choices in videos, training and behavior books, e-books and visuals available. Just because we can does not mean we have too. The following is a list of some that I enjoy re-visiting.

Historically, all reading is educational. Knowledge is empowering, but life experiences are enlightening. Letting go of what we do not believe, evolving, and using what works for us and our dogs—is pure wisdom.

I invite you to visit my websites where you can download handouts, view educational visuals and find connections on animal (and our) wellness.

Dog Talk Training and Wellness Sanctuary, LLC,
    www.dogtalk.com
    www.youtube.com/dogtalkmedia
New England Pet Partners, Inc.,
    www.newenglandpetpartners.org
    www.youtube.com/nepetpartners
Daily Doga Inspirations, www.dailydoga.com
    www.youtube.com/dailydoga
Sharing our Pets, www.sharingourpets.com
Pet Wellness Festival, www.petwellnessfestival.org
Multi-Taskers, www.multi-taskers.org (new and evolving)

Training and Behavior

Aloff, Brenda, Get Connected with your Dog, www.brendaaloff.com, 2008.

Benjamin, Carol Lea, *Dog Smart*, Telemachus Press, NY, NY 2012.

Mother Knows Best: The Natural Way to Train Your Dog, 1985.

Brown, Ali, *Scaredy Dog*, Tanacacia Press, 2009.

Camp, Joe, *Soul of the Horse*, Three Rivers Press, Crown Publishing, 2008.

Campbell, William, *Behavior Problems in Dogs*, American Veterinary Publications, Goleta, CA, 1999 Revised Edition.

Chronicle of the Dog, Association of Pet Dog Training, www.apdt.com, ongoing.

Clothier, Suzanne, *Bones would Rain from the Sky*, Grand Central Publishing, 2009.

Dawson, Richard, *The Greatest Show on Earth*, Bantam Press, UK, 2009.

Coppinger, Ray and Lorna, *A New Understanding of Canine Origin*, Chicago Press, Chicago, IL, 2009.

Dunbar, Ian. Dr., *Dog Behavior*, Howell Book House, NY, NY, 1999. *Before (and After) you get you Puppy*, www.jamesandkenneth.com James & Kenneth Publishers, Berkeley, CA, 1992.

Goodall, Jane, Dr. *A Reason for Hope*, Warner Books, Inc., 1999.

Lorenz, Konrad, *Man Meets Dogs*, Kodansha America, Inc., 1994.

Grandin, Temple, *Animals Make Us Human*, Houghtin Mifflin Harcourt Publishing, 2010

McConnell, Patricia, Dr., *The Other End of the Leash*, Random House, NY, NY, 2008.

Moussaieff Masson, Jeffrey, Ph.D. *How Dogs Have Captured our Hearts for Years, Harper Collins, 2010*

Dogs Never Lie about Love, Three Rivers Press, NY, NY, 1998.

Pryor, Karen, *Reaching the Animal Mind, Scribner, NY, NY, 2009.*

www.clickertraining.com, Don't Shoot the Dog, Revised Edition, 2002.

Reid, Pam, Ph.D., *Dog Insight*, Dog Wise Publishing, Wenatchee, Washington, 2011.

Ross, Maureen, Ross, Gary, *Train Your Dog, Change Your Life,* 1st Edition, Howell Book House, NY, NY, 2001, www.dogtalk.com

Canine Training and Survival Guide, Dog Talk Media, Pelham, NH, 1998,

Rugaas, Turid, *On Talking Terms with Dogs: Calming Signals,* Dog Wise Publishing, Wenatchee, WA, 2006.

Ryan, Terry, *Coaching People to Train Their Dogs*, Legacy, 2008.

Toolbox, Howell, Book House, NY, NY, 1998.

Sternberg, Sue, *Successful Dog Adoptions*, Howell Book House, NY, NY, 2003. www.suesternberg.com

Pet Assisted Therapy

Marcus, Dr. Dawn, *The Power of the Wagging Tail*, Demos Medical Publishing, NY, NY, 2011

Pet Partners *Team Training Manual*, Bellevue, WA, www.petpartners.org, 2012.

Diamond Davis, Kathy, *Therapy Dogs*, Dog Wise Publishing, Wenatchee, WA, 2002.

Reading Education Assistance Dogs, www.therapyanimals.org

Well-Being

Allen, David, *Making it all Work*, Viking Press, NY, NY, 2008.

Covey, Stephen R., *The 7 Habits of Highly Effective Families*, Free Press, NY, NY, 2004.

Chodron, Pema, *Taking the Leap*, Shambhala Publications, Boston, MA, 2009

The Pocket Pema Chodron

Gawain, Shakti, *Living in the Light*, Nataraj Publishing, Novata, CA, 2011

Reflections in the Light, 2003

Jones, Linda Tellington, *TTouch*, www.ttouch.com

Byron Katie, *A Thousand Names for Joy*, Harmony Books, NY, 2007 www.thework.com

Ruiz, Don Miguel, *The Five Agreements*, 2011. Amber Allen Publishing, San Rafael, CA 2011

Segal, Monica, *K9 Kitchen, Truth Behind the Hype*, www.monicasegal.ca.

Snow, Amy, and Sidonis, Nancy, *Acu-Dog a Guide to Animal Acupressure*, Tall Grass Publishers, Larkspur, CO, www.animalacupressure.com

The Well Connected Dog 1999

Tolle, Eckhart, *The Power of Now*, New World Library, Novato, CA, 1999.

Wilde, Nicole, *Energy Healing for dogs*, Phantom Publishing, Santa Clarita, CA 2009

Winn, Raquel, Stretch Your Dog Healthy, Penguin Press, NY, NY, 2008.

Vignettes

Dog Talk Media, www.youtube.com/dogtalkmedia,
www.youtube.com/nepetpartners,
www.youtube.com/dailydoga—Puppy Social, Doggy Diner,
Flowing Training Postures
Dunbar, Dr. Ian, www.jamesandkenneth.com
Dutcher, Jim and Jamie, Wolves at Our Door,
www.wolvesatourdoor.com
Kalnajs, Sarah, *The Body Language of Dogs, DVD*,
www.bluedogtraining.com
Pryor, Karen, Clicker Training Magic, www.clickertraining.com
Rugaas, Turid, *Calming Signals: On talking terms with dogs* and
Barking, www.dogwise.com

Audio

Leeds, Joshua, Spector, Lisa, *Through a Dog's Ear Series, Canine
Noise Phobia Series*—www.throughadogsear.com

Magazines, E-Subscriptions

www.whole-dog-journal.com *Nutrition and Rotational Diet Feeding*
www.animalwellnessmagazine.com

Organizations

Association of Pet Dog Trainers, www.apdt.com
Certified Professional Dog Trainers, www.ccpdt.org
Dog Writer's Association of America, www.dwaa.org

International Association of Animal Behavior Consultants,
www.iaabc.org

International Association of Animal Massage and Body Work,
www.iaamb.org

International Association of Reiki Professionals, www.iarp.org

National Association of Certified Counselors, www.nbcc.org

TTouch, Linda-Tellington Jones, *Tellington Touch*,
www.ttouch.com

Yoga Alliance, www.yogaalliance.org

International Coaching Federation, www.icf.org